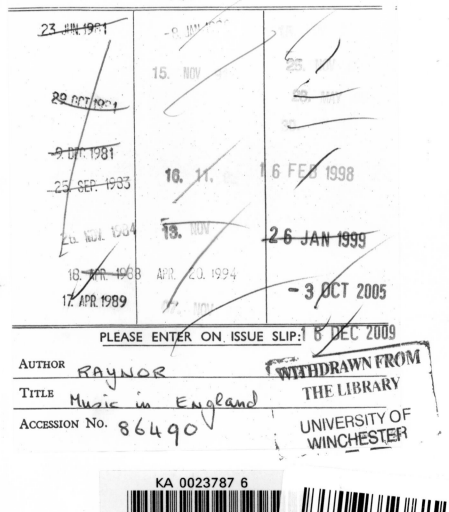

ALSO BY HENRY RAYNOR

Joseph Haydn
Radio and Television
Social History of Music from the Middle Ages to Beethoven
Mahler
Music and Society, since 1815
The Orchestra
Mozart

Contributions to:
Pelican History of Music, Vol. 2
Yehudi Menuhin, by Robert Magidoff (second edition)
Grove's Dictionary (sixth edition)
Encyclopédie de la Musique (edited by Roland Manuel)
Dictionaire de la Musique (edited by M. Honneger)

Music in England

Henry Raynor

ROBERT HALE · LONDON

Henry Raynor 1980
First published in Great Britain 1980
ISBN 0 7091 8356 9

Robert Hale Limited
Clerkenwell House
Clerkenwell Green
London EC1R 0HT

Printed in Great Britain by
Clarke, Doble & Brendon Ltd,
Plymouth and London

Contents

Acknowledgements

Permission to reproduce extracts from published sources in copyright has been obtained from the following: Faber & Faber Ltd, *Music Ho! A Study of Music in Decline* by Constant Lambert; Victor Gollancz Ltd, *My Life of Music* by Henry Wood; Hamish Hamilton Ltd, *At the Piano—Ivor Newton* by Ivor Newton; William Heinemann Ltd, *Bright Day* by J. B. Priestley; Oxford University Press, *The Autobiography of Thomas Whythorne* edited by James M. Osborne, and *National Music and Other Essays* by R. Vaughan Williams; and The Society of Authors on behalf of the Bernard Shaw Estate, *Music in London, 1890–1894* by G. Bernard Shaw.

Illustrations

CREDITS

The British Library: 1; Radio Times Hulton Picture Library: 2, 3, 4, 21, 22, 23, 24, 27; National Portrait Gallery: 5, 6, 9, 10, 11; The British Museum: 7, 16, 17, 18; The Fitzwilliam Museum: 8, 15, 20; The Museum of London: 12, 13, 14; The Royal Academy of Arts: 19; The BBC: 25, 26, 28, 30, 31, 32, 33; Allan Chappelow: 29.

Music Examples

I
English Music

Music, we have often been told, is the international language. The musician writing in Liechtenstein can be understood by players and listeners in Ludlow, Limoges or Leningrad. When we listen to music we are not normally acutely aware of its nationality or of the nationality of its creator, and we feel that we can accept works by composers of all nations simply as music, unconcerned about any characteristics other than those manifested by the mind of its creator.

Everyone, at some time or other, has made use of this argument and has insisted that the 'great' composers, because their works appeal to listeners of all nations, worked in a style which is universal. In a world where Japanese violinists take their places in European orchestras conducted by Indian or Japanese conductors who reveal the character of European or American music with as much honest certainty as conductors born or bred in central Europe, the idea of the universality of music seems to have proved itself to European music lovers who have learned from political experience to distrust the idea of nationalism no less in music than in their political lives.

Nevertheless, the music that we think of as 'universal' is, in reality, a comparatively small body of work composed by a handful of musicians who have worked within certain related traditions. The 'great' composers seem to be capable of speaking to everybody regardless of the listener's nationality, and the subject matter which concerns them appears to develop from a standpoint in a common tradition in which our own lives are rooted. In the later twentieth century the whole of music is open to us in a way that could not be shared by our grandfathers, however eagerly enquiring their minds, but we still tend to listen with some anxiety whenever an Italian conductor embarks upon the works of Brahms, as Toscanini did; we rarely hear Italian or Russian conductors of Bruckner or of Mahler, and we are amazed to remember that it has taken some forty years since Elgar's death to awaken most European conductors to qualities of his music which, to his fellow countrymen, seem both self-evident and incontrovertible. We seem immediately to recognize Russian or Spanish qualities in music even when its composer was not deliberately and consciously writing in a 'national' style in the manner of the great Russian composers of the nineteenth century.

Some music is easily recognizable from its deployment of national traits; other national musical idioms are not easy to learn. The works of Bartók, for example, outraged many listeners for a long time because it was plain that certain passages in his string quartets, for example, are given a place and emphasis that experience and musical precedent tell us are meant to impress us as melody, but Bartók's use of national scales and modes prevent us from hearing them as melody until our ears have grown familiar with the materials that he uses. Anyone who has listened seriously to Indian or to Arab music, for example, is at first baffled by what he hears because the intervals of such music, and the modes which organize them, prevent us at first from hearing anything more than an arbitrary, irrational succession of notes, while it is clear that African music is concerned with rules of behaviour different from those to which European music has accustomed us.

The further we move from a central tradition, the less easy it becomes for us to speak of music as an international language: even a good deal of medieval plainsong is a foreign language to many modern listeners because its melodies grow from the now archaic church modes and baffle expectations taught to depend upon the major and minor structures of European music since the seventeenth century; even as early as the seventeenth century itself, composers of Catholic church music expected by tradition to incorporate traditional liturgical melodies in their own works often found it necessary to convert the old and often very beautiful melodies in the church modes into modern major or minor tonalities.

Thus national music is not always the treatment of specially national subject matter in music drawn from a common international tradition; it is the probably instinctive use of rhythms, harmonies and melodic formulae which, through his inheritance, belong to the composer's ways of hearing and feeling. When Beethoven decided to compose a piece of popular, rabble-rousing music to celebrate *Wellington's Triumph, or the Battle of Victoria*, he characterized Napoleon's forces through the melody '*Marlbrouck se vat'en guerre*' and their British opponents through 'Rule Britannia' tunes which he apparently regarded as characteristically French and English; the victory is further celebrated through the use, in the finale of the work, of the British National Anthem. It would be hard to find anything particularly national in any of this, for the procedures to which these supposedly national tunes are subjected by a composer who was, in musical matters, a confirmed internationalist, are not those of French or English music but those of the early nineteenth-century international tradition. There is, furthermore, nothing idiosyncratically national about the characterizing melodies themselves; the tune which represents the French was granted English citizenship a long time ago as 'We won't go home till morning', and while 'Rule Britannia' is a fine, swaggering, arrogant tune of great vigour and *élan*, written by an unjustly neglected English composer, Thomas Arne, working under the shadow of Handel at a time when specifically English musical characteristics were beginning to be regarded by the up-to-date as rather archaic and musically uneducated. The National Anthem is a song as much at home in Germany as in Britain.

If, therefore, there is a variety of music which we can justifiably call 'English', as there are varieties of music justifiably recognized as Russian, Spanish or Indian, we need to analyze its qualities. Just as English poetry instinctively falls into iambic or trochaic metres, English composers seem equally instinctively to adopt the same metres. A country's language, which predetermines the rhythmic movement of its poetry, and its music seem to be related like chicken and egg, in ways which make it impossible ever to say which came first and gave rise to the other. Before the English language had been fully developed, English musicians and poets were aware of the pleasing rhythmic effects which come from the use of syncopation and the occasional use of an iambic foot in a trochaic pattern, and vice versa; the effect is at least as old as the Agincourt Song and is familiar in Elizabethan music; it was exploited by Purcell and sets modern audiences a little puzzle in 'Sammy's Bath', the second of the Audience Songs in Britten's *The Little Sweep*. We find similar syncopations used by Shakespeare, as when, for example, the dying Antony, struggling for breath in Cleopatra's monument, can speak only in trochees, breaking the expected iambic pattern:

> I am dying, Egypt, dying; only
> I here importune death awhile, until. . . .

and, now in control of his breath, he finds himself able to speak regularly and in iambs. If Shakespeare's purpose in these lines is the dramatic presentation in speech of the dying hero's struggle to gather sufficient breath to say what he has to say and of his success in gathering enough breath to cope with the five iambic feet of "I here importune death awhile, until", he has made the metrical irregularity familiar in English verse into something powerfully expressive. The irregularity is familiar; the Battle of Agincourt, in 1415, was celebrated in the Agincourt Song, with its similar metrical inversion, the use of an iambic foot in a trochaic line (Ex. 1).

The interrupting iambs of the Agincourt Song, of course, falsify the natural trochaic rhythm in which they are placed: we would speak of 'Nōrmăndy̆', 'c̄hivălry̆' and 'En̄glăn̆d'; the displaced stresses forced on to the words by the tune are used for the sake of a purely musical effect, and we are to sing about 'Nŏrmān̄dy̆', 'chĭvālry̆' and 'En̆glān̄d'. A similar pleasure in metrical irregularities is a familiar feature of English music up to the death of Purcell.

The real connection between the inflections of a spoken language —the rise and fall of a voice speaking words of which it is naturally the master—and the melodic style which composers develop to embody and enhance the meaning of the words they use has never been worked out and analyzed satisfactorily. The Czech composer, Leos Janáček, who died in 1928, for example, declared that the melodic style of his operas grew directly from listening to the inflections of his fellow Moravians as they talked; when, in 1926, he visited London and stayed at the Langham Hotel, he noted down the inflections of a page boy's shout: "That's the real England," he remarked to a companion. To Janáček, whose music was originally regarded as difficult, the inflections and rhythms of speech were the raw materials from which the composer could evolve

Ex. 1

Our Kyng went forth to Nor-man - dy With grace and
might— of— chy-val - rye There God for him— wrought
merve-lus - ly Where-fore Eng-londe may call and crye
Chorus
De - o gra - ti - as, Ang - - li -
- a, red - de pro Vic- tor - i - a.

expressive melodic lines. Similarly, Joseph Addison, writing about Italian Opera when it became new and fashionable, noted that one of the difficulties for English listeners was Italian recitative:

> *Everyone who has been long in Italy knows very well, that the Cadences in the Recitativo bear a remote affinity to the Tone of of their Voices in ordinary Conversation; or, to speak more properly, are only the Accents of their Language made more Musical and Tuneful. Thus the Notes of Interrogation or Admiration in the Italian Musick (if one may so call them) which resemble their Accents in Discourses on such Occasions, are not unlike the ordinary Tones of an English voice when we are angry; insomuch that I have often seen our audiences extremely mistaken as to what has been doing upon the Stage.*[1]

A composer is naturally influenced by the speech patterns that surround his ears, and this may be why, for reasons which seem to be beyond analysis, English composers cannot avoid an instinctive tendency to lean towards scales older than the major and minor scales of music since the Renaissance. The modes of medieval music did not demand and fixed pitch for their notes in their varying scale patterns; the modes are varying arrangements of the whole tones and semitones of the scale. Milton, writing in the early seventeenth century, asked in *L'Allegro* for music to "Lap me in soft Lydian airs"; to arrive at the Lydian mode we play a scale beginning on F on a pianoforte keyboard but using only the white keys. The result is a scale with a whole tone between its third and fourth notes, but with semitones between its fourth and fifth, and seventh and eighth notes; the modern major scale puts a semitone between its third and fourth notes, but any arrangement which puts a semitone between the fourth and fifth notes, whatever note it takes as its beginning, is in the Lydian mode. A scale starting on D and making no use of black keys would be in the Dorian mode, and that arrangement of tones and semitones creates the Dorian mode whatever note may be its starting point its semitones fall between the second and third, and sixth and seventh notes. A scale beginning on G, with semitones between its third and fourth and its sixth and seventh notes is the Mixolydian mode. It was natural in this connection, to quote from Milton, the son of a musician who was himself an educated music lover; Milton wished to make poetical use of the view that a composer naturally chose to write in the mode emotionally appropriate to the work with which he was concerned, and thereby achieve the emotional effect he wished his music to have. The Lydian mood is that of music which soothes the hearer into contented happiness, but the armies of Hell, gathering and reassembling after their expulsion from Heaven, move into their new kingdom "In perfect phalanx to the Dorian mood Of flutes and soft recorders"[2], because the Dorian mood is that which inspires courage, resolution and fortitude. The modern major scale, in pre-Renaissance terminology, was the Ionian mode, the minor scale the Aeolian; the Middle Ages rejected the Ionian mode, which it called *modus lascivus*, as emotionally corrupt and debased; the Aeolian mode was rejected as enervating rather than inspiring.

One of the characteristics of English music is a tendency to inflect tonalities from the modern major or minor scales into modality, even when it is the work of a composer whom we do not normally associate with folk-songs and folkish musical traditions. Act II of *Peter Grimes*, the vivid picture of an East Anglian fishing village on a clean, clear, sunny Sunday morning, has sharply-etched, tough music, as clean and fresh as the morning it depicts; it is music in the Lydian mode, as is the waltz song in Britten's *Saint Nicholas* which salutes the birth of the saint. The 'chorale' of the chorus which begins and ends *The Rape of Lucretia* is in the Lydian mode. To look for modal idioms and harmonic inflections in the music of earlier composers, like Vaughan Williams and Gustav Holst, who were actively devoted to folk-song, is, of course, to attend to works by composers consciously influenced by modal idioms, but the same tendency makes itself felt in many of the songs of Peter Warlock composed in the 1920s with little or no cognizance of folk-song but a passionate devotion to Elizabethan music.

English composers of the twentieth century, with traditional tonality weakened as it had been everywhere since the 1860s, when Wagner developed the intense, chromatic vocabulary of *Tristan und Isolde*, found not only the revolutionary styles of modern European music but also the possibility of a recovery of older, pre-Renaissance idioms with the employment of modal harmonies to which they adapted the harmonic grammar of modern tonality. In a sense, this development links modern English music with the world of Purcell in the late seventeenth century for though Purcell was, in his own day and in every sense a 'modern' composer, utilizing in entirely English styles the Italian conventions and idioms which were the progressive music of his period, he had a cavalier attitude to major and minor tonality, using both modes, if it suited him to do so, within a single melody.

The tendency towards modality gives harmony a colour which the listener feels not only in the music of such composers as Holst and Vaughan Williams, but also in much of the more 'modern' and often more astringent music of Britten. The first historical reference to specifically English musical characteristics comes from Giraldus Cambrensis in the eleventh century, and makes particular note of the English style of harmonization. At a time when primitive harmony depended on the intervals of the fourth and fifth, English singers, Giraldus pointed out, instinctively improvised harmonies based on thirds and sixths, officially regarded at that period as illegal discords; this English taste must have struck listeners in Giraldus's day in much the same way as listeners today may be struck by Britten's practice of accompanying a melody by harmonizing it with seconds (in, for example, the third movement of his *Sinfonia da Requiem*), creating a startling manner of reinforcing and underlining a melodic line. Harmony with a basis in thirds and sixths exists for the effects made by its deliberate emotionalism, like an arching melody in nineteenth-century Italian opera moving with two sopranos in parallel thirds or a soprano and a tenor united in parallel sixths. It would really not be too much to suggest that in its early days, as in its later, English music aimed at frank emotionalism.

English music, of course, has kept its individuality through the existence of a time-lag between the appearance of Continental styles and their adoption by English composers. Whatever the precise sound, and even the precise techniques, of early English harmony with its insistence on the use of thirds and sixths, the early polyphonic style worked out by composers at the French monastery of St Martial and at the cathedrals of Notre-Dame in Paris and Compostella in Spain did not reach England or affect English composers until it was established all over Western Europe. When it did so, it adapted the rules worked out and promulgated on the Continent to English tastes in harmony, and exploited the English style within the framework of such Continental disciplines as the motet. To say that English harmony is more sensuous by nature, and more emotional, than the music composed on the Continent is not, perhaps, simply to listen to primitive music with ears conditioned by musical habits acquired from attention to the musical richnesses of later periods; such a conclusion seems to miss the point of what we should, perhaps, regard as a national idiosyncrasy. At the beginning of the fifteenth century, when Continental music had become for a time drily pedantic, English composers such as John Dunstable and Leonel Power effected a romantic revolution in the music of their age by feeding into the Continental style a native, liberating freedom of harmony and lyrical statement.

In the same way, the school of composers which came into prominence in the 1580s and flourished for some fifty years, enabling us to speak justly of a 'Golden Age of English Music', finally worked out the polyphonic style associated at its inception with composers in Burgundy and the Netherlands. They gave the accepted European style, carried from Northern Europe to Italy where it reached its zenith, an English accent and an attitude to words and their declamation which was the result of the maturity and sophistication of English poetry. But it was not until the 1680s and 1690s, and the age of Purcell, that English styles and techniques reunited themselves with Continental practice by catching up with them. It was not until 200 years later, until which time the best English composers had occupied themselves in backwaters, that Parry, Stanford and above all Elgar, were able to master the techniques and idioms of late nineteenth-century music and use them to speak with an English accent in the lingua franca of their own age. Schoenberg, the most influential of twentieth-century revolutionaries in music, was dead before the teachings he had worked out during and immediately after the First World War began to exert an impact on English composers.

The history of English music is not, therefore, an account of a steady development but the story of a series of exciting spurts followed by periods of consolidation followed by periods of stagnation. The great English composers—Byrd and his contemporaries, Purcell, Elgar, Britten and their contemporaries—are musicians who consolidated in their own styles varieties of musical expression new and old, and proving, often enough, oddly successful at the unscriptural task of pouring new wine into old bottles.

The history of music anywhere is inextricably bound up with the history of the purposes for which music was required, that is, with the tastes and preconceptions of its audience. Music, ultimately, is written for the people who want it. French music, for example, was given its *raison d'être* by the absolutism of Louis XIV in the late seventeenth century, which made Paris and the royal court the centre of artistic endeavour as well as of social manners and political action. The French Revolution of 1789 applied to its own purposes the grandiloquence and grace which had been the keynotes of court music in the days of the greatest of French kings. Italian music is inescapably conditioned by the circumstances that made opera not an upper-class amusement but the popular form of drama, the essential theatrical necessity. English music was never thus under the direction of any single authority; even in the 'Golden

Age' of Elizabeth I, English composers expected to make, and were left to make, their main income in the public market where popular taste was the determining factor in their success. The history of English music has, in part, to be the story of public taste and its lack of direction, together with a lack of any general musical education. This, as much as the rarity of musical genius in any society, has determined the story of English music.

II

The Middle Ages

The history of music is inextricably mixed up with the history of the organizations which make music, so that whilst it would be foolish to think of the music of the Catholic Church in England as the beginning of English music, it is natural to think of the establishment of the Catholic Church in England as the beginning of the recorded history of English music. It is easy to think of folk-songs which are connected with pre-Christian fertility rites as instances of music which predates the conversion of England to Christianity, but such songs have survived in forms that have evolved comparatively recently. Handed down orally from generation to generation, they have adapted themselves to musical styles and to versions of their texts belonging to periods long after their original composition; even their texts find time to refer to personalities and incidents belonging to periods far nearer to us than the original purposes of their primitive singers. May Day at Helston or Padstow is marked by the celebration of extremely ancient religious dances intended to ensure fertility, but the music of the dances refers to personalities whose place in history is far more recent. History depends upon records, annals and the evidence they give us, and the early days of European music are recorded for us only by the Church. In the year 580 St Gregory the Great, having codified and organized the music of the Church, modernizing and completing the musical system worked out by St Ambrose (340–397), instituted the *Schola Cantorum* in Rome so that there would always be a supply of trained singers to ensure that the services of the church would always not only be well sung but correctly sung to the recognized, authorized chants which were regarded as an essential part of the service. In 650, less than fifty years after the death of

Saint Gregory, the Abbot of Wearmouth sent to Rome for a singer who could teach his monks "the system of singing throughout the year as it is practised at St Peter's in Rome." Less than a century later, the Council of Cloveshoe (in 747) made the use of the Roman chant compulsory throughout the country.

This naturally meant the creation of identical musical organizations in all monasteries and cathedrals, not only everywhere in England, but also throughout Western Europe. It was the duty of the monks, and of the canons of cathedrals, not simply to say Mass and the Office—the daily forms of prayer contained in the Breviary—but to sing them according to the chant laid down by St Gregory. In cathedral churches many of the canons had external duties which would keep them out of their places in the choir—they might, for example, hold a living some distance away or be involved in administrative work for their bishop or even for their king or temporal ruler, so it became customary for canons to appoint vicars, priests without livings of their own, who do duty in the cathedral choir whenever the canon was occupied elswhere. When the canon was on duty or 'in residence' in the cathedral, the vicar became the canon's servant until it became natural for the vicars to organize themselves into 'colleges'; at Wells, for example, they had their own individual houses and their own Collegiate hall. Naturally, the canons realized that as the primary duty of the canons was the singing of the Mass and the Offices, vicars should be chosen for the quality of their voices and for their general musical ability.

Among the duties of monks had been the education of their own recruits, who were often small boys, and the existence of such educational facilities made it seem natural to them to become educators of other small boys, the sons of friends and benefactors of their order. Such boys were expected, as were the adult members of their order, to join in the performance of the Mass and the Divine Office, so that the enrichment of the music of the church persuaded cathedrals to co-opt boys with unbroken voices and to give them a musical education (which necessarily implied an education in reading and in Latin) so that they could regularly contribute to the music of the services. A song school for such boys was established at York in the year 627. There were cathedrals in Europe—at Salzburg, for example—with song schools cqually old, but in 1083 the *Patrologia Latina* (a book of church regulations) ordered that "in whatsoever school are found boys who can sing, such boys are to be brought up in the song school."

At first the boys sang the same part as the men, singing the plainchant an octave above them. Roughly speaking, between the years 950 and 1150, the beginning and development of polyphony diversified the service music. Beginning with two-part settings, composers quite quickly added a third and a fourth vocal line to the official music of the chant. Music from this period survives in manuscripts from some of the Spanish cathedrals, having reached them from France, where it apparently originated, having first been developed at the Monastery of St Martial and at the Cathedral of Notre-Dame in Paris. A choir book at Worcester Cathedral contains works in the new style, some of them copied from Notre-Dame music, and others, anonymous works probably by English composers exploring the same style, were added to them within a century of the development of French polyphony. The official plainchant remained obligatory, and the new style provided it with counterpoints which were often elaborate, lively and rhythmical while the tenor voice—it owes the name 'tenor' to the Latin verb *tenere* ('to hold')—held resolutely on to the notes of the chant which were often vastly elongated to allow the counterpoints their freedom to dance expressively round them.

The musical organization of cathedrals and monastic churches, and of those parish churches which were served by a college of priests, required a precentor, who had to be a specialist on the liturgy and the music it required; a cantor, who taught the music to be sung by both boys and men; a cathedral chancellor, who took charge of the discipline and administration of the school; and a rector, who functioned as headmaster. The choirs would have seemed strangely disorganized to a modern listener, with the number of boys quite lost among an apparent crowd of men—thirty-six men at York, fifty-four men at Wells, for example, with seven boys at York and twelve at Wells. It was usual that the boys and all the men would join in the singing of the obligatory plainchant when no polyphonic setting was used, and that out of the total number of available singers, a smaller polyphonic choir, accurately balanced, could be formed when it was needed. It seems that a long time passed, and several reorganizations of cathedral statutes were required, before the entire available choir found itself engaged in polyphonic music.

The development of music within the cathedral services demanded by more and more skilled singers, and the increasing use of expert voices of course made practical the use of still more elaborate music. The chant, of course, was formalized and in theory unchangeable, as it had been before any effective system of notation existed, so that, when the Abbot of Wearmouth was able to acquire a teacher of authority from the Pope to train his choir in the intricacies of the Roman chant, the inviolability of what was taught depended upon the ability of the choir singers themselves to remember and accurately reproduce year after year what they had been taught. The oral transmission of music, however determined singers might be to preserve it unchanged, more or less invited the cooperation of any creative instincts the singers may possess. Such creative instincts almost instinctively modified and at times 'modernized' the official chant, extending and elaborating the melismata that were regarded as extremely expressive; in England, naturally, the chants developed national characteristics and, often, a lyrical emotionalism that was specifically English.

As certain Mass chants grew increasingly extended, additional words were extended into them. *Kyrie eleison, Christe eleison, Kyrie eleison,* the opening words of the invariable 'common' of the Mass, each three times repeated, were treated with increasingly elaborate melismata, shapely melodies of as many as thirty or forty notes; the setting of the *Kyrie eleison* authorized "to be sung on solemn feasts" is known as *Kyrie fons bonitatis* because the words *fons bonitatis* (fountain of goodness) were interpolated into the first petition. There is nothing to prove or disprove the notion that such tropes, as the interpolations were called, were fitted into the chant to assist the memory of the singers and to help them keep the free rhythm of the plainchant clear and unanimous.

By the time of the Norman Conquest, polyphony had developed in Northern France and had travelled to Spain. Though most developments in church music roused opposition from the church authorities, the two great masters of the Notre-Dame school of composers, Leonin and Perotin (the first two composers whose names are associated with any specific works) had formulated the first phase of the new style. Leonin's work was apparently written between 1160 and 1180; he seems to have been Perotin's teacher, and his music was collected together in a volume called *Magnus liber organi*, which consists of elaborate settings of music for eighty of the church feasts. *Organum* was the name given to the two-part music, one voice singing the official plainsong and the other providing it with a free, decorative counterpoint above. Perotin wrote *clausulae*, in which two or three voices move against the plainchant, in measured rhythms of their own and sometimes in contrary directions. He also revised his master's *organa*, interpolating *clausulae* passages into Leonin's work. He had the approval, apparently, of the Bishop of Paris for his biggest works, *Viderunt*, for New Year's Day, 1198, and *Sederunt Principes* (the words of the Introit of the Mass of St Stephen's Day) a year later. The Bishop was eager to set up something as likely to excite worshippers as the various dubious ceremonies of popular religion which crowded into the period between Christmas and the New Year.

Though traditional opposition to any elaboration of church music continued, the existence of musical organizations within the church meant that elaborations continued. A Cornish manuscript, apparently from the early twelfth century, gives a hymn to St Stephen in Leonin's *duplum* style, and the Worcester choir book has pieces in Perotin's freer three- and four-part writing which seem on purely musical grounds to be English.

The Continental composers of the period treated thirds and sixths as dissonances, permitted in passing-notes but not in cadences; in English music, thirds and sixths were not merely accepted but regarded as particularly appealing. A structural use of thirds and sixths is in itself enough, in this early period, to suggest that the works which contain them probably originated in England.

But, in addition to the formal organization of cathedral and monastic music, even inside the church as it developed in England, a tradition existed which may have encouraged greater musical freedom than religious authorities really approved of. Giraldus Cambrensis (Gerald Barry), Archdeacon of St David's in the later part of the twelfth century, wrote not so much about church music as about the general musical habits and tastes of the people of Great Britain; the Irish, he explained, were particularly skilful in the playing of instruments, but their skill was rivalled by the Welsh and Scottish. The people of Northumbria, instinctively and without any formal musical training, harmonized the songs they sang, fitting a second part, or descant, to the melody. The Welsh, too, instinctively harmonized their music: "It is their custom to sing in a body, so that you hear as many songs as you can see singers." As soon as Welsh children begin to sing, Giraldus Cambrensis explained, they begin to sing in parts. Whatever instinctive method and style of harmony evolved among such singers in Wales and Northumbria might, by the time Giraldus heard them, have developed from listening to *dupla* in the Leonin style which the common people had heard in church; such an explanation of their musical habits is not entirely impossible if they had been in touch with the latest in musical composition by the time that Giraldus heard them, so that they harmonized the music they heard at fixed intervals of fifths and fourths. But in reality it seems that the English and Welsh had their own sense of harmony, and exploited it in an entirely untutored way simply because they liked the sounds they could make. The English style, at a time when educated harmony was based on sixths and fourths, may have been influenced by Celtic musical habits when it used thirds and sixths as intervals on which cadences come to rest, but the fact is that English music in its early days, chose to follow a more poignant, sensuous direction than that taken by the early polyphonic composers.

The musical establishments which grew up within the church in the period before and after the Conquest are a natural point of departure for any history of English music because they provide us with a firm, factual ground, to which can be added equally objective information about other musical facts, such as the installation of organs in churches and cathedrals and the development of votive services which were not, strictly speaking, within the liturgy; the Mass of the day had its indispensable chant, and the correctness of the chant was, in the views of the authorities, as vital to the validity of the Mass as the use of the correct words, the correct readings and lessons. But a Votive Mass of the Blessed Virgin, sung in her own chapel within the cathedral, was not so narrowly bound by strict musical regulations; it provided an opportunity for musicians to free their ambitions and stretch their style and technique beyond the limitations of what was permitted within the strictness of the liturgy.

The Catholic Church, brought to England by St Augustine of

Canterbury in 597, regarded music with strict Puritanism. Every departure from St Gregory's musical style had to be won with difficulty from the authorities, who only slowly permitted organs, instrumental accompaniment, the use of polyphony and the other medieval developments. Bishop Eude de Sully, however, encouraged Perotin to write *Viderunt* and *Sederunt Principes* apparently not only in the rhythmic, almost dancing style of their period, but also to support the voices with organ and sackbuts and to punctuate the musical phrases with the use of bells; such departures from normal custom were generally opposed. The Celtic Church, however, which had brought music to many parts of Britain before St Augustine's mission arrived, seems to have shared none of the inhibitions which made life difficult for Catholic musicians. In the eyes of the Roman authorities, music was inseparably wedded to memories of Latin, and other pagan doctrines and practices. The Celtic missionaries seem to have acted on the principle that if music added to the beauty and the sense of mystery of any rite, it was good and to be encouraged. It was the Catholic suspicion of music which, in 878, enabled King Alfred to spy on the invading Danes before the Battle of Edginton; King Alfred could enter the Danish camp in the guise of a harpist, as it would never occur to the invaders, aware of the Catholic dislike of music, that a harpist could be a Christian and Catholic King.

Celtic Christians, it seems, believed that music could be sanctified; it was Caedmon's vision of Christ himself which inspired Caedmon to sing his biblical hymns in music which appears to have been in a popular minstrel style. St Aldhelm, the Bishop of Sherborne, who died in 709, attracted a congregation to his sermons by playing and singing to the accompaniment of his harp. The actual music made by Caedmon, by St Aldhelm and the Celtic Church in general, both inside and outside the liturgy, is lost, but it was clearly less austere than the plainchant which became the ideal after the arrival of St Augustine and the later synods and church councils which imposed uniformity on English catholicism. The Sarum Missal and Breviary, the pattern for the variants of the liturgy used in England, belong on the whole to a system of devotion more emotionally subjective than the services originally brought from Rome, and it seems that English musical tradition percolated into the new polyphony of

Northern France through such collections as the Worcester Choir Book.

The next step in the emancipation of music from the liturgy was the development, originally in Northern France, of the motet. Originally, the motet was simply a devotional work, based on some piece, or fragment of a piece, of liturgical plainchant set to words which were not necessarily liturgical though they were religious; they could be treated with greater musical freedom than the words of the liturgy. The tenor voice, the foundation, was plainchant, usually slowed up to allow free-composed voices above it; the top voice, or *motetus*, had its own text irrespective of the words that were associated with its structural foundation chant. A middle voice might elaborate the music of the *motetus* or might be totally independent of it, even having a text of its own; the composition was a 'motet' because of its setting of the words given to the top voice, but its treatment of words—and in the twelfth century it might easily deal with three texts each in its own language—was entirely subservient to its music, so that the words were normally unintelligible; it was the first purely abstract music of which we have any real history. Often enough, the plainchant foundation was no more than a single phrase, sometimes no more than a word or syllable. The motet was music for skilled musicians, so its history began, like the history of all learned music, in church; here it could be put to practical use, filling up gaps in the rite of, for example, the Offertory or the Communion, with music which could stimulate emotion. But it was an interesting field for cultivation by composers, so that the motet technique of composition was carried into secular music wherever there were trained singers to do it justice. Thus it became an aristocratic as well as a religious form, used often with words that had no religious justification at all.

The development of music in England, therefore, had its idiosyncrasies as it proceeded parallel to the history of music in Northern Europe. A motet (probably English) of the late thirteenth century uses as its foundation a chant for the Epiphany—'*Epiphanium Dominum canamus gloriosum*'—while the first tenor sings a text rebuking jealousy (for this is a secular motet with a high moral purpose) and the second tenor's words are a condemnation of slander, the voices coming to rest on triads which were still theortically unacceptable in the harmony of the time; the chant is used only for its first word, repeated several times, as the motet is performed.[8]

The first great triumph of English music, the Reading rota 'Sumer is icumen in', was probably composed between 1280 and 1350 by some musician whose name we do not know; these dates have been established by Manfred Bukofzer, in his *Studies in Medieval and Renaissance Music*. It is a highly developed work in strict counterpoint, a round or canon in which four voices sing a melody in a popular style, in the favourite English trochaic rhythm. The second voice begins the melody when the first has sung its opening phrase, the third follows a phrase behind the second and the fourth when the third has sung its first phrase. Each melodic phrase can be written down, in modern practice, as a phrase of four regular bars, whilst two other voices are laying down a harmonic foundation, called the *pes*, another four-bar phrase, which is repeated without variation.

This spring song, with its springy, dancing rhythm somehow (perhaps simply because people liked it) became a Latin hymn text, '*Perspice, Christicola*', as though the monks of Reading Abbey wanted an opportunity to sing their song in the Abbey Church. Again, each phrase ends on the harmony of a triad in one of its simple inversions, and this is perhaps enough, if we knew nothing else about its provenance, to claim English nationality for it. Nineteenth-century scholars tended to claim an earlier date for 'Sumer is icumen in' than modern scholars will allow, claiming that it was written at least a century before the date we now accept, creating the impression that some English musician in the eleventh or twelfth century had somehow managed to create a piece of music that could stand as a musically and mathematically impeccable example of the way in which music was to develop much later. The time which we now assign to the Reading rota simply puts it in place as a good tune treated with effective counterpoint in the days when counterpoint was a new and lively musical pleasure.

The twelfth century, which saw the development of polyphony and, in the motet, the beginning of abstract music which used words only to stimulate its own expressive purposes, also saw a general expansion, in theology, literature, art, architecture and music. It was the age of early secular song developed by troubadours in the south of France and trouvères in the north, and, a little later by Minnesänger in Germany. There were, we know, songs before this sung to English words by Englishmen, but we know little about them except their names; a few tunes, obviously in later forms than those sung by their creators, have been orally transmitted to us. The troubadours were aristocrats or the employed musicians of aristocrats and the social status of the songs, as well as the wealth of the aristocratic singers and composers, meant that written copies were made of them. Troubadour song was a courtly art, its musicians courtiers; the most celebrated of English troubadours was King Richard I, and what we know of his music was entirely in the fashionable French style; its character and development is not strictly relevant to the history of English music.

Popular English song, as it began to find its way into manuscript, has reached us most often in treatments arranged by later musicians whose taste and ambitions were those of the church music of their period, in versions in a style which probably grew from the motet, with the melody in the tenor between a soprano or alto and a bass. The song '*Angelus ad Virginem*', which the young Clerk of Oxenford sang, according to the Miller of *The Canterbury Tales*, surely existed in a more accessible form than a three-part setting, especially as the Clerk sang it to the accompaniment of his psaltery, "on which he made a nightes melodye so sweetely that all the chambre rong".

Ex. 2

(The melody is in the tenor)

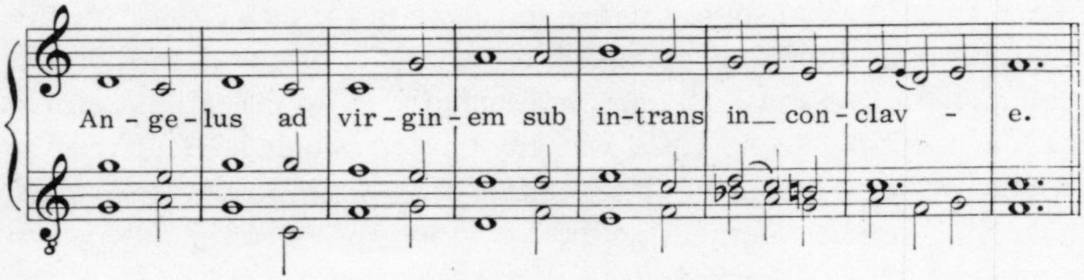

The gloomy intense song 'Worldes Blisse', an expression of deep pessimism which seems rare in the thirteenth century, is an English song for which it is impossible to find a source and it seems not to have been touched by the upper-class troubadour tradition.

Ex. 3

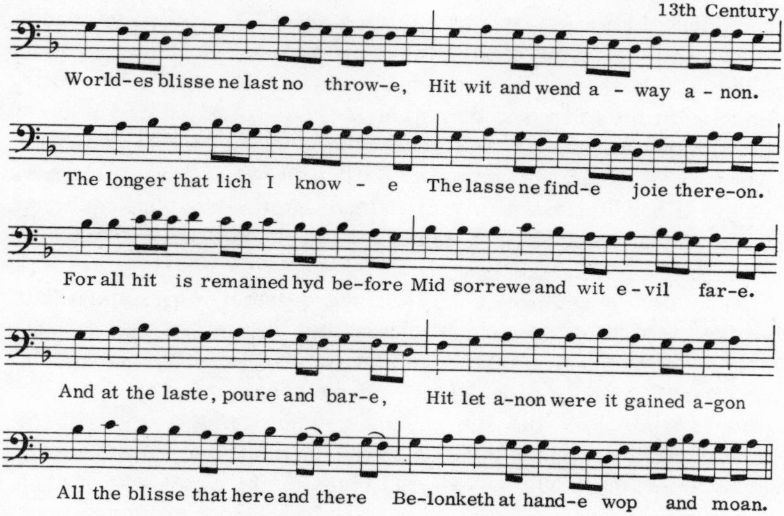
13th Century
World-es blisse ne last no throw-e, Hit wit and wend a - way a - non.
The longer that lich I know - e The lasse ne find-e joie there-on.
For all hit is remained hyd be-fore Mid sorrewe and wit e-vil far-e.
And at the laste, poure and bar-e, Hit let a-non were it gained a-gon
All the blisse that here and there Be-lonketh at hand-e wop and moan.

Dance music of this period survives in a few manuscripts, but the dance music which reached pen and paper belongs, like the troubadour songs, most usually to the upper classes, and more popular dances hardly exist for us as more than names. Even carols, which strictly speaking consist of solo verses and danced refrains for the company, hardly survive from so early a period. Possibly the passionate hostility of the church authorities to popular dancing discouraged the making of written versions, which depended on the interest and enthusiasm of literate musicians.

By the thirteenth century, however, the groups of singers, instrumentalists and entertainers which kings and noblemen recruited for their private chapels and for their general entertainment were groups of all-purpose musicians, for all of them were to some extent trained to sing or play, to juggle, tumble and do whatever their employer wanted them to do. A pay-roll survives from the time when Edward I knighted his son Edward of Caernarvon (the future Edward II) in 1306, when he was eager to create new knights who would replenish the membership of an order seriously depleted by losses sustained in his wars. This pay-roll lists the great number of minstrels in other regular service who were on duty for an unusually spectacular occasion; they were paid a regular salary and provided with official livery. Their statutory wage was 4½d. *per diem*, which a modern authority states as equivalent to £3.75 in today's money. In addition to their salary, minstrels were often called upon to undertake extra duties for which they could expect to receive largesse in the form of a tip or bonus. The profession of a minstrel made him a member of the minute middle class of the Middle Ages. Minstrel, however, was a rather elastic term which must often have included hardly-trained or half-trained entertainers who could not hope for so respectable a remuneration as Edward I's minstrels were granted.[4]

Such instrumentalists did not come together into standardized bodies resembling a modern orchestra but were assemblies of whatever instruments were available and were in the hands of reliable players. The enormously elongated plainchant of the early polyphonic composers and the early motet encouraged not only the development of organs but also of the sackbut, the primitive trombone; the organ could sustain the notes of the slowed-down chant for as long as the composer could ever wish, and players with sackbuts could give a compatible but more than vocal steadiness to the musical scaffolding. The extreme prolongation of the notes of a plainchant theme in many early motets is probably an indication that such lines were not meant for singing but for performance by an instrument. Even the tiny portative organs, which were carried round with a choir to any point in the building where the choir was needed, could provide all the necessary sustaining power. These organs were pumped by the player with his left hand while he played the notes with his right hand.

It was this unswerving sustaining power which made the organ the essential church instrument, and not the later Victorian view that the organ was for some reason particularly suitable for religious music. The 1306 pay list shows that two organists only were paid for taking part in the mass knightings, and that neither of them was directly in the service of the king.

The installation of organs in monastery churches and in cathedrals had begun before the Norman Conquest; Winchester Cathedral, in the tenth century, had an organ which was either one of the wonders of the world or a great, fearsome monstrosity against the roaring of which people covered their ears; for it was described as both. It needed seventy strong men to pump its bellows, its keys were pressed by blows from the fist and it could be heard all over the city. The invention of smaller organs domesticated the fearsome instrument and the organ, once it became manageable, took a general part in music. The organ was not the only or the most important church instrument but simply the most useful when no others were available.

These developments, though little of the music itself, can be traced in church and court archives in England and all over Europe. The troubadour movement encouraged the spread of secular music and the employment of church musicians, or of musicians trained in the church. The part played by music in the lives of ordinary men and women is a matter for conjecture rather than precise knowledge. As long ago as any records can be found, the wealthy had employed their entertainers, who were always, at least in part, musicians. The term '*jongleur*', which was the title of such entertainers in many places, is the word from which we derive the term 'juggler'. The word 'minstrel' derives from the Latin *ministerialis*, meaning an official, minstrels having originally been attendants to the troubadour knights whose services included the duty of accompanying their songs. As resident, liveried retainers in an aristocratic household, minstrels were employed for their ability to entertain an employer and the employer's family in whatever way, from music to comic cross-talk and acrobatics, the employer demanded.

Though itinerant, lower-class entertainers were never encouraged, nobody could prevent their existence. Among their gifts seems to have been that of giving music to exciting stories or to items of news, and their popularity among the common people was often reinforced, if their skill warranted, by the support of the rich and important who could take them into service. Church authorities condemned minstrelsy of this sort as an encouragement of immorality, but just as monarchs like King Alfred and even Charlemagne himself had not only encouraged minstrels, but employed them and collected their songs, not all the powerful were opposed to the sort of entertainment they offered. In 1289 Richard de Swinfield, Bishop of Hereford, made payments to various minstrels, among whom were viol players and a harpist. From the fifteenth century onwards Durham Priory and various other religious houses record payments to minstrels, as though such payments were ordinary enough to be regarded merely as routine expenditure. The lists of minstrels' songs preserved in the Harleian and other collections of manuscripts suggest that at times the minstrels were outspoken and sometimes dangerous critics of political abuses and even of abuses in the church. Indeed, the objections of church authorities to minstrelsy may have been the result of the minstrels' readiness to criticize religious as well as political authority. The profession only slowly became respectable; in 1319, Roger de Mortival, Bishop of Salisbury, warned against minstrels as "upholders of sloth". They were not to be given money or enabled to earn money because they encouraged "slander, back-biting and scurrility". Mortival instructed the clergy under his authority not to pay any attention to their "yelpings". The itinerant minstrels, unprotected by any organization of higher social status than themselves, were an easy target. However, those who found liveried positions under noble patronage were accepted as respectable members of society, and the minstrels' guilds which began to be set up in the fourteenth century gave musicians the type of organization which the people of the Middle Ages could understand and which made them respectable in the terms of later-medieval society. They gradually became as acceptable as the members of any guild which existed to produce goods, to price them fairly and to organize systems and methods of training. The minstrels themselves profited by the imposition of strict professional standards.

A combination of civic pride and social necessity led to the creation of bands of waits or minstrels in the towns. In most towns and cities, waits and town minstrels were the same people; as waits they were official watchmen, using their instruments to give warnings of fire or any other emergency. Their main instrument was the shawm (a shrill-voiced primitive oboe), but they might also have had a sackbut (the early trombone), a cornett or some sort of horn. As entertainers, until Tudor times they kept the same instruments and were granted the monopoly of any public music-making in the town which employed them. This meant that they accompanied the music in the church, were booked to play at every wedding and the jollifications which followed it, and to accompany any pageant, banquet or dance, all at a fixed rate of pay. As the duties such groups undertook as watchmen could not secure a sufficiently high rate of pay for them, these additional privileges were the only way of raising their earnings to a real subsistence level, and anybody who attempted to break their monopoly must have been either an amateur or an itinerant minstrel not qualified to make himself heard because he was not a member of the local guild. Their fees, however, were not high; in 1391, for playing at a municipal banquet in Bristol, the four city waits shared a fee of five marks, and five marks was the sum allowed for the Lord Mayor's wine. Lincoln had a group of waits by 1399, as had Beverley and Norwich among other towns. At about this time, Chaucer was writing *The Canterbury Tales*, but we do not know what future he planned for Perkins, the unsatisfactory apprentice in 'The Cook's Tale', and the Cook never finished his story. Perkins "loved bet the tavern than the shoppe", but he knew that his riotous career as an apprentice was likely to cause him to be "Led with revel to Newgate". If the minstrels marched with prisoners to prison, they were demonstrating to the populace that even at the turn of the fourteenth century crime did not pay. In some places they rang the bell which called citizens to pay their taxes. In Germany they were "Tower Men" who from some convenient vantage point gave warning of the approach of any unexpected and inconveniently large band of travellers; their duties were many and various.

A qualified member of a Musicians' Guild played all its instruments, and though English waits, groups of four, five or six players, usually restricted themselves to woodwind instruments until Elizabethan times, and each was expected to train a limited number of apprentices, we have no certain knowledge about either their repertory or the standard they maintained before the reign of Elizabeth I. Their existence, apart from their utility as municipal watchmen, was simply an acknowledgement of the social necessity of music, so highly regarded that the campaigns of Henry V before 1417, and the negotiations which preceded the Treaty of Troyes in 1421, were accompanied by his Household musicians, a body of twenty-seven clerks and sixteen boys. Among the clerks, the musicians who served the King in France, were four composers—John Burrell, John Cooke, Thomas Damett and Nicholas Sturgeon. The works which were sung in the Chapel Royal (of which these composers were members) in the time of the Lancastrian kings (who enlarged it and saw it gain an international reputation) are known from the Old Hall Manuscript, a collection of 140 choral pieces of church music kept in the Old House at Ware and containing the works of composers known to have been associated with the Lancastrian Chapel Royal. The Lancastrians were musicians themselves, and one of them, though we do not know which, was composer of a *Sanctus* and *Benedictus* simply attributed, in the manuscript, to "Roy Henry".

Ars Nova, the new art which opened a new door into musical progress and reached its highest development on the Continent, affected English music very little. It was primarily concerned with a new and more intricate treatment of rhythm and a new interest in instrumental colour. The composers who are on record as having accompanied the King to France, for example, seem little influenced by it. Some of the music in the Old Hall Manuscript suggests that there were English composers who were training to find their way into a style which exploited Continental intellectual tricks without sacrificing the traditional English delight in vigour of rhythm and the traditional English love of rich, massive musical textures through the traditional delight in English harmonic eccentricities. *Ars Nova* was, so to speak, a highly developed style intended for the delectation of sophisticated audiences which seem to have taken greater pleasure in ingenuities than in direct emotional expression. The English revolution in music came in the works of John Dunstable and Leonel Power. Dunstable, in the service of Henry V's brother John, Duke of Bedford, died in 1453. Power, perhaps older, was a musician in Canterbury Cathedral and then later in Winchester Cathedral; he died in 1445. Their works were known on the Continent, and it is not always easy to distinguish the authorship of some works between them. Power's music can be found in manuscripts at Aosta, Trent, Modena and Munich; a Mass, '*Rex Saeculorum*', is ascribed to Dunstable in the Aosta manuscript, while four of Power's motets are credited to Dunstable in the Trent and Modena collections; much of Power's surviving music, however, can be found in the Old Hall Manuscript. Dunstable's music exists solely in Continental copies, a fact which perhaps explains why some of Power's compositions were ascribed to him, for his was the bigger name in Europe though his tombstone, in St Stephen's Church, Walbrook, in London, mentions him as a mathematician and astronomer, and says nothing of his music; tables of latitude and longitude which he compiled for his patron are preserved in the Bodleian Library; a treatise of his own time mentions him as one of the Duke of Bedford's musicians. As the Duke was more or less permanently engaged in France from 1421 until after Dunstable's death, the absence of any of his music in important English manuscripts may be quite easy to explain.

Both Dunstable and Power were primarily composers of church music; there is no secular music by Power in existence, and as he spent his life singing in the choirs of the two cathedrals associated with him, this is not surprising. But Dunstable, whose precise position and functions at court cannot be ascertained, provided a little secular music. Despite the different routes their careers followed, the two English masters of the first half of the fifteenth century are composers who modernized the English harmonic tradition until it became a style which dominated European musical thought, and at the same time combined it with the rhythmic refinements worked out by the composers of the *Ars Nova*. By 1441 or thereabouts, Dunstable's work and example were accepted throughout Europe. A French poet, Martin le Franc, wishing to pay tribute to the leading composers of his own country, Dufay (*c*. 1400–1474) and Binchois (*c*. 1400–1460), praises them for having accepted and learned from the style of Dunstable:

> The English guise they wear with grace,
> They follow Dunstable aright,
> And thereby they have learned apace
> To make their music gay and bright.[5]

The English style, what Martin le Franc called '*le contenance Anglais*', is primarily a type of thought dominated not by the need to observe academic precedents and ancient rules, or by the mathematical rules of the *Ars Nova*, but by the need for frank emotional expression based on the idea that what matters is for music to sound good; neither Power nor Dunstable went on record as declaring beauty and effectiveness of sound to be of primal importance to music; they simply took the almost unprecedented step of taking care to write music which invariably sounded beautiful. Power, whatever plainsong he may have used in a work, was inclined to concentrate his attention on rich, ornate, expressive melodies in the soprano line of a composition though he never abandoned the delight in effects of grandeur and massiveness. Dunstabie, in such of his works as '*O rosa bella*' (Ex. 4), a secular canzone, and his motet '*Sancta Maria*', liked to build melodies out of notes that form the outlines of chords. The English style cared for lyrical expressiveness and used its unorthodox freedom of harmony to extend the length of musical line between cadences, while creating a sense of movement organized from cadence to cadence, rejecting the style of harmonization in parallel thirds and sixths which had been the conventional unorthodoxy of English music, as well as the standard Continental fourths and fifths which had been the basis of European harmony, in order to extend and make inevitable this sense of movement.

Dunstable's life is, from the point of view of the historian or the biographer, impossible to record in any detail; we do not know how so much of his music was preserved only in Italian manuscripts or whether he was able, at some time, to spend a considerable time in Italy; we do know that his patron, the Duke of Bedford, spent thirty years trying to maintain Henry V's empire in France. But the reference to the gaiety and brightness for which le Franc's poem praises Dunstable's compositions suggests that among the music that influenced him might have been a good deal of the popular English music that is preserved in medieval carols.

Power's music marks, in a way, the end of medieval music and Dunstable's the beginning of the Renaissance, though Dunstable's works do not jettison the techniques of the Middle Ages. His expressive lyricism still exploits the subtle rhythmic ingenuities of the *Ars Nova* composers, but does so without the dogmatic passion for keeping rules which was one of the principal features of *Ars Nova* music. It would be possible to argue that he was the first major composer to judge the effects he made not by their obedience to given rules but by their beauty of sound.

The Old Hall Manuscript and the career of Dunstable show how the increase of patronage by the Lancastrian kings created opportunities for musical ambitions to be realized. Henry IV was a musician remembered for his recorder playing. Henry V enlarged the Chapel Royal so that a permanent body was left in England while a chapel of equal size and ability could accompany him on his campaigns in France; this seems to have inspired the development of Burgundian music because the Duke of Burgundy was present at, and deeply involved in, the negotiations which preceded the

Ex. 4

Dunstable
(Instrument)
(Voice)
Ay las-so me Ay las-so me Ay las-so me
do-len - - - te der-o fi - ni-
- re Per ben ser-vi - re Et le -

Ex. 4 contd

signing of the Treaty of Troyes in 1420. The Duke of Burgundy seems to have been enlarging his own musical forces after he had heard those of Henry V, in emulation of the English King's magnificence. Henry VI was no less musical, until the civil wars after 1453 left little time or money for the cultivation of the arts. The Yorkists, Edward IV and Richard III, both kept up the standard of the Chapel Royal and increased its numbers. At the same time, they followed Henry V in using all the royal musical institutions as a sort of all-purpose group, employing both singers and instrumentalists for secular as well as religious purposes.

Similarly, within the Church there were influences which, by offering increased freedom from liturgical control, encouraged musicians to work ambitiously. The Colleges of Oxford and Cambridge grew up with choirs organized like those of the cathedral and collegiate churches but to a considerable extent free from the day to day control of diocesan bishops, who were often unsympathetic to the musical ambitions of precentors and cantors, while cathedral and collegiate church choirs found themselves increasingly encouraged to sing votive Masses as well as the rigorously controlled Mass of the day. A Votive Mass of Our Lady—in some churches a daily occurrence in the later Middle Ages—could be musically experimental because duty had been done to the compulsory plainchant in the Mass of the day. The Daily Mass, sung in the choir stalls, was the business of the precentor, fourth in rank of the cathedral clergy; any votive Mass was the concern of the cantor, whose preoccupations were almost exclusively musical while the precentor had to be concerned not only with the cathedral music but also with the observance of strict liturgical propriety; it was his business to see that what the *Book of Common Prayer* was later to describe as "the number and hardness of the rules called *Pie*" (which established an order of precedence among the saints to be commemorated on any given day) were properly attended to. The fifteenth century was the period in which the cantor rose to prominence.

The fact that two cathedral cantors became known outside their own cathedrals is in its way a surprising tribute to their eminence. All that is known of the life of Walter Frye is that he was probably Cantor at Ely Cathedral in 1443, a fact which suggests that he might have been a member of the choir at Ely and have risen in the ranks there; in 1447 he is listed as a member of a musicians' guild in London. One of his songs can be found in an English manuscript at Magdalen College, Oxford; the rest of his church music can be found in copies in the Bibliothèque Royale in Brussels, in the Escorial and in Trent; his songs and motets are in manuscript collections at Mellon and Schedel. One of his songs, '*Tant a pour Moy*', was used as a basis for Masses by several Continental composers, and he composed an '*Ave Maria*' which appears in thirteen Continental collections. The presence of a musician from Ely in the membership of a London Guild is no less mysterious than the apparent popularity of his music on the Continent.

Perhaps as much as a generation younger than Frye, Richard Hygons (d. 1509) became Cantor and Master of the Choristers at Wells in 1474. Hygons seems to have been a pupil of Henry Abyngdon (*c.* 1418–1497) who went to Wells Cathedral as Succentor in 1447 after service with Humphrey, Duke of Gloucester, and who died as Cantor of the Chapel Royal; Abyngdon, in 1443, became the first Doctor of Music at Cambridge. Hygon's life was less eventful; in 1487 he was granted an increase of salary in recognition of "his diligence and good service". He became organist at Wells, but there is no record of the date at which he did so. In 1507, perhaps because of advancing years, he began to pay forty shillings a year to his deputy, Richard Bramston, for teaching the choirboys; he died in 1509.

One of his works, a setting of the Latin hymn, '*Salve Regina*', is in the Eton College manuscript, a collection made between 1490 and 1502. During Hygons's time at Wells, a daily votive Mass of the Blessed Virgin Mary was sung in the Lady Chapel, and this became the cantor's responsibility, so that Hygons was paid extra for singing in the Mass of the day sung in the choir; the music of the votive Masses seems to have been entirely his responsibility.

Of course, such works as those mentioned here, and all those which have survived into the twentieth century, are but the small visible signs of what must have been the huge bulk of medieval music. The cantor's work, perhaps because it was principally involved in the provision of music for votive Masses and for vespers, encouraged experiment and exploration. The most profitable experiment of the fifteenth century, from the point of view of the music it produced, was the habit of substituting an unliturgical or even a secular tune for the fragments of plainchant of the decoration of a complete plainchant setting, which had been used as a *cantus firmus* for the composer to elaborate. Such use of secular themes was, like other Continental developments, slow to reach England while songs like Frye's '*Tant a pour Moy*' were seized upon for elaboration by composers on the Continent, like the song '*L'Homme armé*', on which every composer in Europe seems to have based a Mass. Although often enough composers used only a phrase or two from a well-known song to be their *cantus firmus*, the use of what originally had been secular music in church works, shocking as it was to those who could recognize the source of what they heard, added a certain vitality of rhythm to church compositions.

III
Music and the Tudors

Henry VIII was obviously a monster, but he was equally obviously magnificent. His monstrousness lay in his combination of uncontrollable power with a conscience which always conveniently supported the decisions of a powerful intelligence and a corrupt will. It was possible for Henry VIII to win the support of his conscience for the unthinkable and the intolerable. But he was a genuine and serious musician who, though it is extremely unlikely that he composed 'Greensleeves', did compose some songs like the sturdy, unsentimental and rather academic 'Pastime with good company'. He was a skilled instrumentalist, and in an age of galloping inflation, despite his incurable shortage of money, he did his best not to stint his domestic musicians. In addition to maintaining what he would regard as the traditional musical establishment which his predecessors would have found essential both for ceremonial and domestic use, he also recruited string players whose performance could be enjoyed in more intimate surroundings.

The Tudor inflation had a good deal to do with what we naturally regard as the 'Golden Age of English Music'. It created a poor monarchy and a deprived labouring class, but allowed the middle classes and the landowners to expand not only their wealth and power but also their culture. The King, with a more or less fixed income and political aims which, because they were dangerous, were costly, was always poor as a king after he and inflation had exhausted his father's treasury. The relatively new class of agricultural labourers suffered extremely and swelled the number of savagely and fruitlessly punished beggars. The landed gentry, and those whose money came from trade overseas, profited. "As the polite arts are the children of affluence," wrote Dr Burney when he considered the great outburst of musical activity in the fifteenth-century Netherlands, "and dependent upon superfluity for support, it is natural that they would thrive at this time." The days of Henry VIII prepared the way for the explosion of musical genius in the England of Elizabeth I. Henry VIII's tastes, like his choice of composers, was conservative and, at the same time, constructive. His court composers were expected to provide magnificence and colour, but little of the music of such composers as William Cornyshe has much to say to us today. It is restricted both in design and in its harmonic resources, and, like Henry's own 'Pastime with good company', does not put a single foot beyond the musical style of the part-songs written by composers more than a generation before.

The additions to the King's musical establishment, however, were not designed to add to its capacity for magnificence or to increase its power and splendour. It was the gentler, domesticated instruments which became more numerous. Throughout the Tudor period there were reductions in the number of brass players and drummers in royal employment to make room for more keyboard, woodwind and string players. The lists of players involved in great ceremonial occasions, transcribed by Henry Carte de Lafontaine in his book *The King's Music*, indicates the process at work. At the funeral of Henry VII, in 1509, there were two musicians simply set down as "minstrels", three described as "minstrels of the chamber", four players with sackbuts and shawms, twenty-six trumpeters, eight more "minstrels", eleven "children of the Chapel" and eighteen "Gentlemen of the Chapel and singing men". When Henry VIII died, thirty-eight years later, there were twenty "Gentlemen", eighteen trumpeters, five undefined "musytians", four sackbuts and shawms, six "vyolls", fife "fluttes", two "vyalls", a "fyfer", a drummer, a harper and a bagpiper. In addition there were others who did not take part in the funeral procession: the court also housed four lutenists, a virginalist, and three rebec players. This expansion of court music led to a considerable influx of foreign players. All the violists, a lutenist, two trumpeters, two flautists and two organists were immigrants, the violists Italian and one of the lutenists a Fleming.

The process continued in the reign of Mary Tudor; new Liveries were ordered for Italian players in 1555, after Edward VI's short reign had added a harpist, six violists, two flautists and two virginalists but dismissed three sackbut players. By the time of Elizabeth I's coronation, in 1558, six violists who had taken part in Henry VIII's funeral are written down as violinists. The gradual change from ceremonial music to private chamber music continued, slowly but surely.

At the same time, Henry VIII had, like his immediate predecessors, been concerned not simply with the size of his choir but with its musical standards, and it became his policy, followed by his children, to find places in the Chapel Royal for any composer who had won a high public reputation. Henry took care not only of the size of his choir, he also made sure that the Gentlemen, singing men and boys of his chapel were the best he could find, and at the same time his agents had not simply the power to impress boys with good voices but were under command to do so. The system of press-ganging potentially useful boys for the sake not only of their voices but also for their musical abilities, the Chapel Royal as well as for the cathedrals, seems to have been applied with some vigour. Thomas Tusser, the writer on matters agricultural, wrote of his experiences as a choirboy, first at Wallingford Priory, where discipline was severe and punishment both harsh and frequent, and then at St Paul's Cathedral, where Henry VIII's tutor, John Colet, was Dean, John Redford organist-choirmaster and the system far more humane. Needless to say, the King's Renaissance passion for education and learning made him care as passionately for their general education as for their musical training. Erasmus, the great Renaissance scholar, had been a choirboy and his experiences had left him with an ineradicable dislike for church music, but Tusser, who had developed an Erasmus-like hatred for Wallingford Priory, was reconciled to life in the choir by Colet's humanity.

Perhaps for the sake of his prestige, it was necessary for Henry VIII to grab the finest musicians available for his Chapel Royal. In 1518 Richard Pace, the Dean of the Chapel Royal, wrote to Cardinal Wolsey, demanding that the Cardinal handed over his solo boy to the Chapel Royal. The King had shown William Cornyshe, the master of his choir, that Wolsey's chapel was better than the King's, and wrote Pace, only Henry's affection for the great Cardinal prevented him from taking over Wolsey's entire establishment. There were accepted procedures by means of which choirboys might be taken over from a lesser institution into the

King's chapel; even the cathedral choirs were not sacrosanct, but in a tussle between the King and Wolsey over a point of pride, the King was not prepared to use official machinery to get his own way, and the boy was handed over. Dean Pace's letter was dated March 26, 1518; on April 1, he wrote again, reporting Cornyshe's praise not only for the boy's voice but also for the thorough training the child had received from Richard Pyggott, the Master of Wolsey's chapel. Pyggott himself became a Gentleman of the Chapel Royal in 1524 and Deputy Master of the boys in 1527.

Actually, Henry VIII's musicians were people whom the apparently ruthless King treated with a consideration not far from generosity; as the debasement of the coinage lessened the value of their salaries at a time of rising prices, the King did his best to see that their salaries rose to match the cost of living. Pyggott, although a layman, was awarded a pension at the dissolution of the monastery of Coggeshall, was given money from the abbey at Tower Hill and held a prebend at Tamworth. At the same time, he held his post in the Chapel Royal until his death in 1552 and was, apparently, highly regarded both by Edward VI and by the young Princess Elizabeth.

Henry's own song, 'Pastime with good company', is itself music in good company; the part-songs that were popular secular music at the time of its composition were songs in three parts, like the much earlier '*Angelus ad Virginem*', with the tenor carrying the musical weight. The royal amateur composer follows the most satisfactory models that he could find. The most impressive composer of the early part of Henry's reign was Robert Fayrfax (*c.* 1464–1521), appointed Gentleman of the Chapel Royal by Henry VII in 1496). Fayrfax held his post at court in conjunction with that of organist and choirmaster at St Albans Abbey from about 1498 until about 1502. He became Bachelor of Music at Cambridge in 1501 and was awarded his Doctorate in 1506. Seven years later he gained a second doctorate, from Oxford. He became a 'Poor Knight of Windsor' in 1514, and between 1516 and 1519 he seems to have been paid by the court for composing and supplying copies of his music. Then, in 1520, he was choirmaster of the musicians whom Henry VIII took to dazzle Europe at the Field of the Cloth of Gold. Unfortunately for us, most of Fayrfax's music survives not in score but in incomplete part-books. His work for the church is large scale, and set for five voices, with at least one voice missing from most works, so that complete scores have to depend upon conjecture. Fayrfax was obviously interested in music with varied textures; passages of powerful block harmony are broken by elaborately contrapuntal music, and both give way to passages for two voices, after soprano and bass, apparently intended for two solo voices. His Masses are among the first English settings of the liturgy to be unified by the employment of a motto theme used to introduce each movement.

His secular part-songs seem to have little of the ambition that marks his church music, perhaps because they primarily set out to satisfy the taste of their period, and a couple of interesting works are all that remain of whatever instrumental music he composed.

The next generation of composers, that of John Taverner, (*c.* 1495–1543), Christopher Tye (*c.* 1500–1570) and the great Thomas Tallis (*c.* 1505–1585) found, like Fayrfax, that the church demanded their most ambitious work and that the old-fashioned but socially acceptable three-part songs satisfied more or less all that was socially asked from them. Taverner became master of the choristers at Christ Church, Oxford, but in 1528 he was imprisoned for heresy and, after his release, he became one of Thomas Cromwell's agents in the dissolution of the monasteries and was, apparently, responsible for stamping out monasticism in the area round Boston, Lincolnshire. Music seems to have ended for him with his arrest, giving way to a fervent, fanatical determination to advance the anti-papal cause. Taverner composed a little instrumental music —a few *In Nomines*—and a handful of songs, but his greatness rests in the richness and mysticism of his music for the catholic liturgy. Like his contemporary, Tye, he used the song 'Westron Wynd'

Ex. 5a

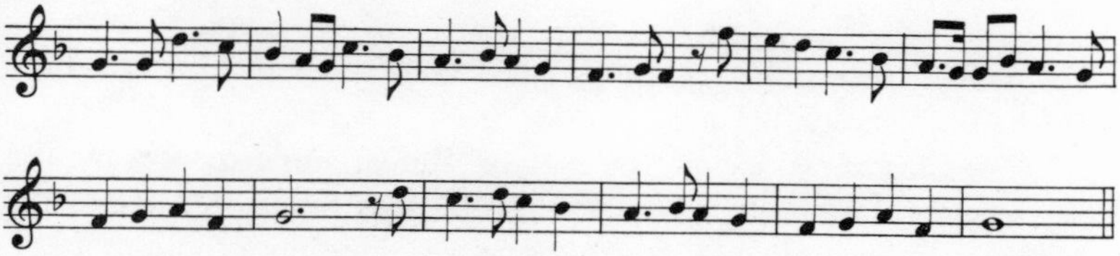

as the *cantus firmus* of a Mass in which depth of feeling is matched by intensity of technical ingenuity, the *cantus firmus* used with mathematical precision, used in full three times in each movement;

it gives rise to a four-note phrase, f, e, d, c, used throughout the work as an *ostinato* which links and unifies the entire composition.

Ex. 5b

This was a technique growing, by Taverner's time, increasingly dear to English composers.

Tye managed, it seems, to remain almost unperturbed by the religious revolution. In 1511 or 1512 he was taken into the choir of King's College Chapel, and became a singing man there in 1527. He was awarded a Doctorate at Cambridge in 1536 and became *Magister Choristarum* at Ely from 1541 to 1561. He, too, based a Mass upon the 'Westron Wynd' tune—music smooth and effective

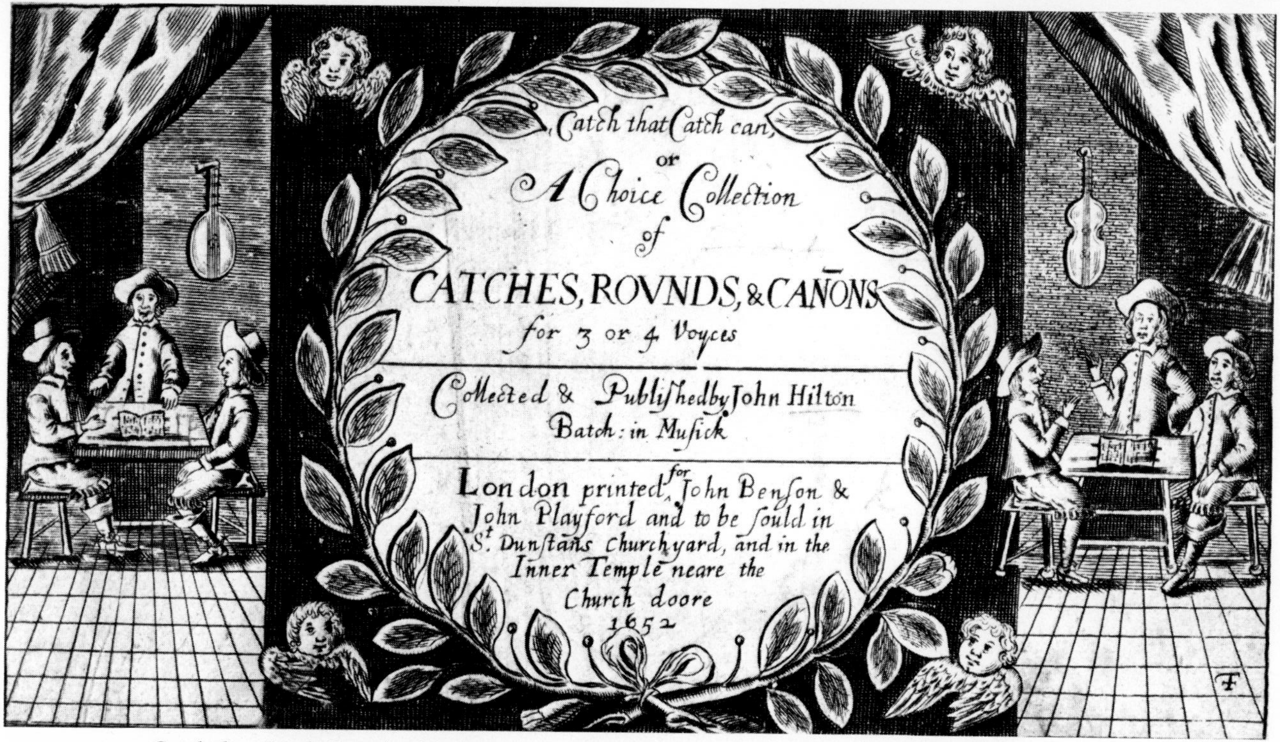

Catch that Catch Can, the title page of a collection of catches published in 1652. On each side of the title a group of catch singers is enjoying itself.

Thomas Tallis

William Byrd

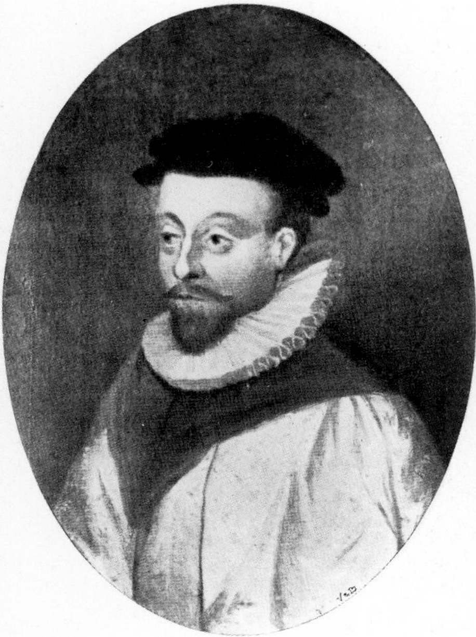

Orlando Gibbons

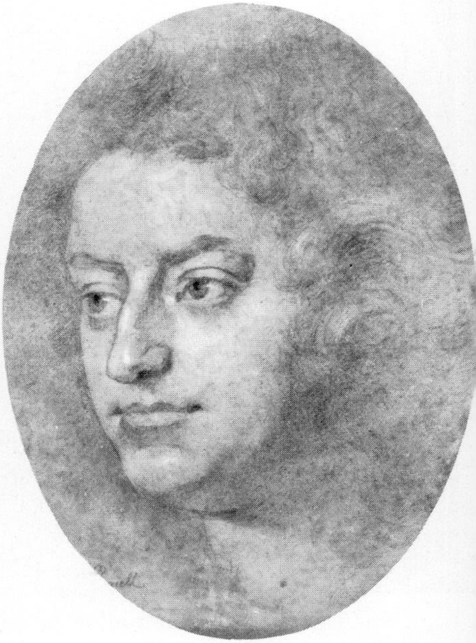

Henry Purcell

The Unton Picture (*detail*: the Masque frame)
Sir Thomas Unton was a courtier and ambassador who died in 1587. Around his portrait are grouped incidents from his career, including this banquet and masque, with a 'broken' consort of musicians surrounded by the masquers. The players have two treble viols, a transverse flute, a lute, a theorbo and a pandora (or bass lute). This was a combination of instruments specially recommended by Thomas Morley in his volume of *Consort Lessons*.

Hogarth: *The Rehearsal*. The singers are learning *Judith*, an oratorio by Michael Festing (?1680-1752), a violinist and composer who in 1727 led the orchestra at the King's Theatre in the Haymarket (the Opera). *Judith* was performed in 1731.

George Frederic Handel

Maurice Greene

Thomas Arne

Musicians in the Coronation Procession of James II (1685). From Sandford's *The Coronation of James II and Queen Mary*, 1687. *Above:* Trumpeters and drummer.

Above left: Choristers of Westminster Abbey.

Above right: The original artist was mistaken; the two sackbut players are not with a player of the Courtall (or primitive bassoon), but with a player of the alto cornett.

Hogarth: *A Musical Party.*

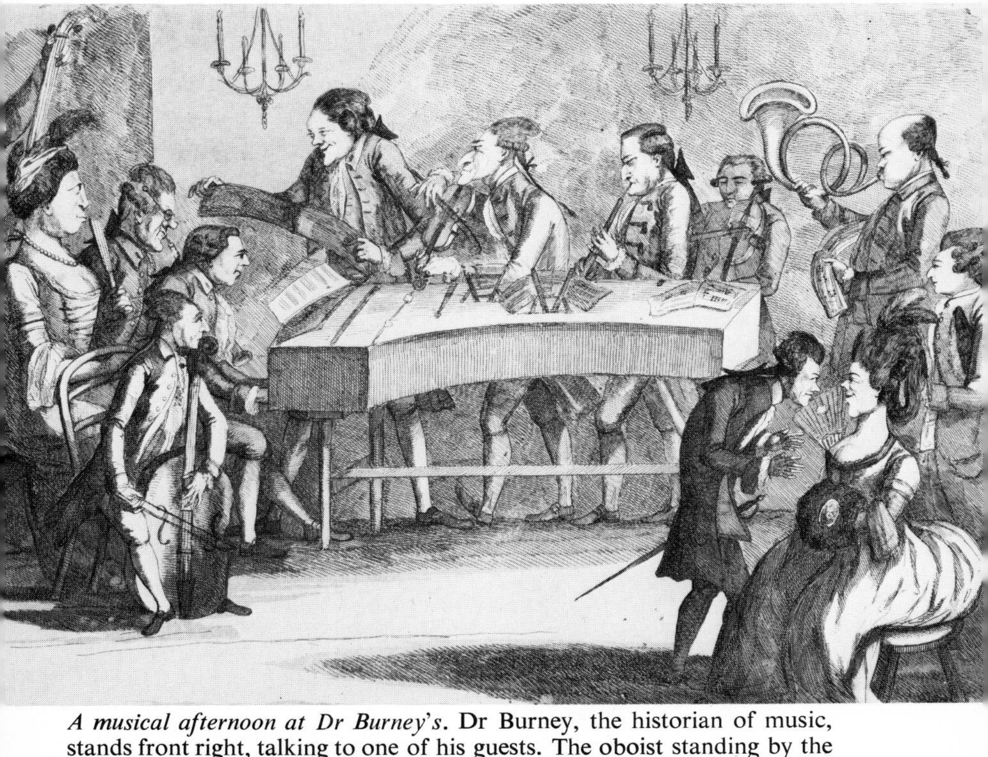

A musical afternoon at Dr Burney's. Dr Burney, the historian of music, stands front right, talking to one of his guests. The oboist standing by the harpsichord keyboard is Johann Christian Fischer (1733-1800). The horn player, who is holding his instrument in an awkward way to show that he has fitted a remarkable complication of crooks to alter the instrument's pitch, is Peltain, a French player well-known in England in the 1780s and 1790s. The caricature is by Loraine Smith.

London Publish'd according to Act of Parliament 1744
J. Maurer delin et Sculp.
A Perspective View of Vaux Hall Garden

The bandstand in Vauxhall Gardens.

in its emotional directness—but the advent of the first English Prayer Book in 1549 seems to have caused no interruption to Tye's work, nor did he suffer any spiritual or musical upheaval in his life and work. His account of the *Westron Wynd Mass* used the melody smoothly, for direct emotion, adapting its rhythm to the Latin text and providing new elaborations for its melody. His work to English text has the same fluency and mellow richness. Tye has been described as Edward VI's music master, though there is no document which confirms his appointment to this post, nor of his appointment to the Chapel Royal, which he himself mentioned in the Preface to his *Acts of the Apostles*, which he dedicated to the young King. This is a cycle of part-songs for four unaccompanied voices, or for lute and solo voice in which the Biblical text is adapted into neat four-line stanzas and the music aims at direct tunefulness; it is meant for domestic singing, and not as a contribution to the English liturgy.

Tye, for all the apparent pliability of his religious convictions, seems to have been a difficult, awkward man. Ordained, he lost a benefice because of his failure to pay tithes, and, according to Anthony Wood, he annoyed Queen Elizabeth by playing the organ in her chapel at too great a length and in a way that did not appeal to her; she sent a verger to tell him that he was playing out of tune, whereupon Tye sent back the messenger to say that the Queen's ears were out of tune. What Tye did, of course, was to compose music for the new Anglican rite in precisely the style he had used for the Latin rite, as did the great Thomas Tallis. A Gentleman of the Chapel Royal under Edward VI, Mary Tudor and Elizabeth I, Tallis had been organist at Waltham Abbey before the dissolution of the monasteries and a lay clerk at Canterbury Cathedral from 1641 until his appointment to the Chapel Royal, undisturbed, so far as we can tell, by religious controversy and agitation. Osbert Parsley (*c.* 1511–1585), according to his tombstone in Norwich Cathedral, was a singing man in the cathedral choir for fifty years; he died in 1585, the same year as Tallis. Parsley was another composer apparently happy to apply the style he had learned as a Catholic to the new rite, and had done so without in any way outraging his conscience.

"Music," wrote Thomas Fuller of Tye, "which received a grievous wound in England at the dissolution of abbeys, was greatly beholden to him for her recovery; such his excellent skill and piety that he kept it up in credit at court and in all cathedrals during his life." Tye has been called the 'father of the English anthem' because his anthems really founded the style which the Elizabethan composers exploited.

The relatively limited amount of secular music, either vocal or instrumental, by the composers whose careers straddled the religious convulsions of Henry VIII's rebellion against the Pope and his son's protestantism, Mary Tudor's return to Catholicism and Elizabeth I's search for an acceptable *via media*, contrasts sharply with the flood of music, both religious and secular, which poured out of England in the second half of Elizabeth's reign. There is a sense in which this flood clearly indicates the extent of the Tudor social revolution. A composer from England or from mainland Europe, Catholic or Protestant, has to earn his living; he did so by writing music that is, so to speak, 'of use'. Therefore composers became church musicians, writing service music and motets, or service music and anthems; this was an established career, and it set the musician into contact with an audience. He was under no compulsion to publish his music—Tye, for example, seems to have had no interest in publishing his music for the Church, either before or after the breach with Rome and Elizabeth I's establishment of a Church of England, but he immediately published his *Acts of the Apostles* as music intended for social, informal, and domestic use among amateur singers. Throughout his life he was a member of the Church, working to glorify its services, paid for his membership and for the work which he did, knowing that the Church would make immediate use of anything he wrote; the *Acts of the Apostles* had to find the singers and players to whom it would be of use, and only publication would enable it to do so.

This, perhaps, more than its intrinsic musical quality, is the important fact about Tye's composition. It was addressed to a new audience for performance under new conditions. It presupposed that there were in England singers and players enough to make viable the idea of a published cycle of religious part-songs, arranged so that they could be performed in a number of ways—in four-part vocal harmony, as vocal solos with lute accompaniment, with the lute filling in for any missing voices, or with lute accompanying the vocal ensemble. Part of its usefulness was its adaptability. The

Acts of the Apostles is the precursor of the flood of songs for educated amateurs which makes it more or less reasonable to describe the fifty years or so from 1570 onwards as a Golden Age. It was the age when English people wanted to make music and sufficient of them were trained to do so to make the publication of compositions a reasonable commercial venture. The music of Henry VIII's court was old-fashioned in sixteenth-century terms; the work of Tallis, the youngest of the great composers whose music was heard in Henry's reign, handles Continental styles and techniques with vigour, intensity and inventiveness but was designed almost exclusively for highly-trained, specialist choirs.

Tye's *Acts of the Apostles* is one of the first works to indicate the existence of what might be called the English market for compositions designed for the use and pleasure of amateur musicians in their own homes, but Tye's work did not immediately inspire other English composers to follow his example. During the reign of Mary Tudor (1553–1558), a great deal of Italian and French music reached this country, to be welcomed (or so it seems) by enthusiastic amateur musicians. The age was dominated by an energetic, adventurous middle class which had gathered money well enough to enjoy its leisure with music, to buy and to study instruments and to enjoy part-singing; imported music fed the taste for music as a domestic pleasure and, in the second half of Elizabeth's reign, English composers had reached a situation which they could supply what was needed. The demand for church music continued undisturbed, and the call for secular instrumental music offered another outlet for composer's energies. The English composer did not necessarily have to find a private patron who could employ him and keep him in conditions which would encourage him to work ambitiously; few of the English composers depended on private patronage because the middle-class amateur market provided them with the equivalent financial reward but left them free to work in their own way. The members of the Chapel Royal, for example, held their positions whilst holding other posts as, for example, cathedral organists and choirmasters; it seems that the Tudor monarchs, Elizabeth I in particular, regarded membership of the Chapel Royal as a way in which the work of good composers could be subsidized even when such composers were known to spend a good deal of their time elsewhere.

Tallis, Tye and Parsley, secure in traditional positions, worked through the religious revolution as though, musically speaking, there was no essential difference between a church ruled by the Pope and a church ruled by a King under an Act of Supremacy, or between the Catholic liturgy and the Prayer Books designed and revised by Archbishop Cranmer in 1549 and 1552. Tallis and Tye, musicians of great authority and reputation, and the more obscure Parsley, living in the provinces far from the centres of power and controversy, seemed to be quite oblivious of the doctrinal points at issue though men enough lived by them and died for them. Naturally the Church of England, like the Catholic Church, had to fight out the perennial battle about the position of music in worship. Just as the Council of Trent, in the 1560s, seemed likely to forbid polyphonic music in the services, and had almost decided to do so while at the same time banning the use of the organ and other instruments to accompany a choir, and to forbid the use of Masses with any secular *cantus firmus,* many Anglican authorities were equally eager to achieve a total simplification of music in cathedrals and collegiate churches. The struggle between the claims of music and the desire for primitive simplicity was at least a thousand years old by the time that there was a Church of England to consider the rights and wrongs of the polyphonic style as a handmaid to religion. Erasmus, who had learned as choirboy to hate music, declared, "There was no music in St Paul's day, but words were pronounced then. Words seem to mean nothing nowadays. . . . If people want music, let them sing Psalms, and not too many of them."[6] And there were plenty of later authorities among the Anglicans who hoped to see the end of polyphony and all other music elaborations. John Marbecke (or Merbecke) (*c.* 1510–*c.* 1585) was one of the two organists of St George's Chapel, Windsor, whose earlier works had been conventional settings of liturgical texts. In 1550, only a year after Cranmer's first Prayer Book had been compiled, he published his *Book of Common Prayer Noted* to organize all the music the Church of England would need. Marbecke found a style of more or less modernized plainchant into which he adapted many of the traditional Roman chants and in which he composed many more, using notes with four time values but remaining within the medieval modes. Cathedral music was, however, a powerful vested interest and composers, usually engaged to control the choirs for which they wrote, continued to apply to the *Book of Common Prayer* the musical style which their predecessors had developed for Latin services. Five years after the accession of Elizabeth I, in 1563, Convocation debated a resolution to order the removal of organs from churches; Bishop Burney's *History of the Reformation* says that the resolution was lost by a single vote. The Anglican attitude, however, finally coalesced into something essentially more traditional that its extreme Protestant wing could tolerate, but by 1594 Richard Hooker's *The Laws of Ecclesiastical Polity* reached what have been ever since the essential Anglican formulations:

Musical harmony is a thing which delighteth all ages and becometh all states; a thing as seasonable in grief as in joy; as decent being added unto actions of great weight and solemnitie as being used when men must sequester themselves from action. The reason hereof is an admirable facilitie which musique hath to express and to represent to the mind more inwardly than any sensible mean the very standing, rising and falling, the very steps and inflections every way, the turns and varieties of all passions whereunto the minde is subject.[7]

Therefore, as a source of inspiration, music has its place in worship though nothing can be more 'pestilential' than bad music; it is good music that has its secure place in worship.

But by the time Hooker's book reached its readers, a crisis in English music had been passed. Elizabeth's religious attitude, at least insofar as such matters as music, ceremonial and the use of a formulated rite are concerned, was essentially conservative and traditionalist, and though in 1559 injunctions were issued limiting the extent of music and ceremonial in the services—music must never be allowed to obliterate the words—she nevertheless insisted that services in her own chapel should be sung with organ accompaniment on normal days, and on feast days by sackbuts and cornets. She had been Queen for only two years when, in 1560, she issued commissions allowing all boys, except those of St Paul's Cathedral and of her own chapel, to be impressed into cathedral choirs, and in 1580 she allowed the impressment of boys from St Paul's.

The impressment of choirboys shows that there was a shortage of trained musicians especially noticeable in the younger end of the profession, and musicians throughout the reign were therefore agitated about prospects for the future. There was no general educational doctrine about the need for music teaching and the towns, where there were grammar schools, tended to follow puritanical ideas and devote whatever education was available to subjects which could be regarded as practical. In Protestant Germany, Luther's dominating position insisted on the value of music as a subject for study as well as a delightful practical skill, but in England, while music flourished in some schools, in many others it slipped almost entirely out of the curriculum. In 1589, for example, the governors of Christ's Hospital, where singing and instrumental music had been fostered, decreed that no boy should be apprenticed to a musician except "such as be blinde, lame and not able to be put into any other service." Thirty years later the retired actor, Edward Alleyn, founded the school which eventually became Dulwich College, insisting that mattins and evensong be sung in the chapel daily as they were at Westminster Abbey and the Chapel Royal; but Alleyn's ambitious musical plans ran counter to general trends, conflicted with the puritanism of south-east England and the demand for practical education, so that although the College of God's Gift (Alleyn's name for his foundation) employed organists of considerable authority, like Benjamin Cosyns, music never featured so prominently in the school as its founder had intended.

With musical education thus declining, musicians in the 1570s and 1580s began to ask how standards could be maintained in cathedrals and elsewhere as the current musical staff of such institutions retired or died. At the dissolution of the monasteries, all professed members of religious orders received a pension which Henry VIII took the trouble to pay very punctiliously. But as well as professed monks and nuns, the monasteries employed workers of all sorts, including musicians; we simply do not know how many musicians were thus employed, or under what conditions, and we do not know what became of them. If the great churches, as well as the monasteries, lost their music, the necessity for any sort of strict, advanced musical training would vanish, for it was the great churches with their choir schools which provided advanced musical education.

The situation was described by Thomas Whythorne (*c.* 1528–1596) in his *Autobiography*. Whythorne, apparently in his forties, had published his *Book of Songs and Sonnets* in 1571; it was the first surviving book of madrigals published for some forty years, and his *Autobiography* seems to have been written some five years later. As Whythorne's *Songs and Sonnets* are composed for three, four and five voices, they have earned their composer the title 'Father of the English madrigal'. Twenty years later he published a book of duets, for treble and bass, for two trebles or for two equal voices; each of his books has a wordy preface, that of 1591 explaining the various ways in which the music can be performed with instruments or with an instrument replacing one of the voice.

Whythorne was sent to New College School and then to New College by his uncle, who died before Whythorne had completed his education. The young man, not really qualified for the musical career which was his aim, began to earn his living as a tutor and confidential servant in the homes of prosperous middle-class people, the new gentleman of the Elizabethan period, living always in terror of the widowed mistress, or the unmarried daughter of the scheming housekeeper who could entice him into matrimony. The publication of his *Songes for Three, Fower and Fiue Voyces* won him the right to specialize in music, and he became Master of Music in the private chapel of Matthew Parker, Archbishop of Canterbury. Parker encouraged him to write church music, so Whythorne set to work on the Archbishop's own translation of the Psalms into metrical verse. His *Autobiography* comes at the crisis of cathedral music and analyzes its causes. Whythorne's English is quirky, with a sixteenth-century addiction to exhaustive lists, and it is written in an 'orthografie' of his own devising which has the strangely un-English merit of complete phonetic consistency, but for the sake of ease in reading it needs to be reduced to normal illogicality.

> *In Time past* [he wrote] *music was chiefly maintained by cathedral churches, abbeys, colleges, parish churches, guilds, fraternities etc. but while abbeys and colleges without the universities were suppressed, then went music into decay. To speak of music in houses, you shall understand that divers noblemen and women, in times past, imitating the Prince, would have organists and singing men to serve God after the manner of that time in their private chapels. But that imitation is also left. Then for such as served for private recreation in houses, which were for the nobility* and

worshipful, were no less esteemed than the others, till *that time the rascal and scum of the profession, who be, or ought to be, called minstrels (although nowadays many do calle them musicians) these, I say, did and do make it common to every jack, going about to every place for the same purpose.*

Now I will speak of the use of music in this present time [Whythorne continued]. *First for the church, ye do see and shall see it so slenderly maintained in the cathedral churches and colleges and parish churches, that when the old store of musicians be worn out which were bred when the music of the church was maintained (which is like to be in short time) you shall have few or none remaining except for a few singing men and players on musical instruments, of which ye shall find very few or none that can make a good lesson of descant, and yet these would be accounted musicians although there be none worthy of the name except they can make a song of two, three and four parts and so upward according to the true rules thereof.*[8]

Since the coming of Christianity, the church had been the centre of musical education and of 'learned' composition; now there was a diminishing and ageing band of properly trained musicians and no recognized means by which the supply could start to flow again. On the other hand, there were 'speculators' who could neither play nor sing but who could slavishly observe the rules of composition and, so to speak, compose only in the abstract but still claim to be the musical superiors of those who could play and sing from a score.

In 1581, a pamphlet by Thomas Case repeated Whythorne's lament for the decay of traditional musical learning, and in 1597 Thomas Morley's *A Plaine and Easie Introduction to Practicall Musicke* mourned that "musicke, by reason of the negligence of its professors, is almost falled into the nature of a mechanical art, rather than to be reckoned among the other sciences."[9] Morley's book is set out in question and answer form and purports to be the lessons given by a skilled teacher to a mature but ardent student who finds himself in social disgrace because he cannot sing from a part-book after supper at a friend's house; host, hostess and fellow guests looked at him in amazement, as though wondering where he had been to be brought up in such ignorance. The passage is one on which a good deal of conjecture about the 'Golden Age of English Music' has been based, but perhaps Morley was only exaggerating the desirability of musical knowledge as a way of advertising his text book. We understand his strictures on the state of music a few years before the Golden Age, and the earlier laments of Whythorne, as we read the book; in order to sing after his supper, the student has to learn all about music, so that by the time he reaches the end, and we reach it with him, he cannot only read music but can also write it according to the accepted rules. Its doctrine is that music has its grammar and accidence which can be mastered by any intelligent, diligent student, and that to be a musician means not only the ability to read a vocal line in a part-book or to pay one's recorder or viol accurately; to be a musician is to understand and to know how to use music's various resources. The student is, of course, unlikely to write anything of value, just as teaching him his letters will not really make him an epic poet, but at least he will write something musically literate.

Our information about private patronage in Elizabeth's England is not so null and blank as is our information about such aspects of musical life as the musical organization of the theatres; though there is not a great deal of information about the patronage offered by the wealthy, only complaints that those who could afford to do so enticed useful choirboys away from the organizations that needed them; at times, even singing men were taken from cathedral and collegiate church choirs into private service. One highly musical family was the Petries, who lived at Ingatestone Hall, in Essex. Friends of the great William Byrd, the Petries were Catholics who, despite their religion, had bought themselves church lands at the dissolution of the monasteries; they later joined the Church of England. When Byrd visited them, in 1559, John Petrie, the head of the family, paid six shillings and eightpence to bring the boys of St Paul's Cathedral to sing at Ingatestone. The boys returned a year later to sing at the wedding of Petrie's daughter. When Byrd visited the Petries, five musicians were brought from London, and the family account books make a note of the prices, and cost of repair, of the instruments available for them to play—organ, virginals, cittern, lute and viols. Payments to itinerant musicians—waits, a Welsh harpist and minstrels—are mentioned from time to time, but the only professional musician at Ingatestone Hall was 'John the Frenchman', apparently the family's music master and general musical expert.

The Kytsons, of Hengrave Hall, Suffolk, were music lovers on a much grander scale. Their collection of instruments, carefully catalogued, included six viols, six violins, a case of seven recorders, four cornutes, an archlute and a lute, a bandora (or pandora) and a cittern, two sackbuts, two oboes, a curtal (primitive English bassoon) and a lyserden (bass cornett). There were also two flutes, a pair of "little virginals", a wind instrument "like a virginals", a "great pair of double virginals" and a "pair of great organs; in the church". There was vocal music for ensembles of four, five and six parts, one collection specially mentioned as Italian, and a considerable amount of instrumental ensemble music, mostly in dance forms. Among the professional musicians connected with the Kytsons was John Wilbye (1574–1638), possibly the most exquisite perfectionist among English madrigal composers, who lived at Hengrave Hall from 1595 to 1628, when he retired to live in considerable affluence; he had the lease of the Kytsons's best sheep farm, and he owned property at Diss (his birthplace), Bury St Edmunds and elsewhere in Suffolk. In Wilbye's case, patronage worked well. There were also Edward Johnson (whose dates are unknown) and Robert Johnson (*c*. 1583–1633); the two may have been relations. Edward Johnson wrote some of the music played before Queen Elizabeth on her visit to Lord Hertford in 1591, contributed to East's Metrical Psalter, was made Bachelor of Music at Cambridge in 1594 and contributed to *The Triumphs of Oriana*, the collection of madrigals presented to Elizabeth I in 1601. Robert Johnson was appointed one of the lutenists of James I in 1604 and remained in royal service into the reign of Charles I. He wrote not only vocal works but also keyboard music and music for viols.

IV
The Golden Age

The Golden Age of English music, to which Tudor social and musical developments led, was relatively short-lived. In a sense it was, like the parallel Golden Age of English Drama, little more than an interlude between political and religious convulsions. The Spanish Armada failed in 1588, and its failure seems to have created an unusual and splendid self-confidence. By the early 1620s, the cracks in English society which Elizabeth I had hidden by papering over, had showed themselves to be extremely deep and extremely wide both in religion and in politics, and the great creative period was over. The Golden Age of music was co-terminous with the Golden Age of the theatre, although music did not fall so steeply as did the theatre in the closing years of James I's reign.

Certain Elizabethan characteristics are, perhaps, essential to any golden age: creative self-confidence is one of them. The creative artist, in an age of creative self-confidence, can feel that both he and his patrons and his audience in general are moving swiftly and purposefully to a generally approved goal; his artistic presuppositions are shared by the vast bulk of his audience, and his personal idiom does not, by its nature, exclude anyone as the personal idioms of, say, a Delius, an Elgar or a Vaughan Williams exclude those who are out of sympathy with natural grandiloquence, pantheistic meditation or traditionally-minded progressiveness. In a golden age, creative artists work inside, and serve, a tradition which is still open enough to allow each of them his own personal style of utterance; he can fulfil himself within the general tradition which is wide enough and inclusive enough to allow space for development in every direction.

At the same time, as composers were working in the same

inclusive style and in an idiom which united them to their audience while remaining elastic enough to permit them great individuality, they were never left without an audienoe. An attachment to the Chapel Royal provided a considerable number with a basic salary, and there were other court posts available, for it was possible for a composer to hold a post at court and yet be attached to other institutions. For example, Thomas Weelkes (?–1623) described himself in his volume *Airs or Fantastic Spirits*, published in 1608, as a "Gentleman of His Majesty's Chapel, Bachelor of Music and Organist of the Cathedral Church of Chichester".

It is hard to tell, from the information we have, the extent to which composers profited from the publication of their works. The publication of music was at least potentially a profitable business; this is clear from the amount of music in all forms that has survived —church music, madrigals and other concerted vocal works, consort music and, after 1612, keyboard works. The relatively late appearance of *Parthenia, or the Maydenhead of Musicke, The first musicke that ever was printed for the Virginalls*, seems to have been due to the difficulty of reproducing the ornate keyboard style of the period with proper accuracy and clarity. *Parthenia*, printed from engraved copper plates, must have been an expensive book, just as the virginals was an expensive instrument to own. We know that the entire first edition, apparently 1000 copies, of John Dowland's *Third and Last Booke of Songes or Ayres*, in 1603, was sold out in the year of publication and that his *First Booke of Songes* (1597) went into a second edition in three years and reached a fifth edition in 1613. His *Second Booke* was equally successful. Dowland (1563–1626) was apparently Irish, and as young man travelling in Germany he became a Catholic; his conversion seems to have been responsible for the fact that he spent most of his life until the late 1590s in Europe, where his reputation as a virtuoso lutenist stood extremely high. In 1588 he became a Bachelor of Music at Oxford, and received the same degree at Cambridge at some time within the next ten years. He applied for court employment from Elizabeth in about 1594, but was without official employment until, in 1612, he became one of King James I's 'Musicians for the Lutes'. To what extent he profited from the success of his music with publishers, or whether the profit was all theirs, it seems impossible to determine.

In 1575, Queen Elizabeth had granted Tallis and Byrd (who were perhaps, master and pupil), a licence which gave them a virtual monopoly of printed music in this country; there was, of course, some typically Elizabethan wrangling with the printers when the two monopolists declared that their licence gave them control of lined manuscript paper. But in 1577 the two told Elizabeth I that in spite of their licence they were losing money in Royal service; Byrd in particular claimed that his duties at the Chapel Royal made it impossible to attend to as many pupils as he expected, and that he had sacrificed a good salary as organist of Lincoln Cathedral in order to serve the Queen. Elizabeth silenced their complaints by granting them a profitable lease.

Possibly neither Tallis nor Byrd knew how to make the best of their monopoly. Thomas Morley (1557–1603) seems to have become organist of St Giles, Cripplegate, in 1588, the year he graduated as Bachelor of Music at Oxford, then he seems to have been organist of St Paul's Cathedral. He became a Gentleman of the Chapel Royal in 1592, and in 1598 he was granted a licence to print music and music paper for twenty-one years. Working through professional printers to whom he 'assigned' work for publication, he was responsible for the appearance not only of his own music and that of other English composers but of anthologies of works by foreign musicians, most of them Italian.

A golden age, and there have been very few, also earn its title by exploiting every style available to its composers and by developing familiar styles in music that is memorable, original and revelatory. The English Golden Age had everything except dramatic music, and though it invented little except the lute song, it carried everything it touched to a high, idiosyncratic point of development if not to a conclusion. If the climax of grandeur and sonority came early, in Tallis's '*Spem in Alium*', his motet for eight five-part choirs (that is, for forty real, independent, contrapuntally motivated parts), it was Byrd, the Catholic, known to be a catholic in spite of his membership of the Chapel Royal and his music for the Anglican Church (knowing that his huge set of *Gradualia* for the catholic services was unlikely to be heard in England and must exist as a private act of devotion, and, perhaps, of penitence for his compromise with the schismatic Church of England) whose music often seems to express intensities of deeply personal, tragic religious devotion. Apparently Byrd's catholic music was known on the Continent, where several English composers who remained catholic chose to work. Among them were Richard Dering (*c*. 1580–1630) and Peter Philips (*c*. 1565–1640), and such composers seem to have spread Byrd's reputation in catholic Europe.

By the 1580s, the direction that was music was to take in the Church of England had become clear. The Marbecke setting survived and remains to this day a viable treatment of the Anglican services, but the danger of inevitable war with Spain, Queen Elizabeth's own cautious conservatism and the genius of the musicians who handled the still relatively new text gave Elizabeth's church its own, personal, unmistakable devotional way. There was no English Luther, whose passion for music and whose power as leader of a successful revolution insisted that the musical tradition should be preserved: the English musical tradition, so to speak, preserved itself by modifying itself to meet the demands of the new Middle Way.

Not only Byrd but a variety of other composers used Latin texts when, it seems, the Latin language appealed to them; only Byrd chose to make any comprehensive collection of Latin liturgical settings. The music of the Church of England grew apart from that of the Roman Catholic Church, not through any careful design on the part of the new church and its composers or of the Queen, but by virtue of the developing character of the Church of England itself. A vast amount of settings of the Prayer Book services and anthems came into being because the Anglican Church had its traditional musical organization but no traditional repertory of its own. It was natural for organists and choirmasters to deal with the texts which had to be sung, especially since their treatments of frequently heard texts would bring their work to general public notice. The only specific Anglican invention came in the anthem, which first found its ways into services before the death of Henry VIII, but which was not given its appointed place in the services until the 1662 revision of the *Book of Common Prayer*, after the Restoration of Charles II, fixed its position. The prose writers and apologists of the Church of England gave the Church a way of sober, dignified music which became the voice it adopted for its music. It was Morley who was responsible for the most effective innovation, the 'verse anthem', with a solo voice alternating its music, often verse by verse, with the choir; other anthems, without solo voices, were designated 'full anthems'. Morley's setting of Psalm 139—'Out of the Deep'—is one of those new works which seems to have come to life without the need for experiment or any process of trial and error. Byrd, too, wrote verse anthems, and the style developed until, in Orlando Gibbons's 'This is the Record of John', it achieved one of the outstanding masterpieces of English music. The text is the investigation of John the Baptist by the priests and Levites sent to enquire into his teaching and authority; the solo voice is that of a counter-tenor, accompanied by viols; the choir is unaccompanied. Gibbons, like other later composers, found new texts for anthem settings in the words of the Prayer Book collects themselves.

Outside the cathedrals and the few collegiate churches, there was little Anglican church music. The parish church in town or in the country had little or no music except that to which the psalms were set in metrical translation. The 'Old Hundredth', a tune exceptionally popular in England, is typical in its slow, stately dignity, of the music which the average English congregation associated with church-going.

The music brought into being by the development of the Church of England was impressive; it included settings of the services written in short form or extensively, as 'full' settings at first and then in 'verse settings', analogous to the 'full' and 'verse' anthems. The works of the composers we know as the English madrigalists are, perhaps, more startling because they do not carry on a tradition or follow a precedent. Between 1530 and 1587, only one book of secular part-songs was published—Whythorne's *Songes for Three, Fower and Fiue Voyces*, which appeared in 1571. Between 1587 and 1630, eighty-eight collections of pieces for vocal ensemble appeared, containing not far from two thousand separate works; many more remain in manuscript. The term 'madrigal' is applied to all this music, though composers like Morley carefully distinguished between madrigals, balletts, canzonets and other forms which are now regarded as lighter than true madrigals. There was nothing in the Italian madrigal denoting any special seriousness; the canzonet could be lighter to the point of frivolity, while the *ballett* (often, from its refrain, known as a 'Fa-Ia') was a vocal dance form based on the Italian *Frottola*.

In his secular vocal music, as in his work for the church, Byrd was the composer most concerned with intensities of emotional expression, often achieved through elaborate and sometimes disturbing cross rhythms. Byrd's style, in secular as well as in religious music, often led him to build considerable works out of motives drawn and developed from some grand, eloquent, regularly formed tunes, imitating and repeating these motives in the voices that are not immediately concerned with its statement.

Byrd and Morley provided the aesthetic justification for the musical style. In 1611 Byrd published his last major collection of works. The title-page reads: "*Psalmes, Songs and Sonnets:* some solemne, others, joyful, framed to the life of the words: Fit for Voyces or Viols." Music, to Byrd and his contemporaries, did not simply express the emotions of the poetry it set; it grew out of the words.

> *You must have a care that when your matter signifieth ascending, high heaven and such like, you must make your musicke ascend: and by the contrarie where your dittie speaketh of descending, lowenesse, depth, hell and such others, you must make your musicke descend, for it will be thought a great absuditie, to talke of heaven and point downwards to the earth.*[10]

The idea of music feeding directly from words in this way applies not only to the idea of motion, like the movement 'up' and 'down' to which Morley draws attention as being something so obvious that it hardly needs saying; 'speed', for example, and 'slowness' give rise just as immediately to illustration (just as Bach, a hundred and fifty years later, puts down the mighty in his *Magnificat* by sending them crashing down a clear octave). Insofar as a composer makes such illustrative patterns integral to his musical design, the passion for direct illustration is anything but an unsophisticated way of doing what seems to be entirely obvious. Thomas Weelkes's contribution to *The Triumphs of Oriana*, 'As Vesta was from Latmos Hill descending', is a madrigal for six voices; it continues with the words "She spied a maiden Queen, the same ascending". Of course, 'ascending' and 'descending' give rise to patterns of falling and rising figures, not only to a descent of more than an octave in its tenor, and to a similar, light-footed climb (would Elizabeth I have allowed herself to appear breathless as she made her way uphill?) but to a passage in which the ascending Queen is greeted by shepherds coming first "two by two" and then "three by three", and the number mentioned is the number of voices involved. This apparently over-literal treatment of words works admirably—just so long as the composer was able to think of text and music as a single entity and not as two separate forms, one demanding subservience of the other—because these composers lived in an age which delighted in expressive language no less than in expressive music.

This literalness in treatment was not restricted to the madrigal and the secular forms of ensemble for voices; it applied no less strongly, and with the same possibilities for eloquence, to religious music, and to emotive words, as well as to those suggesting movement. The sixteenth piece in the first book of Byrd's *Cantiones Sacrae* warns the Christian to be watchful so that his Lord, at the second coming, will not find his follower sleeping. There is a passage full of the haste with which the Lord may return; it refers descriptively to the cuckoo and considers the plight of any sleepers, any *dormientes*, whose eyes seem to shut in spite of themselves and their good intentions; the music explains that they cannot, however much they will to do so, bestir themselves.

Ex. 6 Byrd

The art is not so much the adornment of words or the use of a text to give music some necessary motive power; it is a complete union of words and music sharing the same expressive life.

We have found it convenient since the days of the composers themselves to speak of their ensemble vocal pieces as madrigals. Byrd's secular vocal music was collected in three volumes, which he himself named: *Psalmes, Sonnets and Songs of Sadness and Pietie* (1588), *Songs of Sundrie Natures* (1589), *Psalmes, Songs and*

Sonnets (1611). Morley published his *Canzonets* for three voices in 1597, his *Madrigals* for four voices in 1594, his *Canzonets* for four voices in 1594, and his *Balletts* for five voices in 1595, distinguishing between the different types of work by the titles he gave them.

The crucial date for England, however, was 1588. Until then, apart from Whythorne's 1571 collection, there was no new or even recent music available for enthusiasts, but in the quarter of a century which followed an enormous number of madrigals (to use the term generally, as English composers used it) came into print. The first volume was an anthology, *Musica Transalpina*, collected by Nicholas Yonge, a London business man who may also have been a singing man at St Paul's Cathedral. Yonge's dedication explains that

Since I first began to keep house in this citie, it hasth been no small comfort unto me, that a great number of Gentlemen and Merchants of good accompt, (as well as this realme as of foreine nations) have taken in good part such entertainment of pleasure, as my poor ability was able to afford them, both by the exercise of Musicke daily used in my house, and by furnishing them with Bookes of that kind yeerely sent me out of Italy and other places, which being for the most part Italian songs, are for the most part for sweetness of Aire verie well liked of all, but most in account with them that understand that language. As for the rest, they either do not sing at all, or at the least with little delight. And albeit there be some English songs lately set forth by a great Maister of Musicke, which for skill and sweetness many content the most curious; yet because they are not many in number, men delighted with varietie, have wished more of the same sort. For which cause I have endevoured to get into my own hands all such English songs as were praise-worthie, and amongst others I had the hap to find in the hands of some of my good friends certaine Italian madrigals translated most of them fiue yeeres ago by a Gentleman for his private delight (as not long before certaine Napolitans had been Englished by a very honourable personage, and now a Counsellor of estate, whereof I have seene some but never possessed any). And finding the same to be well liked, not only of those for whose cause I gathered them, But with many skilfull Gentlemen and other great Musicians, who affirmed the accents of the words to be well mainteined, and in the descant not hindered (though some fiue notes altered), and in everie place the due decorum kept: I was so bold (being well acquainted with the Gentleman) as to entreate the rest, who willingly gave me such as he had (for of some he kept no copies), and also some other more lately done at the request of his particular friends.

The demand for madrigals, in other words, preceded the published supply, and *Musica Transalpina* contained fifty-seven works, including a setting by Byrd of Italian words (a poem by Ariosto retranslated, in Yonge's book, into English). Lassus, Marenzio, Palestrina and Ferrabosco the Elder (who worked in England from 1562, when he was nineteen, until 1578, when he returned to Italy leaving his children behind, one of which, Ferrabosco the Younger, was to make a great reputation as a composer), as well as lesser masters, were represented, and though the English translations have no particular lyrical merit, Yonge brought out a second volume in 1597, offering another twenty-four works.

If Byrd's madrigals achieve the greatest emotional power allied to the most adventurous techniques, Morley's the most wide-ranging appeal, and those of Wilbye and Weelkes the greatest stylistic perfection, one of the wonders of the period is not the creation of masterpieces by a handful of outstanding composers but the large number of musicians who found in the madrigal a natural, unstrained mode of self-expression. We can turn to music of relatively obscure composers—Bennet, Ward, Bateson, Ford, Pilkington, Johnson, Farnaby, John Cooper (the first English musician who found it advantageous to impersonate a foreigner and who preferred to be known as 'Coperario') among others—as well as to the real Italian, Alfonso Ferrabosco (1543–1588), who had settled in England by 1562 and left his family in England when he returned to Italy in 1578, and his son, Alfonso Ferrabosco II (1575–1628), who wrote not only vocal music but also music for viols which reached a very high stature in what was really an almost entirely English form. The 'English Madrigal School' continued at least until 1622; the last survivor of the great period, Thomas Tomkins (1572–1656), one of the contributors to *The Triumphs of Oriana*, seems to have written little during the last half of his life; Tomkins's work rivals that of Byrd in emotional intensity.

The composers of madrigals, however, regarded themselves as

all-purpose composers writing works 'fit for voices and viols'. Instrumental music, however, divorced from words and voices, and written apart from the dance, not only grew up but won popularity along with the madrigal. The habit of playing viols in consort, or in 'broken consorts' of mixed string and wind instruments, seems again to have preceded a traceable repertory for the instruments. The viols' effective range was more or less that of the human voice to which it was analogous. The viols, tending to huskiness of voice, were not athletic, and their upper reaches were not developed, so that vocal part-music could sound natural and graceful when played by them; none of them developed a solo repertory of its own.

The earliest purely instrumental music in this country, as elsewhere, owed a great deal to the general style of the motet. It exploits the motet's tendency to use words as a mere abstract, often unintelligible prop for music that is entirely abstract. Instrumental forms, as they first appeared apart from the social necessities of dancing, often adopted a plainchant theme as a *cantus firmus* round which the various instruments played; some or all of the antiphon *Gloria tibi Trinitas*, sung at Vespers on Trinity Sunday, was the most popular source for instrumental explorations, particularly in the form in which the antiphon appears in Taverner's Mass, *Gloria tibi Trinitas*, as it appears sung to the words of the *Benedictus*, "*In Nomine Domine*"; this given *cantus firmus* melody remained

Ex. 7

popular as a framework and point of departure for instrumental works from the time of Henry VIII until that of Purcell, and though a number of composers wrote *In Nomines* without the plainchant theme, in Taverner's or any other treatment, the term always meant a work in which a theme was treated to contrapuntal, *faux bourdon* or *cantus firmus* type elaborations. Scholarly treatments of this kind had originally been the preserve of church music, and the handing over of the *In Nomine* to instruments and the secular world as a more or less abstract form of self-expression indicates as clearly as anything in Elizabethan and Jacobean music the growing self-confidence and independence of secular composition.

The Fantasy, or Fancy—the terms are interchangeable—indicates that the music follows not any prescribed form of treatment but simply its composer's imaginative bent. To Morley, in his *Plaine and Easie Introduction,* "The most principall and chiefest kind of musicke which is made without a dittie is the fantasie, that is, when a musician taketh a point at his pleasure, and wresteth it as he list, making either much or little of it as shall seeme beste in his own conceit. In this more art is shown then in any other musicke, because the composer is tide to nothing but that he may adde, diminish, and alter at his pleasure."[11]

The term fantasy itself, however, dates back, so far as surviving examples show, to the time of Taverner and a work composed by him apparently in the 1530s. Tye left a couple of dozen or so fantasies, all close to the *In Nomine* in style. When the Italian fantasia reached England, English composers, easily influenced by anything that came from Italy, found a new freedom in a marriage between their traditional instrumental music and the Italian style. The opening and closing sections became fugal so that the central sections, for the sake of contrast, became homophonic, and the various sections tended to adopt contrasting tempos. The *In Nomine* aimed at a completely seamless texture, the various themes evolved by its counterpoints coming into prominence before the *cantus firmus* had reached its cadence so that the music moves to its conclusion without pause or interruption, while in a fantasy the composer made definite breaks between sections, sometimes marking each of them with a cadence and a double bar before setting off again on a new, though allied, section.

There was never an impassable gulf between the 'art music' of the great composers of the 'Golden Age' and its popular music. Taverner, Tye and others found the plaintively beautiful melody of the 'Westron Wynd' folk-song capable of inspiring a richly devotional setting of the Latin Mass; Gibbons, in a work larger in scale than most of his secular music, married the London street-traders' cries and songs to a string *In Nomine* which would be satisfactory music without the five voices which interpolate authentic street-sellers' calls, beggars' pleas, a town crier's announcement and a chimney sweep's song into its grave, polyphonic texture. Dering (1590–1630) used many of the same 'cries' in a similar composition as well as basing another on what he called 'country cries'. Snatches of similar melody find their way into the fantasies and other instrumental pieces of Byrd and his contemporaries. In the words of A. L. Lloyd, "During Elizabeth's time and for a while after, the new high-art music which had grown up mainly as a result of the secularization of church music, absorbed a good deal of popular song and dance melody into itself."[12] In a six-part fantasy, Byrd uses the tune we know as 'Greensleeves' as well as 'Walsingham' and other allusions to popular tunes. It was possible, as it has rarely been possible since and as it had not been possible before, to think of Elizabethan and Jacobean England to be united in culture as well as in its assertion of national independence.

The cultural unity is evident in the Fitzwilliam Virginal Book, which by its nature was a collection of music made by well-to-do musicians, not the compilation of professional musicians who might have wished to put easy-going, catch-penny music at their disposal for the sake of its popular appeal. Of the two hundred and ninety-seven pieces contained in the collection, a large number seem to have been given the title Fantasy as the most convenient label available for an abstract instrumental work, and a large number are not content with simple allusions to popular melodies recognizable through the artistic treatment they are given; they are treated to elaborate variations in the advanced contemporary style; in keyboard arrangements, for example, using instruments which had no sustaining power, this inevitably meant elaborately decorative figurations playing round what, in songs or strings arrangements, would be long sustained notes (Ex. 8). Byrd alone, in *Parthenia*, is represented by variations on 'The Carman's Whistle', 'John Come Kiss Me Now', 'All in a Garden Green', and 'The Woods so Wild' amongst other folk-songs; 'The Woods so Wild' turns up again in the fantasy *Ut-re-my-fa-sol-la*, a duet piece in a style familiar to Elizabethans, in which one player repeats the first six notes of the scale, ascending and descending, as a ground bass in very slow notes, while the second player treats them to elaborate variations; 'The Woods so Wild', in this work, is discovered to go happily in counterpoint with another popular song of the time, 'The Shaking of the Sheets'.

Ex. 8

The madrigal was transformed into later styles, as was the fantasy, but the great days of virginal composition lasted from about 1560 for a hundred years and, like many other things in English music, was transformed by the Restoration of the Monarchy, and the personal tastes of Charles II. The other glory of the 'Golden Age' was the lute song, which flourished for no more than a quarter of a century. Songs with lute accompaniment go back at least to the reign of Henry VIII, but the lute parts of such early songs are really transcriptions of music for other instruments or for voices. In 1597, Dowland's *First Booke of Songes or Ayres* was published. Four years later Thomas Campion (1567–1620) published *A Booke of Ayres, set foorth to be song to the lute orpherion, and base Viol.* Dowland's songs, though their ideal performance asks for no more than a single voice and a lute, were published with optional vocal parts to make them accessible to any vocal ensemble. In 1622, John Attey (?–1640) published the last collection of lute songs, and with them the usual wise precaution of optional parts for the other members of a quartet of singers, and then the form fell out of use. Between 1597 and 1622, however, composers were content to publish such works primarily as solo songs.

The lyrics which gave rise to this spate of music brought an established tradition to its culmination. Though most of Chaucer's poetry exists independently of music—Chaucer was not primarily a lyric poet—John Gower noted that "the Land fulfilled is over all" with Chaucer's "ditees and songes"; this statement preceded Caxton's printing press, so it can only mean that Chaucer's verses were passed around verbally, like folk-songs. Tudor poets expected their words to be sung even when they seem to us to defy music. Donne, often a knotted and convoluted poet, declares that he is "two fools, For loving and for saying so In whining poetry", but realizes that, "When I have done so, Some man, his art and voice to show, Doth set and sing my pain." The younger Ferrabosco set his poem 'The Expiration', for example. The poet did not feel that his lyrical work was complete until it had found acceptable music. The poets were not yet aware of hackneyed themes, and if Donne's intense individuality, for instance, seems too explosive to marry a smooth melodic line, it would have been difficult almost to the point of impossibility for Donne's contemporaries to have thought of his lyrics without music. The novelty of the lute song in 1597 was not the setting of words to melody—the obvious thing to do with verses, after all, was to sing them—but the use of a single voice in a solo song with instrumental accompaniment rather than the use of four or five or six voices in a performance of the after-dinner sort for which the madrigal composer worked; the solo accompanying instrument was ideally to be played by the singer himself. Byrd's songs, characteristically long-breathed, intense and balancing intensity with scholastic, technical depth, preferred accompaniment by a consort of viols. His elegy for Tallis, 'Ye Sacred Muses', begins contrapuntally—the instruments weaving a pathetic web in madrigal style which allows the singer, when he enters, a considerable freedom of declamation, but it develops into a passionate vocal expression of grief with the viols, at the end, following the singer's lead.

Few of the lute songs go so far as even to consider such complexity; they offer freshness and directness of melody against an accompaniment that is usually harmonic, as though the natural thing to do is to work out the harmonic implications of a melody rather than to treat its melodic properties as a subject for counterpoint. To Campion and to several of the other song composers, the lute song seems to have appealed as an escape not from the intensity of polyphony but from its technical complexity. Campion, as an amateur composer—he was a physician by profession—may have felt himself to be ill-equipped for work in more intricate forms. When Campion grows technically adventurous, he does so through experiments in rhythm as in his Catullus setting, 'My sweetest

Lesbia', a song in which his determination to reproduce in notes the quantitative rhythm of Latin poetry puts his song into a strait-jacket.

Campion's metrical experiments are an indication of the unity of music and poetry in the minds of both poets and composers. Because it was necessary to the composer to ensure the vitality of each poem, they were concerned with a freedom of declamation within the pattern of the music. Even in the strophic songs with the simplest harmonic accompaniment designed, almost, for the merest strummer, the poem is left room to breathe for itself and to live under its own terms. Even the most sophisticated songs by John Dowland and John Daniel (1565–?1630) never constrain the poem although, in a sense, the aim of Dowland was to create, within the limitations of the solo song, a richness of texture comparable to that of the madrigal but in terms of the lute itself. Both were expert lutenists, Daniel at the court of James I, and Dowland for a time at the court of the King of Denmark, and both had international reputations. In the hands of such players, the lute was capable of accommodating polyphonic music; in Dowland's more ambitious songs, the madrigalesque interplay of voice and accompaniment almost invites the suspension of established rhythmic and melodic patterns as further emotional enrichments and intricacies. The slow songs are often pavanes, the faster songs galliards, the dance forms lifted, so to speak, like waltzes by Chopin, into abstraction but, like all the music of their period, they are never a great distance from folk-song. Dowland's speciality was the expression of melancholy, like the motto he punned on his own name—*Semper Dowland, semper dolens* (Always Dowland, always doleful). His song '*Lacrime*' ('Tears') became enormously popular as an expression of a mood which seemed to be deep in the consciousness of the period (Ex. 9). For all its artistic freedom and subtlety of expression, it is perhaps as near as music can be to an expression of the mood of *Hamlet* and *Measure for Measure*, and it is more often referred to than any other music of the period in the age's literature and drama. Dowland himself arranged it as seven Pavanes, each more desperately sad than the last, and it exists in a remarkable number of instrumental arrangements and adaptations by Dowland's contemporaries.

The world of keyboard music at the time was one of often extrovert brilliance. The keyboard instruments for which the composers

Ex. 9 Dowland: *'Lacrime'*

Slow
1. Flow, my tears, fall from your springs,
2. Down, vain lights, shine you no more,
Ex - iled for e - ver let me mourn Where
No nights are dark e - nough for those That
night's black bird her sad in - fa - my sings, There
in des - pair their lost for-tunes de - plore, Light
let me live for - lorn.
doth but shame dis - close.

wrote often imposed extreme difficulties on their work and on that of the player who attempted it. The instruments offered no possibility of great power or spectacular display; there was, as well, no possibility, except when writing for the organ, of sustained tone, 'long' notes or extended melody. To create the impression of sustained tone, of extended notes held as long as the composer would wish, he was compelled to invent elaborate figurations which emphasized the required note, so to speak, by leaving and returning

Ex. 10

to it, as Byrd did when using '*Lacrime*' as the subject for a fantasy. The virginalist composers seemed inexhaustible in their ability to devise decorative filigree work to compensate for their instrument's shortage of breath.

Keyboard instruments were unusually costly in themselves, and players who were willing to equip themselves so expensively might easily have been taken to be endowed with rarefied, exalted tastes, providing occasion, or at least excuse, for musical intellectualism. But the music provided for players who were apparently wealthy and aristocratic amateurs blessed with good education was never remote from the general taste of the period. Byrd's keyboard music included, as well as fantasies based upon popular songs, elaborately worked, precisely written dances and a musical battle characterizing rival armies, the marching and counter-marching, appropriate trumpet calls, evocations of the sound of guns and clash of swords. The real, historic John Bull (1562–1628)—oddly enough, his portrait shows a slim, serious-looking, Italianate Renaissance gentleman—was for a time organist of Queen Elizabeth's chapel, doctor of music at both universities, the first Gresham Professor of Music and active at court until 1614, when he removed himself without leave to the Continent and became organist of Antwerp Cathedral. According to Antony Wood (1632–1695), historian to Oxford University and an enthusiastic chronicler of musical events, "he did in that dishonest manner steal out of England through the guilt of a corrupt conscience, to escape the punishment which notoriously he had deserved, and was designed to have been inflicted on him by the hand of justice, for his incontinence, fornication, adultery, and other grievous crimes." Bull, Wood noted, was "possessed with crotchets as many musicians are". But he was an international celebrity for his skill as a keyboard player, and in an age when the way for a keyboard player to become famous was to demonstrate legerity, neatness, precision and grace, he composed not only a handful of choral works probably imposed upon him by his long service in the Chapel Royal, but a wealth of virginal pieces of spectacular difficulty to perform but not to understand.

For all their passion for music and the pleasure they took in writing, the Elizabethans left us with less knowledge of the part played by music in the theatre than would be helpful. We know that actors and their apprentices were taught to sing, and that the presence of a good singer capable of strumming his own accompaniment on a lute was always a signal to Shakespeare to add a sung lyric or two to comment on the action. The apprentice who played Lucius, Brutus's page in *Julius Caesar*, could be trusted in this way to prepare the atmosphere for the appearance of Caesar's ghost after the quarrel and reconciliation with Cassius. The original player of Ophelia had a good deal of singing to do, and Desdemona has her Willow Song. Such musical comment on the action, offered by the characters involved in the action, is an obvious enrichment of drama. Nevertheless, even the musically gifted among the players cannot take time off to play consort music as an aphrodisiac for Orsino, in *Twelfth-Night*, or to march and countermarch, playing oboes beneath the stage as "The god Hercules, whom Antony loved, Now leaves him." Actors are not likely to be available to become musicians in Cordelia's camp and play soothing music to ensure that King Lear wakens from madness into serenity, nor can they be responsible for the variety of drum and trumpet calls which are part of every Shakespearean battle. The staff of a theatre must have included musicians, some eight or even ten of them, who provided all the music needed except dramatically placed songs.

Who these players were, how they were recruited, and under what conditions they joined the various actors' companies are things outside the existing records. There is the nameless boy in *Measure for Measure*—his part in the play is too brief for him to deserve a name—who lives at the moated Grange simply to sing, "Take, O take those lips away . . ." to the deserted Mariana; he must have been an apprentice, and an acting apprentice or we should not have been likely to hear his voice; instrumentalists were not actors and did not, except in scenes of unusual pomp, show themselves upon the stage.

Similarly, we have no clear notion of their repertory. We can track down Sir Toby Belch's catch and the fragments of song that Falstaff sings from time to time; the lyrics which slip into the action exist in settings which could well be those actually sung in the original productions; there could have been two apprentices in the company in 1599 capable of singing Morley's setting of 'It was a lover and his lass' (going straight into the song without any hawking or spitting). But we have no idea as to the identity of the strain with "a dying fall" which fed Orsino's love for Olivia, just as we do not and cannot know the dance music which so neatly fits the sonnet by which Romeo and Juliet got to know each other.

The only certain fact is that the theatres had their own musicians, usually incarcerated in the top gallery, over the balcony stage. Sometimes the London or Southwark waits, remembering their monopoly of public music-making, seem to have taken action against them, and the theatre proprietors seem to have paid the statutory fine, in these circumstances, without much repining. Perhaps, sometimes, the theatres used the local waits as their orchestra; when the Citizen who makes a nuisance of himself in Beaumont and Fletcher's *The Knight of the Burning Pestle* takes his new wife to the theatre, he demands that the waits of Southwark be brought to play to make up for the theatre's lack of oboes and "stately music", and nobody seems to be outraged by his demand.

The boys' companies (of the choir schools of St Paul's and the Chapel Royal) are referred to in *Hamlet*, because they so upset the First Player of the company which makes its way to Elsinore to play before the Prince of Denmark because the children's companies had won enthusiastic public audiences and were, apparently, responsible for the lack of patronage which sent the professional players on tour. The boys' companies had their own, and seemingly very accomplished, musicians. In the professional companies, at least some of the instruments belonged to the theatre. Philip

Henslowe, whose daughter married the actor Edward Alleyn and who owned the Rose Theatre and the Theatre in Newington Butts as well as more questionable establishments like a bear pit, and who became Alleyn's partner in the Fortune and Hope Theatres, kept a diary of day-to-day expenses; from this it seems that some of the actual instruments in use were the property of the players themselves, while other instruments were bought for them by the theatre. There are references to the buying of a sackbut, two trumpets and a bass viol, some of which they bought from, or through the instrumentality, of, one of the Royal musicians.[13]

By the turn of the sixteenth century, however, Morley seems to have begun to interest himself, as publisher, on music for the theatre. In 1599 he published *The First Booke of Consort Lessons*, an anthology of six-part works, for an ensemble less frequently provided with music than a four-part consort; it was described as for "... the treble lute, the pandora, the cittern, the base flute and the treble viol." Philip Rosseter (?1568–1623), who succeeded to Morley's licence for music printing, published a collection of *Lessons for Consort* in the same year as Morley's volume, as did Anthony Holborne, whose title was *Pavans, Galliards, Almans and Other Short Aers.* The more colourful broken consort (that is, of mixed winds and strings) offered a wide range of tone colours that could be regarded as appropriate to almost any stage situation that demanded music. Such a consort did not, however, exhaust all possible theatrical demands: when Sir John Falstaff entertained Doll Tearsheet at supper at the Boar's Head, in Eastcheap, he booked "Sneak's Noise" to provide the music, and a "noise" was a brass ensemble, distinct from the "musitians" who were booked to escort Juliet to her marriage to the County Paris. But Shakespeare's company must have had brass players to play trumpets, and these were probably the same players who dealt with other incidental pieces; any trained musician was, in the sixteenth and seventeenth centuries, able to play a variety of instruments.

The *Consort Lessons* of Morley and Rosseter might equally well have been designed with an eye on the demands of the waits, who in several cities were renowned for their quality. When the Royal Exchange was opened in the City of London, the City waits were ordered by the Queen to make music from its balcony every afternoon for the entertainment of the citizens, while the waits of other cities seemed to make occasional tours; those of York were paid for performances in Nottingham in the June and September of 1597, as though on the outward and homeward journeys of an extended tour. The Norwich waits went on Sir Francis Drake's 1596 expedition against Cadiz, taking with them "three new howboys, one treble recorder and one saquebut". Probably they took strings with them too, for only four years later, when the comedian Will Kemp danced a Morris from London to Norwich in 1600, he was greeted at his destination by "such Waytes . . . few cities in our realm have the like, none better. Who, besides their excellency in wind instruments, their rare cunning on the Vyoll, and Violin; their voices be admirable, every one of them able to serue in any Cathedrall Church in Christendoome for quiristers".[14] We do not know what the waits played, but until 1600 and the arrival of suitable printed music, they probably had their own arrangements of the popular tunes of the day.

V
Music and Political Turmoil

To describe the English 'Golden Age' as a prolongation of the styles and attitudes of Renaissance composition into a later period would be to simplify musical complexities beyond anything justifiable. Even the use of the phrase 'golden age' itself might be contested, for it was entirely an age of change. The changes which manifested themselves in Italy in the first two decades of the sixteenth century moved Italian composers towards the baroque style, a startling revolution; and were present in English music, where they worked less startlingly, as though they were the product of an innate conservatism slowly yielding to the inevitable.

We could, for example, argue that the fantasy exploited by the English composers of the 'Golden Age', held in its alternation of homophonic and polyphonic sections, as well as in its alternation of slow and fast episodes, the beginning in English music of the baroque notion of contrast as a structural element in music, as a manifestation of the concerto principle as the baroque composers of sixteenth-century Italy understood it. Of course, the development of the verse anthem and the verse service in Anglican Church Music can be seen, without distorting the evidence they provide, as the development of an English baroque in minds naturally conservative and traditionalistic in outlook.

The other strand from which the Continental baroque style developed was a new passion for just, precise and declamation which would reinforce the poetic quality of a text, point its rhythms and establish the pattern of its intonation. The early experiments of Florentine composers, which led to the operas of Peri and Caccini in 1597 and 1602 were, so to speak, the rebellion of the text against music. English composers never permitted that rebellion to succeed, but the English Lute song was often allowed sufficient freedom to allow poetic rhythms, and the life of the text to determine musical form. Opera, with the concerto, became the essential forms of the baroque period, but English composers were not drawn to opera. The triumph of early Italian opera was really the triumph of Italian recitative, and recitative never triumphed in England. The Jacobean composers found themselves satisfying an official demand for the masque, a form designed originally to show the greatness of the monarch; in the words of James I, "These outward and indifferent things will serve greatly for allurements to the people to embrace and follow virtue." The masque was essentially an action carried out with the greatest lavishness and magnificence in the presence of the king, celebrating his power and justice, and the unity he brought to his realm. The splendour of a show which embraced music, scenic design, verse and action was attractive enough to force its way into the commercial world of the public theatre, so that such plays as *The Winter's Tale* have scenes in which the appeal of the masque is exploited, and *The Tempest* contains a genuine masque scene in the entertainment provided by Prospero to mark his acceptance of Ferdinand as a suitable suitor for his daughter's hand. The commercial theatres, however, could not attempt to rival the lavishness of dance, design, costume and decoration achieved in the court masques of the first Stuart Kings. The masque did not, however, evolve into genuine opera but, indirectly and in increasingly popular styles, became a way to ballad opera, musical comedy and the modern musical, all of which use music and dance as decorations of a primarily spoken drama. The English more or less decisively rejected opera in the early, formative years of the form.

The masque normally accepted music not as the vehicle of drama, which is what opera became in the hands of Monteverdi, when in 1607 he composed *Orfeo*, but as a pleasant decoration to spoken drama except when, in the hands of a playwright, it was used to make a dramatic point. The stage drama was, often enough, necessarily trivialized and limited by the need to accommodate song and dance. The dance music through which Romeo and Juliet work out the sonnet that marks their first meeting is music embodied in drama; the music and dance of the sheep-shearing festivities at which we find Perdita and Florizel cannot be more than a decoration, enjoyable but adding little to Shakespeare's tale of forgiveness and redemption. Once it lost its foundation in court propaganda, the masque naturally contained enjoyable music and charming dances, but it did not deal in the emotional intensities of the drama or offer anything to disturb its audience. Opera, as a new art form, reached England with the strictly classical aesthetic which it had developed to advance among intellectuals in Florence as a means of recreating the glories of ancient Greek tragedy. It set out to convey the points of intensity reached in the discussion of events enacted off-stage.

To the Florentine pioneers of opera, the drama of Shakespeare and his contemporaries must have seemed, however remarkable the poetry and the rhetoric it embodied, crudely sensational, rejecting not only the classical disciplines of dramatic art (to which opera clung devotedly), but also the 'unities' which insisted that drama could enact only such events as might have occurred in a time equivalent to that of the performance, in a single place which the stage could represent, and admitting no sub-plots or extraneous events. English drama was not only unclassical but it vulgarly (in the eyes of the classically minded) exploited such shocking incidents as the killing of Desdemona, the duel of Hamlet and Laertes, the blinding of Gloucester and even the cooking and eating of the enemies of Titus Andronicus.

The neo-classical masters of primitive opera, intending to recreate what they believed to be not only the spirit but also the style of ancient Greek tragedy, accepted music as something parallel to the poetry of the classic tragedians, a meditation on the events of the drama meant to draw a moral from them. English audiences, brought up in a tradition through which Shakespeare and his fellows had achieved work of the highest imaginable standard in which character and significance are revealed through and in action rather than in its later consideration, never totally succumbed to the lure of the classics. Because the English theatre had developed its own style and techniques, evolving from an original crudity and sensationalism to tragic and comic forms of unusual effectiveness and richness, adaptability and power, opera in the early stages of its career, and, indeed, until the end of the baroque period had little to offer audiences which found in the theatre the sense of form, the emotional expressiveness and the richness of comment at which the composers of the early operas aimed. In addition, the English theatre gave its patrons a wider world than the composers of early operas wished to explore; it had, for example, room for comedy and wit in tragedy, for sub-plots to offer their own reflection, true or distorted, of a main theme. To the Continent, a century or so later, English drama of the great age was a barbarous form, while opera, a development from classic drama, seemed to the English to be a static and unnatural form.

England, therefore, lacked opera until the 1690s. Two isolated works by Blow and Purcell made English opera feasible, although their example was neither followed nor developed. The masque, played at court or in the houses of the rich, more often than not used music simply as the theatre used it but on a larger scale. Shakespeare, at the end of his career, was prepared to experiment with the masque, as he did with Prospero's "insubstantial pageant" in *The Tempest*, or in other words, to use it is an attractive adjunct to the real business of drama. Though Ben Jonson wrote lines in a court masque marking them to be sung as recitative, they seem to have worried nobody and impressed nobody, perhaps because a court masque was written not only to glorify the monarch but also to provide an opportunity for everybody present to dance; the masque was normally, despite its lavishness in settings, costumes, designs and machines, the curtain-raiser to a more conventional social evening. Milton's *Comus*, produced at Ludlow Castle in 1643 with an elaborate and attractive score, is a masque in that it demands settings, costumes and dancing, but it asks for little more than a minimum of singing and is complete in itself, hardly encouraging its audience to end in a general jollification, so that it is a moral drama rather than a masque as the term was generally understood; in the early eighteenth century, when it became extremely popular in the public theatres with music by Arne and rival settings by others, Milton's poem was changed and expanded to provide more lyrics for singing.

Henry Lawes (1596–1662), the son of a vicar choral at Salisbury Cathedral, was a pupil of John Cooper, who called himself 'Coperario'. Lawes became a member of the Chapel Royal in 1626; in 1634 he provided the music for *Coelum Britannicum*, a masque by Thomas Carew apparently responsible for Lawes's appointment as music master to the family of the Earl of Bridgewater and therefore for the composition of *Comus*. The score, like all Lawes's music, shows that he was aware of the operatic revolution in Italy,

Ex. 11 Lawes: *Comus*

Sweet E-cho sweet-est Nymph that livst unseen
Within thy air-y shell by slow Me-ander's margent green
And in the vi-o-let embroider'd vale Where the love-lorn
Nightingale Night-ly to thee her sad song mourneth well.
etc.
etc.

and that he was prepared to take from the new style such tricks of rhythm, declamation, orchestration and harmony as he felt to be useful to his purposes, but he was not swept away by delight in novelty.

Lawes's other works include paraphrase settings of the psalms for voice with thorough-brass accompaniment—another sign of the influence of modern music from Italy—a set of psalm paraphrases for three voices, and songs from contemporary plays and poetry. Like Milton, the poets of the period were all delighted to have their texts handled by Lawes because he was scrupulously precise in dealing with the scansion and prosody of the words he used. His normal style pitched itself somewhere between the simple declamation of recitative and the lyrical expressiveness of his English predecessors, and this stylistic devotion to the legitimate claims of poetry was probably more than anything else responsible for Milton's admiring sonnet:

> Henry, whose tuneful and well-measured song
> First taught our English muse to scan.

Milton, really, was too good a musician to have escaped with so extravagant a compliment unrebuked—Campion (who was poet as well as composer), Morley, Dowland and all their contemporaries set out to care for poetry but not with Lawes's concern for semi-recitative types of declamation—Lawes was the product of a new age which was prepared to accept poetry, and not music, as the determining factor in the making of a song.

Thus English music moved into a new age without what, in Europe, was the most startlingly effective element in the new music; the masque did not grow into opera, and English opera was a later a rival. The other arm of the revolution, however, which established the new, vertical conception of harmony as a series of chords working towards a cadence but gaining tension and expressiveness by postponing its arrival, became a part of English technique with comparatively little difficulty; they had already begun to move towards that concept when composers first decided that such forms as the lute song would be more effective if the fundamental bass line were played by a viol and thus given sufficient weight always to be within a listener's awareness.

A similar hardly conscious movement towards new techniques began to be felt in cathedral music, although works written for the church are the least likely to be affected by changes in style. William Child (1606–1697) trained as a boy in the choir of Bristol Cathedral, and became one of the organists of St George's Chapel, Windsor, in 1632; the Chapel Royal was disbanded in 1643, and Child lived as a music teacher, composing church music for his own pleasure until his reinstatement in 1660 at the restoration of Charles II. The music which he wrote during the interregnum shows no awareness that its composer was slipping into a new style, and his music is most impressive when it is least consciously affected by the new music. After the Restoration, when Charles II's tastes demanded innovations—anthems with overtures and orchestral ritornelli, a rhetorical treatment of texts and the other baroque developments, Child seems to have remained a pre-Civil War composer, moving only slowly and apparently unconsciously towards new ideas.

William Rogers (1614–1698), the son of a choirman at St George's Chapel, became organist at Christ Church, Dublin, and spent the years of the Civil War and the Commonwealth as a music teacher in Windsor. He made his reputation with a set of *Airs* for four violins and organ and, after the Restoration, became organist of Eton College and a lay clerk at St George's Chapel. In 1669 he went to Magdalen College, Oxford. Rogers, too, was a transitional composer, writing naturally in the rhetorical, harmonically motivated style while keeping his feet firmly in the Anglican tradition, effecting a short-lived but often impressive compromise with the new age.

It is the nature of church music to cling to tradition and to depart from it only slowly. Other forms of music changed more rapidly, the madrigal more startlingly by requiring accompaniment. At first this accompaniment was from a bass which could be figured to show the harmonic development of the work. In a short time, English composers were moving along the route first explored by Monteverdi in his publications after 1605, accompanying madrigals with free-moving, independent instrumental parts. The madrigal, however, was coming to its end. In 1602, Sir Toby Belch, Sir Andrew Aguecheek and the clown Feste, sitting up late and drinking, woke up Olivia's household by singing a catch and rousing not only the night-owl but also the steward Malvolio; there were three to share the singing, so a catch was the obvious thing for them to sing. A catch was a round or canon for three or more voices; apparently it took its name from a corruption of the earlier Italian *caccia*. It was very rarely serious in its subject matter, and it presupposed that its singers would be expert enough to make their effects by careful counting and precise timing, for it won its comic effects from the way in which words, repeated from voice to voice, came from its singers in ludicrous, humorous and, after the Commonwealth, often obscene combinations, the comic inappropriate phrase fitting into, and gaining prominence from, rests in the other parts of another part. The rudery of the words made the catch into music for gatherings of men, and it became the custom to perform with actions, for dramatic effect and increased fun. The Georgian Parliamentary Catch, for example, had singers who stood at the cry of "*Order! Order!*", pointed out their 'colleagues' at the words "*I shall name you!*" and generally set out to have an amusing time (Ex. 12); however, inaccurate counting of rests or any uncertainty of rhythm was likely to rob any catch not only of its often admirable musical neatness but also of its effective humour. The catch was an odd combination of verbal horseplay with musical neatness, and William Hayes, organist, composer and secretary of The Noblemen's and Gentlemen's Catch Club, founded in 1761 and meeting during Parliamentary sessions, who collected several volumes of catches said in his Preface to the first (1763); "The Catch in music answers to the Epigram in poetry, where much is to be exprest in a very small compass, and unless the turn is neat and well pointed, it is of little value." The catch continued to be sung until the mid-nineteenth century, but it seems to have begun at the start of the seventeenth century with Sir Toby Belch; the first collection of catches was published in 1609.

The previous age had been one of exceptional talents not only in the field of music, and there is a sense in which the most startling talent of the new age belonged to the past and was all his life a survivor. Thomas Tomkins (1572–1656) was a pupil of William Byrd and organist of Worcester Cathedral until the Commonwealth suspended cathedral services. His madrigals and church music are not only masterly in technique; they have great intensity of expression and seem to be the last, belated, outstanding music of the 'Golden Age'. It is only in his church music that he departed from established precedent, for as well as 'short', note-by-note settings

Ex. 12

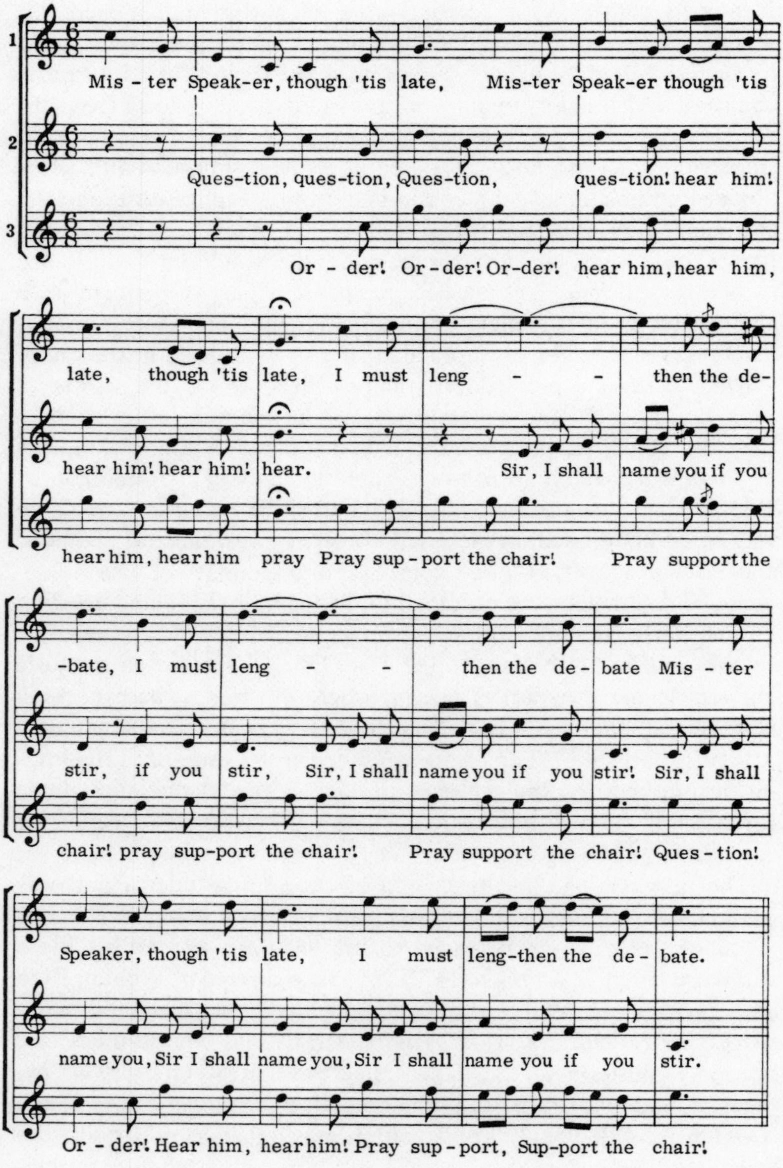
1
2
3
Mis - ter Speak-er, though 'tis late, Mis-ter Speak-er though 'tis
Ques-tion, ques-tion, Ques-tion, ques-tion! hear him!
Or - der! Or-der! Or-der! hear him, hear him,
late, though 'tis late, I must leng - - then the de-
hear him! hear him! hear. Sir, I shall name you if you
hear him, hear him pray Pray sup-port the chair! Pray support the
-bate, I must leng - - then the de- bate Mis - ter
stir, if you stir, Sir, I shall name you if you stir! Sir, I shall
chair! pray sup-port the chair! Pray support the chair! Ques-tion!
Speaker, though 'tis late, I must leng-then the de - bate.
name you, Sir I shall name you, Sir I shall name you if you stir.
Or - der! Hear him, hear him! Pray sup - port, Sup-port the chair!

of the liturgy (a style explored occasionally by earlier composers), he composed verse anthems and verse services, not only using solo voices but also giving independent, freely-moving parts to the accompanying organ. One potential great master, William Lawes (1602–1645), the younger brother of Henry, wrote music for broken or mixed consorts of instruments, often evolving music more colourful and harmonies more daring in their use of dissonance than can be found among any of his contemporaries. His music seems to exceed that of his age in its emotional expressiveness. Like all musicians of his period, he worked with words and voices; at the Battle of Chester, in 1645, as an officer in the Royalist forces, he was killed by a stray shot from the Parliamentary lines, leaving behind him work which had a considerable influence on the music of the Restoration composers in its harmonic and instrumental adventurousness.

After the political antagonisms of King and Parliament reached breaking point in 1642, there were no more Court masques, the theatres were closed and, after 1646, Church of England services were proscribed. In many places, organs were torn down from the churches which had used them. Puritan soldiers marched through Worcester carrying with them the pipes of Tomkins's organ and making probably hilarious noises by using them as trumpets. In other places, organs and church plates, and sometimes even service books, were destroyed. But in St Paul's, York Minster and both Lincoln and Durham Cathedrals the organs, though silenced, remained undamaged, and Cromwell, with the other authorities, did their best to prevent the occasional outbreaks of destructiveness. Nevertheless, the proscription of choral services and the wanton destruction of service books put an end to the English musical tradition, endangered ever since the dissolution of the monasteries; mercifully, the end was only temporary.

Cromwell himself was at least something of a music lover, and, as a matter of fact, few of the leading Puritans objected to music as a thing in itself though they were surprisingly ready to nose out anything they considered to be an abuse of music—its use for any purpose on the Sabbath, in church choirs, in theatres. Even William Prynne, author of *Histrio-Mastix*, the most embroiled attack on such abuses, wrote to justify the value of music once such abuses had been wiped out:

That music of itself is lawfull, usefull and commendable, no man no Christian, dares denie, since the Scriptures, the Fathers and generally all Christian, all Pagan authors extant, do with one consent averre it.[15]

Driven out of church—commonwealth services permitted no music but the unison chanting of psalms—and the theatres, music found other places in which to make itself heard. In many inns and taverns, organs removed from churches were set up in the largest room, which thus became a public music room, though the tavern-keeper did not employ musicians but depended on outsiders to offer their services to entertain his patrons. Thus the dispossessed theatre musicians, made what living they could, or at least, so a pamphlet of 1643, *The Actor's Remonstrance*, explains.

Our music, that was held to be so delectable that they scorned to come into a tavern for less than twenty shillings salary for two hours, now they wander with their instruments under their cloaks —I means, such as have any—into all houses of good fellowship, saluting every room where there is company with, "Will you have any music, gentlemen?"[16]

Though the church lost its music, and though music for some twenty years lost the invaluable training that had been given to church musicians, and though musicians lost their work in both the church and the theatre, the range of public performance was extended; the choirs of Oxford colleges, for example, continued to make music together as the executant foundation members of music clubs. There was sufficient enjoyment of, and sympathy for, music in Commonwealth England for William Davenant, who in 1639 had been licenced by Charles I to build and run a theatre for drama, music and dancing, to attempt in spite of Puritant prejudice to make the theatre active again. Knowing that his licence was secure, Davenant persuaded the Commonwealth Government to allow him to stage musical entertainments. In 1656 Davenant presented *The First Day's Entertainment at Rutland House*. The nature of the entertainment was hardly dramatic and less than operatic. In the first part, after a concert of appropriate music, actors representing Diogenes and Aristophanes argued the value of public entertainment; a chorus, instrumentally accompanied, ended the first part.

The second part again began with appropriate music, after which a Londoner and a Parisian discussed the rival merits of their cities; the concluding music, like the opening music, illustrated the tastes of the rival cities. The 'Entertainment', for which each member of the audience paid five shillings for a seat, was followed after a very brief interval by an opera first performed in Davenant's theatre in Dorset Gardens, *The Siege of Rhodes.* The libretto was by Davenant himself, the music by Matthew Locke (1630–1627), Henry Lawes, Captain Henry Cooke (1616–1672), Charles Coleman and George Hudson; Davenant's libretto suggests that the text was written simply as a play, and that the music was an afterthought added to the play without any adjustments simply to increase the chance of production. The third of Davenant's ventures before the Restoration was a 'presentation' with words and music, in the style of *The First Day's Entertainment,* called *The Cruelty of the Spaniards in Peru.* This was followed, again after only a short interval, by another opera, *Sir Francis Drake.* The two later works, like *The Siege of Rhodes,* depended for their music on a team of composers.

There might have been a real foundation for English opera if Davenant had been both clear in his own mind and seriously concerned about the musical side of his venture; he might, for example, have given any one of his composers authority to control the work. As it was, a year after the production of *Sir Francis Drake,* Charles II returned to England and the Monarchy, the Church and the theatres were all restored, and the Dorset Gardens Theatre could settle down to making money in the way Davenant understood best. New tastes, new fashions and a new society starved the English opera to death in its infancy. Opera, wherever it established itself in Northern Europe, was the special delight of kings and princes; Charles II, with insufficient money to indulge himself with such expensive toys, found his entertainment in the public theatres. The failure of the Davenant type opera to survive was so total that we have no idea how his team of composers attempted to deal with any of the problems which were to bedevil opera in England until 1945; we do not know if the entire texts were sung or whether there was spoken dialogue; these were the subject of hot but often amusing controversy when Italian opera was at last established in England half a century later.

VI
The Restoration

Charles II, when he became King after years in exile, brought to England tastes and a social policy which involved important musical changes. The great influence on his life, apart from his sense of the monarchy and of himself as King of England, was Louis XIV and King Louis's conception of monarchy, which, in truth, came to dominate the political thought of most of Europe. The French language became the international speech of courtesy and high civilization. Opera and drama became the propaganda of monarchy, so that music became, in French thought, a decorative, social art, not an introspective type of expression. Music dealt with grandeur and pageantry on the one hand, and in charm and relaxation on the other.

Charles II, perhaps not quite consciously, brought with him many similar attitudes as well as a conviction that this duty to reign possibly included the duty of compromise over anything that he considered inessential to his primary duty. He had his Chapel Royal, the traditional centre of his musical establishment, and he had his domestic music; this naturally included ceremonial instruments, the trumpets and drums without which royalty would have been musically unrecognizable. For his domestic music he recruited a more or less all-purpose string orchestra in emulation of Louis XIV's *Quatre-vingt Violons du Roi*, and soon came to employ them usually as two groups of twelve serving in alternation and free, when they were not on duty at court, to augment their salaries with other work. John Banister, the leader of Charles's string orchestra, was sent to France to study the work and organization of the *Quatre-vingt Violons*, but by 1672 found himself despite his official post free to organize and present concerts in his own home to audience which simply paid for its seats. Banister's house, in Whitefriars, had a large music room planned to reproduce the conditions of a tavern music room, and the concerts given in it more or less every day were advertised regularly.

The organization of the King's string orchestra, with its offer of a good deal of freedom and the possibility of a wider sphere of profitable action, was motivated only by Charles's poverty. Charles II had a considerable regard for his musicians but usually left them with their salaries in arrears. Louis Grabu, whom the King himself appointed to the royal music, had to appeal for the payment of admitted arrears in salary to save himself from arrest for debt; the Treasury owed him the better part of six hundred pounds. Samuel Pepys, in 1666, noted in his diary a meeting with John Hingston, one of the best known of the King's musicians; Hingston told him how the King's harpist, Evans, had died from want and had been buried "at the alms of the parish" although Evans was something of a celebrity.[17]

Banister's concerts were advertised punctiliously, not with details of their programmes but with information about any artist who might be regarded as specially attractive, and it is clear that they were at least reasonably profitable, for it was not long before other concert promoters began to advertise rival attractions at other venues, usually taverns.

By the 1680s, when the western end of the Strand was being developed and York House was built (more or less where Charing Cross Station stands now) and named after the Duke of York who was to become James II, a group of musicians arranged that York House should include a public music room available for hire. Thus York House became the first centre of London concert life. Events there came under no general musical or artistic management, so that concerts were arranged purely for the sake of profit rather than with any thought of musical standards or other artistic criteria in mind. Perhaps because the writers who devoted most space to his development were convinced conservatives who saw in the growth of public concerts an attack on English musical traditions and the domestic chamber music of the old consort, we may have inherited a jaundiced view of the early public concert; while Thomas Mace, in *Music's Monument* (1676), offered the plan of a music room of his own design, the audience sitting in rising tiers round a central, curtained space, with the performers tucked away behind the curtain, he was at pains to deplore the listeners' dependence on professional performance and to prove how quickly, and with what combination of pleasure and ease, any young person could learn to play the recorder. Roger North (1653–1734), who was Attorney-General to James II, wrote a *Memoires of Musick,* a history of the development of music from the time of the Ancient Greeks until 1728, as well as a variety of more or less incomplete and scattered manuscripts about the art, in which he grumbled at the public concert as a cheap betrayal of music for the sake of profit. There was, he held, no worthwhile co-ordination of programmes, no real management, and no effective discipline among the players, who jockeyed for prominent positions on the platform and did everything they could to draw attention to their own efforts and abilities. Musicians, North declared, seemed to be present on the platform only to find some way of shining at the expense of others and, consequently, at the expense of the music itself.

But, of course, as the first room in London specifically planned as an auditorium for music was part of an expensive, fashionable, modern development, it began the process of social exclusiveness which has bedevilled English music ever since. An audience gathered in York House had to pay high prices because the rent of the concert room was high. A concert for people capable of paying high prices carried with it various accompanying conditions; the right clothes, the right manners and the right social ambience became as important as the actual music heard, so that the factitious alliance between music and social eminence was formed. Although concerts continued to be given in taverns until the nineteenth century, the music rooms in which they were given were rented by the evening for whatever society intended to make music. The various concert halls—Hickworth's Rooms (where the young Mozart and his sister played), the Hanover Square Rooms, the centre of concert life from the 1780s until 1860, St James's Hall in Piccadilly, and the Queen's Hall—were all places where the well-to-do gathered and their support was essential.

Thus, the reign of Charles II accelerated the processes by which music in England was sung and played for, and given to, the English people. The King could not, even if he had wanted to do so, have worked as Louis XIV worked in France for the creation of a national opera, finding and making an English Lully (the Italian composer who was the real musical creator of French opera) out of Blow or even Purcell, and it was probably to Purcell's advantage that neither the King nor his ministers could make external, artistic demands which might have dominated his creative life. Charles II's taste, for clear, vigorous rhythms and singable tunes, was taken into account by Purcell and by everybody else who wrote music which might be heard by the monarch, but so was the popular taste for massive choral sonorities, which does not seem to have been shared by the King. Charles enjoyed the sort of music, in the Chapel Royal and anywhere else, to which he could beat time. He sang 'a plump bass' and was apparently always happy to slip off his majesty and take part in duets, but he could not afford the theatre, the spectacular performers and designers or any of the exorbitantly costly business of a Royal Opera. The financial settlement of the Restoration, intended to settle him comfortably on the throne beyond the need to quarrel, like his father and grandfather, with his Parliaments over grants of money, left him only poorly off as Kings go. He loved the theatre, so he shared the entertainments of his subjects; he enjoyed music, but he could not afford to organize it as he wished it to be organized; his string orchestra was halved for the sake of economy.

In a sense, therefore, only the reconstituted Chapel Royal directly expressed Charles II's musical tastes, and its reconstitution was treated, at the beginning of the reign, as a matter of great urgency. Choirboys had to be recruited and trained, the surviving men re-assembled and vacancies filled. As Master of the Boys, Charles appointed Henry Cooke, one of the composers who had worked on Davenant's operas. Cooke had some reputation as a composer in the Italian style, but he had fought and attained the rank of Captain in the Royalist army and it seems that his royalism influenced his appointment. He was, however—this is something shown by the results of his work—an efficient and sympathetic teacher, and his musical ideals were not far from those of his King. With a warrant to impress young boys with good voices, he collected the number he needed, among them Pelham Humfrey (1647–1674), a brilliant, apparently conceited youth whom the King sent to study in France and Italy in 1664; when he returned three years later, Pepys, a passionately enthusiastic amateur musician, seems to have been both annoyed and amused to find the young man completely indoctrinated with French musical ideas and professing a complete inability to see anything of value in any other music.[18] Humfrey started to compose while he was still a choirboy, and even his early work showed his determination to write emotionally and achieve music of real intensity. When Captain Cooke died, in 1672, Humfrey succeeded him as Master of the Boys, so that he was Purcell's teacher, Purcell (1659–1695) having been admitted to the Chapel Royal choir by Cooke; Purcell's father and uncle were both gentlemen of the Chapel. Cooke also recruited John Blow (1649–1708), apparently early enough for the boy to have been in the choir at Charles II's coronation in 1661. Among other boys collected by Cooke were Michael Wise (1648–1687) and William Turner (1651–1740). The boys were encouraged to compose, so that Blow, for example, is known to have written anthems sung in the Chapel Royal as early as 1663. Turner and Wise made an equally early start; Blow, Turner and Wise joined together in the composition of what, from its joint authorship, has come to be known as the 'Club Anthem'.

In addition to unusually gifted boys, Cooke recruited adult singers from the cathedrals of Salisbury, Lincoln and Worcester, and from St Paul's Cathedral, because at the Restoration only five of the adult members of the Chapel Royal survived. In November 1660, only five months after the Restoration, John Evelyn noted in his *Diary*, "Now was performed the Service with Musique, Voices etc. as formerly."[19] Matthew Locke (1630–1677) was not only an interesting and vigorous composer but a writer on music whose pamphleteering style is as vigorous as his music; Locke found it hard, normally, to find anything to admire, and the new Chapel Royal did not, at first, strike him as particularly admirable. "For more than a year after the reconstitution of the Chapel," Locke wrote in a typically controversial, hard-hitting pamphlet which he called *The Present State of Music Vindicated*, "the treble parts had to be supported by cornetts and counter-tenors, there being not one lad, for all that time, capable of singing his part readily." Even the King himself was sometimes obviously dissatisfied. Pepys wrote about one Sunday (October 14, 1660) on which he attended the Chapel Royal, "where Dr Croft made an indifferent sermon, and after it an anthem, ill sung, which made the King laugh."[20] The encouragement which both the King and Captain Cooke gave to the child composers of

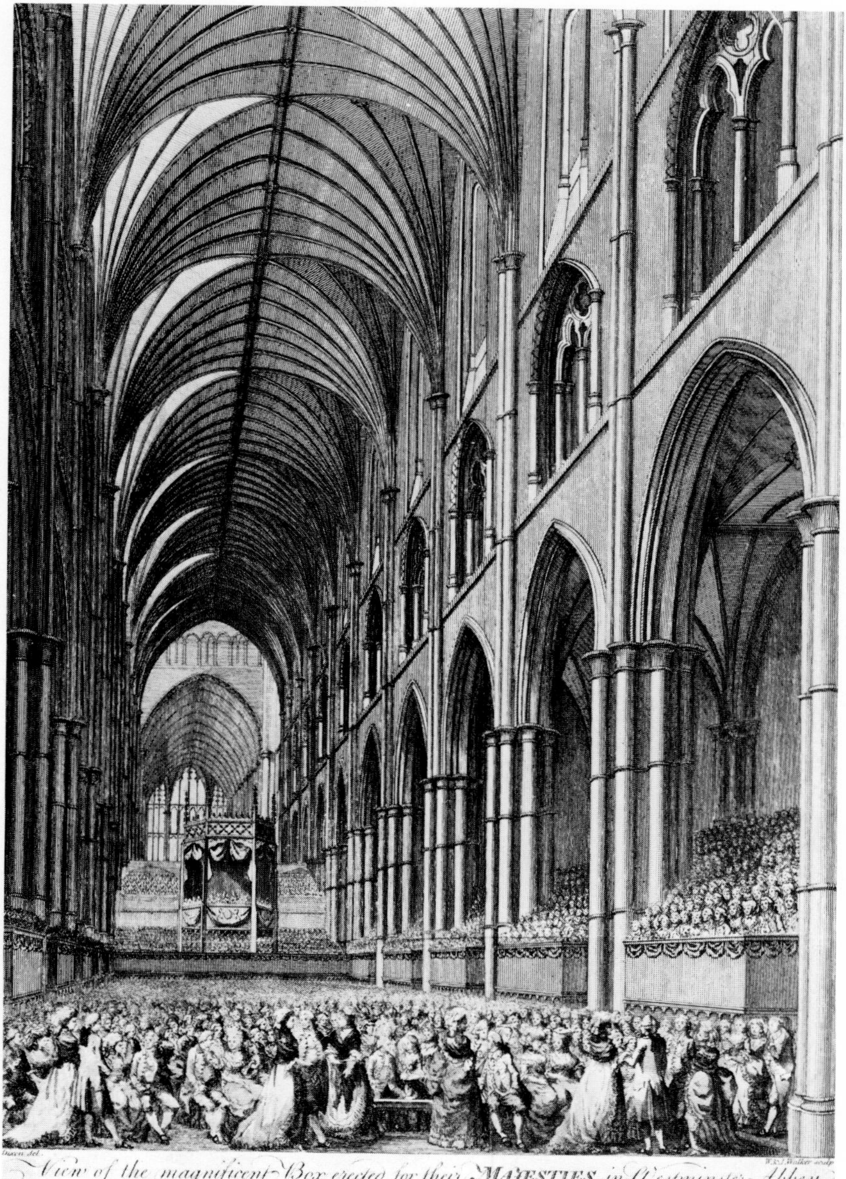
View of the magnificent Box erected for their MAJESTIES, in Westminster Abbey
under the Direction of Mr. JAMES WYATT, at the Commemoration of HANDEL.

Westminster Abbey during the Handel Commemoration of 1791. The audience is facing the West End, and the imposing structure over the Rood Screen is the Royal Box built for the Commemoration. The Handel Commemorations were the first musical events organized for a "mass audience".

Zoffany: *The Cowper and Gore Families.* Aristocratic amateurs – a singer stands with music by the harpsichord – in the 1780s.

A Cambridge concert in the 1780s.

Hubert Parry

Charles Stanford

Arthur Sullivan

Edward Elgar

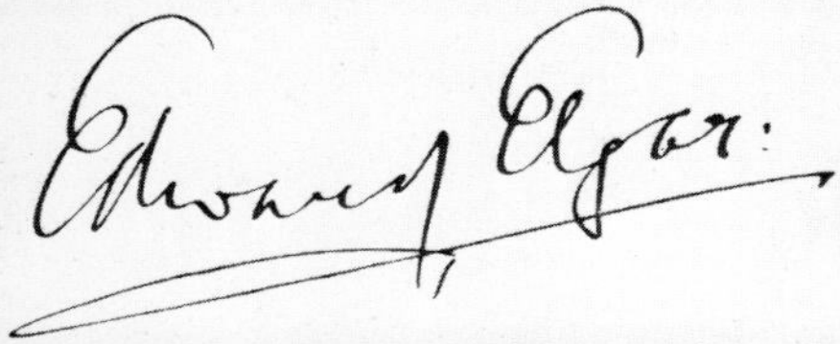

Frederick Delius

Ralph Vaughan Williams

Edmund Rubbra

The changing social atmosphere of the Promenade Concerts: Sir Henry Wood conducting in the Albert Hall, 1942.

Sir Charles Groves conducting at the 'Last Night of the Proms', 1976.

John Ireland

William Walton

Michael Tippett

Benjamin Britten

Richard Rodney Bennett

the Chapel was due, apparently, as much as anything else, to the destruction of some of the Chapel's music books and the King's anxiety to introduce a new musical style specially designed to celebrate the occasions on which he heard the service in his Chapel.

Thomas Tudway (*c.* 1650–1726) was taken into the Chapel Royal in the first or second year of the reign, and he became organist of King's College Chapel in 1670. He is best remembered for the collection of Tudor and Jacobean cathedral music which he assembled between 1714 and 1720, and in the notes to this he discusses the changes which the King introduced.

> *His Majesty, being a brisk and airy Prince, comeing to the Throne in the flow'r and vigour of his age, was soon, if I may say so, tyr'd with the grave and solemn way, and ordered the Composers of this Chappell to add symphonies, etc., with Instruments to their Anthems, and thereupon established a select number of his private music to play the Symphonies and Ritornellos which he had appointed.*

Tudway pointed out that "the King did not intend by this innovation to alter anything in the Established way. He only appointed this to be done when he himself came to the Chappell." Naturally, perhaps, the presence of the King should add a special splendour to the church rites. But whatever damage had been done to the music library of the Chapel, new music was supplied and the boy composers, too young to have any real experience of the older style, supplied it by falling in with the King's wishes and "produced their composition in this style; for otherwise it were vain to hope to please the King."

Writers have, perhaps too vigorously, suggested that Charles II's composers brought frivolity into church music, intending by doing so to please a frivolous King. What really happened, of course, was that the King's wishes were those of the liveliest, most up-to-date and creative of his Church composers, and that the anthem, therefore, became a completely baroque form, a sort of miniature cantata, with solos and instrumental interludes; in a typically baroque way it intensified expressiveness sometimes to the point of sentimentality, never abandoning the use of the massive sonorities which belonged to the English tradition but using them in new contexts and in passages of planned contrast. From Humfrey to Purcell and beyond there are, for example, elaborate *alleluias* which remember

Ex. 13 Blow

that the word is an expression of joy; they intensify verbal sorrows no less remarkably. The sense of shuddering dread which enters Purcell's setting of the 'Funeral Sentences' as well as the sense of

Ex. 14

Purcell

personal desolation and dread which the music expresses, were no less objectionable than a rollicking *alleluia* to anyone whose idea of what is seemly is drawn from the work of Tallis, Byrd, Gibbons, Tomkins and the old school of English church music.

What Charles II induced his composers to do was to introduce a specifically Chapel Royal style with strings as well as organ accompanying the choir, in several linked short movements, with an overture and with ritornelli between the movements, there was room for a good deal of vocal virtuosity. Obviously, the composers themselves relished the opportunities which the Chapel Royal anthem gave them; often their music suggests that they would have risen with delight to the opportunity of writing for a still larger band, and Purcell, in particular, must often have indulged a moment's grumbling at the restriction of his resources at points when he seems to be eager to bring in trumpets and drums. There are moments at which his violins break into fanfare-like figures, the instruments doing the best they can to be trumpets and drums. But insofar as the Chapel Royal style spread, it did so because it expressed the religious feelings of the period and also because many of the Chapel Royal composers wrote for other cathedrals, where the repertory was either depleted or at least partly destroyed. Both Blow and Purcell, for example, wrote for Westminster Abbey, where both were organists; Turner worked at St Paul's Cathedral after spending some time at Lincoln after he had left the Chapel Royal; Wise was for a time organist and Master of the choir at Salisbury Cathedral. Perhaps the new style would have spread more slowly if there had not been some destruction during the Commonwealth of the traditional resources of the choirs. To put the result in the most humdrum terms, to bring it completely down to earth, concerts were becoming too expensive for a large part of the population, even if that large part was not forced by its social situation out of concert life; their acquaintance with modern music, if they were acquainted with modern music, came from the Church.

The second string to the Restoration composer's bow was work in the theatre. Although Davenant's style of embryo opera died as soon as the embargo on the theatre ended, naturally the new Restoration society created by the passing of the Commonwealth and the relaxation of Puritan restrictions required new dramatic forms based on the new theatre design of a picture stage behind a proscenium arch, and both the new theatre and its new music took on the duty of presenting a reflection, slightly distorted, slightly exaggerated, of the realities of the new society; this new aspect of dramatic reality grew up in the plays of William Wycherley, in the 1670s, before Wycherley was disgrace for a freedom of speech and manner which are, in reality, an almost puritanical criticism of England's first 'permissive society'. Wycherley abandoned drama after the theatre was purified, its manners and language brought under restraint. Congreve and Farquhar, among others, were willing to be reformed and carried on the often hilarious analysis of a corrupt society.

Social comedy, however, made relatively few demands on the composer; naturally he would provide an introduction or overture, there would be 'act' music to bring the audience back to the right receptive mood, and the composer would set any incidental songs to appropriate music. But the nature of the plays themselves precluded the demand for any more elaborate music; the theatre composer—who was almost every composer of the age whose reputation attracted the attention of a theatre manager—came into his own in the more serious drama which, in the 1680s and 1690s, became the most prominent exemplar. The serious drama, in which we find the 'heroic style', avoided the mixture of comedy and tragedy which had come naturally to the Elizabethan and Shakespearean theatre; if the request of the dying King Lear, "Pray you, undo this button" comes to a modern audience (as it apparently came to their Jacobean forerunners) as a moment of heart-rending pathos, a Restoration audience would probably have found it as pathetically lacking in proper tragic dignity as Sharples's offer of whisky and soda to Lieutenant Pinkerton. The Restoration style demanded that expression should walk always on the heights, that seriousness should never be mixed with the comic or the everyday, and that consistency of characterization might, when necessary or when the opportunity arose, be sacrificed to grandeur of expression.

Dryden's personal dedication to a form of drama depending on grandeur of expression led him to his own attempt to work out the principles of English opera; in 1671 Charles II had induced the actor, Thomas Betterton to visit Paris and study the works of Lully; Betterton had induced the poet Shadwell to translate Lully's *tragédie-ballet*, *Psyche*, into English, and the translation was given music by Matthew Locke, and in Shadwell's version, with Locke's music, *Psyche* was produced at Betterton's theatre in Dorset Gardens. Two years later, Betterton paid another visit to Paris, hoping to find a French company he could bring back to London; instead, he returned with Louis Grabu, a minor composer who had for some time found favour with Charles II, although Pelham Humfrey had characteristically said that he would soon give Grabu "a lift out of his place" in the Royal music. Grabu had got himself into a legal tangle in 1674, apparently over the hire of scenery from the King's Theatre, in Whitehall; he used it in the French Theatre in London, but failed to return it by the specified date and fled the country. When Betterton brought Grabu back to England, he set the French composer to work with Dryden on an English opera, *Albion and Albanius*, an allegorical work the heroes of which were Charles II and his brother James, Duke of York, the later ill-fated James II; this was to be the forerunner of an even more magnificent piece, *King Arthur*. Unfortunately for Grabu, Charles II died while *Albion and Albanius* was in rehearsal.

Dryden, however, having turned his hand to an opera had found himself compelled to consider the principles on which he must work, and these must be suited to the nature of the English language. Opera, he decided, was a special form of theatre designed to give splendour to scenes of specially heroic character or to scenes of supernatural importance; gods and heroes might sing while others spoke, and supernatural episodes would demand the additional power of music; to give music to the words of mere unheroic common men and women would debase both the music and the type of drama to which it was wedded. Equally, to give music to scenes of common life would rob the music of its force and the scenes themselves of their credibility. Thus he wrote opera in which music was reserved for those scenes which he believed to be consistent with its nature, and these were the important scenes of the work; commonplace dialogue could be dealt with in prose. This was a form which he called 'dramatic opera'.

There remained, of course, the so-far insoluble problem of English recitative. Whether the *King Arthur*, produced at Dorset Gardens in the early summer of 1691, was the libretto he had first thought of for Grabu six or seven years before we do not know; it is dramatic opera with spoken dialogue, but all its great scenes demand music, and the action is designed to include as many musical scenes as possible. Dryden explained that what he had written was a libretto for an opera, not a spoken drama to which music had been added. "The Numbers of Poetry and Vocal Music are sometimes so contrary," he wrote in his Preface to *King Arthur*, "that in many places I have been obliged to cramp my Verses, to make them rugged to the Reader that they may be Harmonius to the Hearer." But music belonged by its nature to what is elevated in style and emotion, so that what he called 'dramatic opera' demanded few approximations to the style of Italian *recitativo secco*. Music was for gods, demigods and heroes, and for their exalted sentiments; otherwise it was better left alone. *King Arthur* can be, and has been, produced as opera without spoken dialogue through trimming and rearrangement of Dryden's plan, for the poet kept the music in more or less self-contained blocks needing no interruption by speech.

Therefore, the drama accepted music as a way of reinforcing the emotional effects of words, larger-than-life acting and elaborate scenic effects. To the theorists, the drama was at its most powerful when it became what Wagner was to call, a century and a half later, a *Gesamtkunstwerk*, a union of all the arts in which none was given predominance over the others. It had always been natural for Ophelia to sing in her mad scene and for Desdemona to sing a sad love song before her murder, for music supplied dimensions which speech might miss. But the Renaissance writers went further. It became natural to add to suitable plays any opportunities for music which the original author had neglected. Thus Purcell could give us the (to us) unwieldly masterpiece, *The Fairy Queen*, adding a masque to each act of Shakespeare's play *A Midsummer-Night's Dream*. If the result overflowed the time available for a theatrical performance, as *The Fairy Queen* does, the original text can be cut to make room for the masques and anti-masque with which it is embellished; insofar as the version of the play remaining deals effectively with the Oberon-Titania story (it is not really interested in the quartet of human lovers, or in the 'mechanicals' ' conscientious amateur dramatics) nobody would be dissatisfied, for the music, Purcell at his most splendidly inventive, was apparently motivated by suggestions from the disfigured play.

Because Charles II never resurrected the court masques which had been the great artistic events of his father's and grandfather's reigns but patronized the public theatres, and because the type of theatrical art which reached its highest point in the work of Dryden and Purcell, *The Fairy Queen* and *Dioclesian*, or in the Middleton version of *Macbeth* (with, it seems, Shakespeare's play cut (and the cuttings lost) to make room for the musical scene of Hecate and the witches, with music of which we know little), a great deal of the drama which occupied the public theatres for the last four or five years of Purcell's life was drama with masque. It was drama at its most expansive and expensive, therefore, it was played to well-to-do audiences, whose tastes it exactly suited. Pepys, of course, had ceased to comment on the shows he saw before *The Fairy Queen* was produced in 1692 (he had less than four years to live), but his opinion of *A Midsummer-Night's Dream* was recorded when he saw the play on September 29, 1662—". . . the most ridiculous, insipid play that I ever saw in my life." In 1692, it probably needed Purcell's additions to make it enjoyable.

The period, in most musical memories, is naturally and inevitably dominated by Purcell. He inherited a powerful English tradition and married it happily to more recent French and Italian styles; his melodic gift was one of the most powerful and wide-ranging that any composer has deployed, his sense of the orchestra as he knew it unsurpassed, and his sense of harmony—nourished by tradition and by modern music—often almost breath-taking. It was natural when Jeremiah Clarke's 'Trumpet Voluntary' was rediscovered and became popular, that the work should be attributed to Purcell, though Clarke (*c*. 1674–1707) wrote other attractive works. Purcell wrote every type of music—from canons of such shockingly schoolboyish obscenity that early editors, assembling his work for the belated Complete Edition which began in 1876 and is not yet complete, felt compelled to fit them to new and unobjectionable words, all the way to church music of great power and strength; from songs which range from impassioned eloquence to others that roister with unrestrained high spirits, to court and occasional odes which musically redeem the fulsome silliness of their texts on to the last riches of the English fantasia and its marriage to the new baroque sonata. He handled them all with unfaltering craftsmanship and equally unfaltering sympathy for their texts and purposes; it was the composer's duty to be able to give himself fully to every task that came his way, and Purcell did so. It is our loss that much of his music does not fit into our pattern of musical performance.

John Blow, who became organist of Westminster Abbey in 1668 and relinquished the post eleven years later to make room for Purcell, returning to the Abbey after Purcell's death, almost rivals his amazing contemporary in choral and vocal music. Like Purcell, he was involved in the setting of odes and welcome-songs for royal and public occasions, but he wrote little instrumental music and only one work for the stage. He falls short of Purcell in his range of technical resource and in the ability to bring freshness, spontaneity and excitement to routine compositions. He lacked Purcell's power of finding genuine emotion, and therefore genuine invention, for such things as the highly artificial round of court duties. What he provides is good, honest, clean and strong, but it lacks the Purcellian ability to lift the routine task to the level of genius. He provided incidental songs for half a dozen stage works, but his one piece of dramatic music, the opera *Venus and Adonis*, is not Drydenesque and admits no spoken dialogue; historians believe it to have been written between 1680 and the death of Charles II in 1685. Without the masque-like characteristics of spectacular scenes and dances, and is a remarkable fusion of masque-like decorative qualities with true opera, and it has grace, beauty, invention and wit. Like everything that Blow did, it is inevitably overshadowed by Purcell's music; Purcell, in *Dido and Aeneas*, composed a true opera in the sense that the term has held always except during the ascendancy of Dryden; in composing it, Purcell solved the literary and musical problems of recitative which kept English opera in the doldrums until the rise of Benjamin Britten.

The circumstances of *Dido and Aeneas* suggest that it should be an eccentric work. It was written in 1689, apparently as an indirect celebration of the 'Glorious Revolution' of the previous year. It was written to be performed by the pupils of a girls' school in Chelsea run by Josias Priest. The details of the first performance are neither clear nor detailed though certain characters—Aeneas himself, one of his crew and the men of the chorus—must have been outsiders. We do not know if they were professional singers imported for the occasion; if that is so, Aeneas has to do little to justify his fee, and the sailor who sings a callously sarcastic farewell to the girls of Carthage has, so to speak, more jam on his bread than the hero himself; we do not know who was the first Dido, though it seems unlikely that her farewell, one of the greatest tragic outpourings in music, should have been written for a girl, however nicely she could sing. Marvellously enough, the little that Aeneas has to do is enough to establish him as a hero whose reluctant desertion of Dido causes the work's catastrophe.

The apparently insoluble problem of English opera, before and after *Dido and Aeneas* until modern times, was that of a free-flowing, natural style of recitative which does justice to the words and to the situation of the moment. Elgar, in *The Dream of Gerontius*, found a convincing free arioso style which could live a full musical life along the lines of Cardinal Newman's poem after more than a century in which composers had looked for Italian or German models of declamation. Blow, in *Venus and Adonis*, almost succeeds in avoiding the need for recitative. He thinks in terms of little, rather disconnected scenes, lyrically self-contained like tableaux. Purcell anticipates Elgar in finding an easy, flowing arioso style which accepts every invitation to deal expansively with emotive words and phrases, giving them all the expressiveness he can. In Purcell's opera, Dido's first entry establishes her as a personality and suggests her

Ex. 15

ultimate tragedy; she is the dominating personality of the work, and the music immediately explains the devotion in which her people hold her.

Nahum Tate's libretto, read without music, would suggest none of the work's quality to a modern reader unfamiliar with the habits of a Restoration poetaster, but Tate's language was a brand of poetic speech which came quite naturally to Purcell, and even Tate has his moment of glory in the song of the sailor leaving Carthage and its girls for fresh adventures and other girls:

> Drown their entreaties with vows of returning
> But never intending to visit them more.

The composer co-ordinates this cheerful, easy cynicism into the pattern of the work and makes an almost Shakespearean contrast between it and the anguish of the principal characters. Dido's final aria, her farewell to life, remains one of the great unforgettable moments in all opera. Like many of Purcell's finest emotional songs, it is set on a 'ground', an unvarying bass phrase over and against which the voice sings phrases which go their own way, not inviting a cadence or a pause when the ground suggests one, and the two coalescing only at the last moment, when there is no more to be said.

Purcell's masques, or semi-operas, perhaps, cannot be recovered in the form their composer created for them, as part of evenings of 'total theatre' with spoken drama interleaved in the music and double plots, spoken and sung, reflecting each other. Even the various court odes and welcome-songs do not fit easily into our twentieth-century musical life, splendid as most of them are, and the texts which motivate them are not easily taken seriously. In 1694, for example, the Queen's birthday was celebrated with the singing of *Come all ye Sons of Art*, the last and most perfect of the odes which Purcell wrote for that celebration; it is difficult not to smile at, for example, the lines of the bass song which attribute to Queen Mary's care the survival of her husband amid all the dangers of battle:

> These are the sacred charms that shield
> Her darling hero in the field,
> Thus she supports his righteous cause

And to his aid immortal powers she draws.

A year later, the birthday of the Duke of Gloucester, Queen Anne's sickly child who was to die long before his mother, inspired a birthday ode *Who can from joy refrain*, in which there is a brilliant and invigorating duet for soprano and trumpet:

Ah, how pleased he is and gay
When the trumpet charms his ear.

The Odes for Saint Cecilia's Day, of course, are less likely to provoke mirth. Their poetry is typical of the occasional verse of the late seventeenth century and it provides everything the celebration needed, from the counter-tenor aria, ''Tis nature's voice' to the massive, splendid chorus, 'Soul of the World', in the magnificent *Hail, bright Cecilia.* To look at Purcell's ceremonial odes from the point of view of the extravagance of the compliments they pay to royalty is to miss their point; they exist, and their words were strung together to provide their composer with the proper opportunities to make effects that were expected of him. *Come all ye Sons of Art*, after a three-movement Overture for strings, oboes, trumpets, bassoons and drums, has an opening chorus, a counter-tenor duet calling on trumpets to use their eloquence, and later demands of the flute and violin to take their part; the sentiments are conventional, but the music is startlingly alive. The conventional sentiments simply set the composer free to give his work vivid colour; these words are not a libretto but simply a musical convenience.

Purcell was master of every aspect of his art. Just as his orchestra exploits the individuality of all his instruments, so that his fantasies and *In Nomines* both end a tradition and lead the way to new developments; he was master of the old style which, perhaps, he came to know intimately when, as a very young man, he was official copyist at Westminster Abbey, and he was master of the styles of his own period, English, French and Italian.

VII
Handel and Hanoverian England

Purcell died in 1695. Handel (1685–1759) arrived in England in 1710, not at that time expecting to settle here but believing that a visit to England would be profitable; he had been told by various Englishmen who had heard and admired his work in Italy that he would find a welcome in London where, belatedly, efforts were being made to establish Italian opera. In 1705, Thomas Clayton (*c.* 1670–?) had composed *Arsinoe, Queen of Cyprus,* to an Italian text translated into English; *Arsinoe* was produced at the Drury Lane Theatre and was successful enough to encourage Clayton to set Joseph Addison's *Rosamund* in the same style in 1707; *Rosamund* failed so completely that Addison never, in later years, had much good to say of opera, but Clayton's songs in the work were published and he continued to try to make opera a force in the London theatre. Circumstances and perhaps, his own lack of talent defeated him, but in 1711 two considerable works of his, *The Passion of Sappho* and *The Feast of Alexander*, were heard in London.

Blow remained the most considerable composer in England, writing good, strong works which did nothing that startled the upper-class audience. The series of big theatre works which had occupied most of Purcell's time during the final years of his life had no one to carry it on, so that a move towards opera was opportune, but Clayton's models were not those which would help him to write for English audiences. Recitative was a problem; how were English words to be treated in a recitative style, as mere conversation linking and motivating musical set-pieces? Clayton seemed unaware that the problem existed, though it was the unnaturalness of recitative applied to the French language that had been the start of Lully's nationalization of opera in France. Clayton simply set

English words as though they were Italian, apparently unaware that English audiences found recitative, Italian style, either boring or funny, and continued to do so until Arthur Sullivan won an easy laugh in H.M.S. *Pinafore*, with the recitative dialogue between Captain Corcoran and his crew in 1878.

Addison, a major literary figure in his own lifetime, convinced that Italian-style opera could do nothing of value for an English writer, decided that for the same reason opera could offer little of value to English audiences until—though he did not imagine that this would ever happen, an English composer found a style of declamation growing as naturally from his own language as recitative grew from Italian.

> *The recitative in every language* [he wrote] *should be as different as the Tone or Accent of each language; for otherwise, what may properly express a passion in one language, will not do it in another. Everyone who has been long in Italy knows very well, that the cadences in Recitativo bear a remote affinity to the Tone of their voices in ordinary conversation; or, to speak more properly, are only the Accents of their language made more musical and tuneful.*[21]

Opera, to Addison, was naturally Italian, and when, in 1710, Handel came to England for the first time, it had begun to seem that Italian opera, in its own language, was a way to success. Handel had been appointed *Kapellmeister* in Hanover in 1710, had spent the summer following his appointment there and then, perhaps because the Electoral Prince of Hanover, his new employer who was to become George I of England, had closed the Opera House his predecessors had maintained, Handel was on leave in England from the November of that year. Clayton's attempt at Italian opera had been followed by the successful introduction of an Italian repertory, sung wholly or partly in Italian, largely by Italian singers; Italian singers, at any rate, played the leading roles. *Rinaldo*, which Handel produced at the Queen's Theatre in the Haymarket, the regular London opera house, in February 1711 (four months after his arrival), was an instant success and immediately published, though without its recitatives; Queen Anne met the composer and, according to his first biographer, Mainwaring, gave him valuable presents and an indication that he would be very welcome to return to this country. He was away for eighteen months, but returned in the autumn of 1712 with another opera for London. He had established himself with English royalty, with the aristocracy and with the limited audience of intellectuals who, with the aristocracy, were the audience for Italian opera; he became part of the fairly numerous, influential colony of German musicians who found music in England profitable. After all, his patron in Hanover was simply awaiting his call to the throne of England.

On his return, Handel composed opera as a freelance for companies and managements to whom he had no other responsibility. He was appointed Music Master to the Royal Family, was supported by the Earl of Burlington and by the Duke of Chandos. Chandos was the one English nobleman to maintain an orchestra and choir comparable to the sort of *Kapelle* Handel knew in Germany, and Handel contributed to its repertory; its *Kapellmeister* was another German musician, Johann Pepusch, who was to have his own influence on English music. At the celebrations for the signing of the Treaty of Utrecht, in 1713, Handel provided the settings of the *Te Deum* and *Jubilate* used at the service in St Paul's, ousting the works by Purcell usually used on such occasions, and won himself a pension from the Queen; he was too shrewd a man to plunge into an English adventure trusting to no more than his popularity for survival.

Handel was what the eighteenth century regarded as a completely professional composer. By the time he was twenty he had trained himself to qualify for a position comparable to Bach's in his native Germany; he had moved to Hamburg to compose opera and had been successful; he had travelled in Italy, mastering Italian styles of instrumental and vocal composition, so that for the rest of his life, the composition of Italian chamber cantatas was a sort of relaxation for him. In England he mastered the choral style of Purcell and, as a composer at Cannons, the Duke of Chandos's residence at Edgware, he accustomed himself in the 'Chandos' Anthems to English church style and the setting of English words, while in *Acis and Galatea* he wrote a work in the style of the English 'Pastoral'; national styles of music seemed right and natural to him, so he studied and mastered them.

Handel's music was, so to speak, naturalized long before he found it advisable to take up English citizenship, and while he was studying the major English styles, he wrote the sets of concertos, Op. 3 (the 'Oboe' concertos) and Op. 12, published in 1734 and 1739 respectively. Because the English 'Music Clubs', who were his steadiest patrons for such works and for his opera overtures, preferred the form of concerto popularized by Arcangelo Corelli, Handel expanded but never strayed far from the Corellian models.

But until the mid-1730s, Handel's principal concern was with Italian opera, provided by Italian librettists and sung by Italian singers. He worked first as Musical Director of the Royal Academy of Music, employed by an aristocratic management which functioned from 1719 to 1728; then, as partner to the Swiss Jacob Heidegger, he made himself the rival of another aristocratic management, the Opera of the Nobility; and finally, after 1732, he took command of his own company. He was not the only composer whose music was used by the Royal Academy of Music; other composers imported to provide works, like Giovanni Bononcini, scored successes as resounding as Handel's; but none of his operas ever failed, and as musical director and principal talent scout he was paid a salary for his work as well as a fee for the operas he provided, his position was to say the least favourable.

Baroque Opera, as Handel knew it, was a firmly binding form. Action took place off the stage on which it was narrated in recitative; recitative led to an aria in which the new situation was discussed; the singer of the aria left the stage, a further passage of recitative followed, leading to another aria, and so on until the end of the act demanded a chorus. When Dr Johnson defined opera as an "exotick and irrational entertainment", he was thinking of the operatic tradition which Handel served, and knew no other, for any improbability or wonder which could give rise to a passage of notable music was accepted, and naturalism as the modern theatre understands it was firmly eschewed. Even the chorus might be no more than the principal singers announcing a unanimous conclusion at the end of a passage of action. Duets were rare, and larger ensembles never attempted; the plot proceeded in recitative and the aria to which recitative led was invariably a *da capo* which took the situation no further forward because its function was the emotional expression of a single situation; for all the eloquence and beauty of his arias, Handel (a superb melodist) never intended his arias to carry the plot further.

Nevertheless, Handel was a dramatic composer within the limitations of the form, which he seems to have accepted unquestioningly. The sequence of keys which his operas follow, for example, is designed for dramatic effect as well as for musical expression. Acts and even whole operas are designed with the idea of key relationships and key contrast, round a main tonality, always in mind. He found a good deal of unexpected variety in the *da capo* aria itself. Cleopatra's gorgeous aria 'V'adoro pupille' in *Julius Caesar*, for example, is interrupted by recitative from Caesar (played, like all the great heroic roles in baroque opera, by a *castrato*) before the *da capo* sign is reached.

The audience, however, was basically the wealthy, 'high society' audience which had invested money in the Royal Academy of Music. The average theatre-goer, who had grown up in the theatrical tradition descended from Shakespeare and the Elizabethans, was unmoved by its rigid pseudo-classicism. It was used to action on the stage, to a style of acting in which battle, murder and sudden death were unblushingly represented, and to a style which mixed emotions; a good performance of *Hamlet* is, after all, very funny at points; *opera seria* was always as serious as it could be. At the same time, English audiences, which admired the *falsetto* singing of countertenors, was not equally impressed by the *castrati* who were the supreme attraction of Handelian opera; to the English, the *castrato* was usually something shockingly unnatural, to be dismissed with repulsion or passed off as a dirty joke. Handel's more or less unsurpassable melodic gifts makes aria after aria in opera after opera a matter of delight, but to Handel's potential wider audience, opera was no more than the "exotick and irrational entertainment" soon to be dismissed by Samuel Johnson. In 1728 the Royal Academy of Music failed, having through bad management exhausted such of the funds subscribed to it as it had been able to raise; the failure was not Handel's, for none of the operas (more than a dozen scores) which he had written for it had been a failure. In partnership with Johann Jacob Heidegger he went into management on his own account, following the policy of the defunct Royal Academy. A rival company again organized by the aristocracy opened its doors and Heidegger seceded to the new Opera of the Nobility, so that Handel found himself unwillingly involved in Georgian politics. The Opera of the Nobility was supported by Frederick, Prince of Wales, and therefore opposed to everything supported by George II, so that Handel appeared to be the composer of an unpopular establishment which supported the cynical corruption of the Prime Minister, Sir Robert Walpole. Two organizations dividing the limited audience for opera between them could not survive, and Handel was left, because of Heidegger's desertion, without a theatre until he arranged with John Rich, the owner of the theatre in Lincoln's Inn, to present opera there.

He had, apparently, begun to see that something would have to be done about opera itself if it were to win a really popular audience, but his attempts to widen the scope of *opera seria* with works like *Parthenope* (1730) simply antagonized the faithful without winning any new supporters; the real enthusiasts wanted opera as they had always had it in the past, and a cheerful, genial work did not appeal to them. But for two evenings a week he carried on his own seasons apparently determined to watch the Opera of the Nobility destroy itself. He began to increase his popularity with the middle classes by employing more English singers, who were, anyhow, cheaper than Italian stars. In 1736 he became friendly with the Prince of Wales, writing *Atalanta* to celebrate the Prince's marriage and providing the anthem for his wedding, but found that by doing so he had lost the King's support. By the time that he had vanquished the Opera of the Nobility he was the only successful opera composer left in London, but he had no funds with which to float a new season, and not even enough money to form an advantageous partnership.

His seasons at the Lincoln's Inn Theatre had, of course, left him with time on his hands, and two evenings of opera each week were barely enough to both keep him and the company for which he was responsible. Since 1727 he had been a British citizen, but he had rarely appeared as a composer of music to English texts—*Acis and Galatea*, the Chandos Anthems and the various ceremonial Royal anthems were his only works with English words; but after 1732 he turned to English oratorio to make use of the theatre during Lent, when opera was forbidden. In 1732, Aaron Hill, the writer who had translated *Rinaldo* for the opera book issued with Handel's first English success, had written an often quoted letter to the composer suggesting that Handel should be resolute enough to "deliver us from our Italian bondage; and demonstrate that English is soft enough for opera when composed by poets, who know how to distinguish the *sweetness* of our tongue from the *strength* of it."[22] Handel had taken Hill's advice so far as to attempt English oratorio, an invention of his own quite unlike the Italian oratorio he had composed in Rome in 1708. It was through the new English oratorios that the English people took him to their hearts, and though he only slowly abandoned opera, the reception of his new oratorios showed him that they had conquered a new audience for him.

In his operas, Handel had worked with great technical resourcefulness through a style which he did not seriously modify or change. Once or twice in the operas, notably in *Julius Caesar*, Handel had exploited powerful choral Masses, but the oratorios integrate powerful, dramatically motivated choruses into their action wherever such integration is dramatically justified. The oratorios use *da capo* arias only when the static *da capo* aria seems to be the appropriate form, justified by the dramatic situation; singers are otherwise occupied with a wide variety of song forms. To all intents and purposes the oratorios are dramas which do not happen to be staged; the exceptions are *Israel in Egypt*, which is a choral epic rather than a drama, and *Messiah*, which is meditative or reflective. Both were, at first, dangerous works because they use the words of the Bible although they were sung in the theatre, and this, to puritanical English eyes, was sacrilege. Even the other oratorios, the texts for which were moulded into eighteenth-century verse paraphrases, were regarded as dangerous. *Messiah* was first performed in Dublin in 1742, and at its first performance, and afterwards until its popularity had established it, it was billed simply as 'A Sacred Oratorio'.

Oratorio succeeded totally while Handel's operas succeeded only with the limited opera audience. His oratorios were dramatic in a direct way, unlike his operas, for though nobody acted on the platform, the music indicated the action that was imagined, so that they met the English understanding of what is essentially dramatic. But their chief point of appeal seems to have been the popularity of the stories they tell. The classic myths and the reworkings of classic and Renaissance adventures, which had provided composers with opera libretti since the turn of the sixteenth century, were familiar to the upper-class admirers of the form as they occupied their places in the theatre, but the Old Testament stories—*Saul*, *Samson*, *Solomon* and the others, paraphrased into very formal English verse—

were part of the inheritance of the English people as a whole. The least successful of Handel's oratorios was *Theodora*, in which the composer's invention flagged no more than it had done in *Saul* or *Samson*; *Theodora* abandons the Bible to tell a story from early Christian history. Nowhere else in Europe was so much stress laid on the reading and study of the Old Testament as in England; the Church of England alone sets lengthy passages of the Old Testament to be read as the First Lesson at Mattins and Evensong day by day, so that these stories, sometimes shocking and sensational, sometimes stirring, sometimes extremely moving, had become an English birthright, and in some way the people of Britain—a small, not overpopulated country which had become so successful that it could see its success as a mark of divine favour—could identify themselves with the tribulations and triumphs of the Israelites.

Turned into the polite, sub-Augustan verse of the mid-eighteenth century, or into the sub-Miltonics of *Samson*, Handel had a wealth of material which he exploited with a full-blooded appreciation of its dramatic quality. He saw the oratorios as divided not into parts but into 'acts', used whatever song forms seemed appropriate to the moment's situation and used the chorus dramatically as the voice of the nation whose adventures he was chronicling. In *Saul* he expanded the orchestra to a size greater than that used in any of his operas, choosing instruments for the appositeness to the situation, with trombones as well as trumpets, and with a carillon for passages of victorious jubilation. It is possible to stage the oratorios effectively—comparatively recently *Samson* was given a dramatic production in London—but Handel never envisaged them as other than concert works.

The upper-class opera enthusiasts were, on the whole, relatively cool about oratorio; it had none of the social glories which had won their allegiance to opera. Those who felt the Old Testament stories to be too holy to be used for entertainment were totally opposed. But in discovering a fundamentally dramatic form which aroused English sympathies, Handel created something which became essentially English to the extent that for more than a century it imposed upon English composers both a subject matter and a style; it is the sad accident of history that few of them were capable of living up to its demands. Handel adopted a style for oratorio that was already growing old-fashioned when he created it, so that in his work the final stages of the baroque style continued in England in the strange perversions of Handel's style which inflated Handel's music with 'additional accompaniments' that robbed it of its lithe, athletic grace and created the notion that all Handel's work is unrelievedly monumental.

There was, of course, no composer who was Handel's equal, though there were some who deserved better than the oblivion to which Handel's success condemned them. The Church of England, sunk into Erastianism, cared very little for its splendid musical traditions. Among church musicians Maurice Greene (1695–1755), organist of St Paul's Cathedral, was a composer whose interests spread far beyond his choir and organ loft. Greene not only composed effectively for the Church; his pastorals, *Florimel, or Love's Revenge* (1734), *The Judgement of Hercules* (1740) and *Phoebe* (1748) are not only theatrically effective but also beautiful, inventive music; his oratorios *Jephtha* and *The Force of Truth* are equally fine. Greene was active in every area of English music, but he set himself up in opposition to Handel and was crushed for doing so rather by Handel's supporters than by the great immigrant himself. William Boyce (1710–1779) is remembered for his early symphonies rather than for his church music; he too composed effectively for the theatre and, after his hearing failed, he occupied himself in making a monumentally important collection of English church music. Thomas Roseingrave (1690–1766) became a renowned virtuoso organist and the first organist of St George's, Hanover Square, in London. Disappointed in love he became unbalanced rather beyond the point of mere unreliability, and his creative gifts seemed to wither away. There were, too, provincial composers like the mysterious Mudge, whose Christian name was possibly Richard and who may have been a clergyman in the neighbourhood of Birmingham. Mudge wrote quite powerful and often unusual music; he published a set of concertos for two violins and strings in the 1750s, bringing an obbligato trumpet into the orchestra of the first of the set and a harpsichord or organ into the sixth, an unusual work which, at the climax of its slow movement, brings in voices to sing Byrd's *Non nobis Domine*; it is not merely the mysteriousness of Mudge which makes his music interesting, for technically he could handle unconventional materials convincingly and he was capable both of high spirits and of a sombre intensity.

Charles Avison (*c.* 1710–1770) was organist, composer and teacher in Newcastle-upon-Tyne and composed for choirs and music clubs in his own neighbourhood. Several of his works have escaped the oblivion which fell on the music of his contemporaries. William Stanley (1713–1786), the blind organist, also remains not completely forgotten.

Obviously, even those with no gifts other than hindsight can see that Handel's obstinate refusal to abandon Italian opera until it had almost ruined him was a foolish neglect of other areas in which he could have worked successfully and in greater freedom. When, in 1728, the Royal Academy of Music was on its last legs, John Gay brought out *The Beggar's Opera*, writing the necessary lyrics to the tunes he had selected for his work; these were arranged by Johann Pepusch, a musician who had a quite untypical interest in the music of the past. Pepusch did well by the materials he was given—folk-songs, traditional popular songs, and songs by recent and present contemporaries like Purcell and Handel himself—indeed, the work turned out to be one of the most successful works in English theatrical history. It was satirical in the way that the English like their satire, as a fundamentally genial bashing of every target, and almost every head, in sight. It 'a had a go at' Sir Robert Walpole, the Prime Minister, once in the person of MacHeath, the highwayman who had two 'wives' just as Walpole had a wife and a mistress, but more than once Walpole becomes a reflection of Peachum, receiver of stolen goods, informer and gang leader; at another time, Peachum deliberately recalls the audience's mind to Jonathan Wild, the 'thief-taker' who was also, like Peachum, the brains of criminal organizations; MacHeath is sometimes Jack Shepherd, the highwayman. *The Beggar's Opera* is topical and it finds a place for everything. It has delightful, innocent tunes like 'Golden Slumbers kiss your eyes' wedded to which are works that are anything but innocent:

> "Oh Polly, you might have toyed and kissed,
> By keeping men off, set them on,"
>   "But he so teased me,
>   He so pleased me—
> What I did, you must have done."

Pepusch's treatment of the airs brings them all into the eighteenth century, but with simplicity and taste; however, under the satirical bombardment of topical ideas and personalities there is a satirical treatment of opera itself, its manners, *mores* and oddities shown in the marriage of melody and words, and in the rejection, by the Beggar who is the supposed author of the piece, of recitative; in the Prologue, the Beggar declares that he will not have recitative because he will have everything natural. At the end of the piece an odd, unmotivated *deus ex machina* rushes on to the stage where MacHeath is in the hangman's cart and waiting for death, shouting "A reprieve! A reprieve!" and all ends with the sort of happy illogicality to which opera audiences were quite accustomed. This, after all, is *The Beggar's Opera*, not 'the beggar's drama'.

Gay's masterpiece—two hundred and fifty years after its first production—still holds the stage, and still seems pertinent to our way of life. Its general derision applies itself readily to twentieth-century habits and is permanently a triumph. It is structured to carry no greater weight than comes from the expression of an immediate response to a situation reached in spoken dialogue; it is settled in the area which Dryden had called 'dramatic opera'. To the average English theatre-goer, it seemed through its spoken dialogue to be a rationalization of the form which Handel served, a humanization of a form which they often did not understand. The system of key relationships, tempo and colour relationships and contrasts, and so on, through which Handel gave his operas dramatic momentum, were not immediately apparent to his London audiences, who simply and rightly felt, without knowing why, that Handel was a towering genius who achieved more satisfying results than his rivals. The looser form which Gay and Pepusch had adopted became the kind of English musical theatre which formed English dramatic music until Balfe's *The Bohemian Girl* (1843), Wallace's *Maritana* (1845) and the 'Savoy Operas' of Gilbert and Sullivan after 1871. Genuine operas like Arne's *Artaxerxes* (1762), *opera seria* in English, its libretto translated from the Italian and set by a composer of real quality, turned out to be only a sort of sport in English theatrical history.

The musical theatre became not simply pleasurable but indispensable after 1737, when the Licensing Act restricted spoken drama to the two theatres royal, in the Haymarket and at Drury Lane, and thus left the other theatres to do the best they could with the various English forms of musical theatre, throwing in, perhaps, a spoken play as a free curtain-raiser or after-piece. The result was the uproarious success of *The Dragon of Wantley*, the libretto by Henry Carey, himself a reasonably successful theatre composer, and the music by the German-born John Frederick Lampe (1703–1751). *The Dragon of Wantley* looked at Handel's most recent works, *Arminio* and *Giustino*, and through them at all the anomalies and illogicalities of opera and slyly edged them into utter absurdity; Handel, who was one of its targets, is said to have laughed uproariously at it. After an unimpressive production at the Little Theatre in 1737, it was taken over a year later by the great John Rich, at Lincoln's Inn, and even scored more performances than *The Beggar's Opera*. In a sense, Gay and Pepusch, Carey and Lampe laughed opera out of serious theatrical consideration. The two pairs of collaborators each produced a sequel to the great hits, but failed to repeat their original successes.

It was Thomas Augustine Arne (1710–1778) who succeeded best among the English competitors of Handel. Arne became a Roman Catholic, and was therefore without the alternative of steady, reasonably remunerative work for the established Church. This meant that his reputation and main source of income depended upon the work he did for the theatre; his instrumental works and his songs and cantatas for the concert halls and pleasure gardens contain a good deal of fine music, but the economic conditions of the period did not make it possible to live by such works although they often seem to be of a higher general level than his music of the theatre on which he depended; often, he simply did not bother to turn out anything but routine music for a routine play with routine words and routine situations. Arne was capable of first-rate dramatic music—it is not simply the familiar eighteenth-century musical idioms which made his setting of Milton's *Comus* appeal to modern audiences and win more response than that of Lawes—but there were obviously times when he simply could not be bothered and went through the motions of composition with an almost obvious lack of interest. Modern audiences insist on singing his 'Rule, Britannia!' as part of the jollification which annually ends the London Promenade Concert season, but few people have followed his work further. It is not for purely musical reasons that he has had a bad Press ever since the 1780s, a very little time after his death; he seems to have been an unpleasant man whose scandalous sexual life did not—as scandalous sexual lives often do—prompt his contemporaries to shocked admiration. Arne married the soprano Cecilia Young, who refused to return to England with him after his successful season in Dublin; his tireless amorous career had, apparently, no passion but only a callous, cool greed, and after the collapse of his marriage it remained active and remained chilly. He was avaricious. Dr Burney, the historian of music, who had been his apprentice, castigated him for extreme stinginess in their dealings together; Arne set his pupil to compose scores which he himself had promised and offered no remuneration to the young man who had done the work. Capable of great originality, with a highly developed sense of orchestral colour, a superb melodist, he found it only too easy to churn out music lacking in every quality of character except infallible technical assurance. He was obviously a splendid teacher whose singing pupils filled a large area of the eighteenth-century stage, and he insisted, even when his pupils had become celebrities, on every penny of his percentage of their fees.

Nevertheless, whatever his flaws of character, even many of his most casual theatre scores contain songs or orchestral movement in which the music is utterly delightful. With Purcell, he was a genuine influence upon Handel's English style, especially in later works like *L'Allegro, il pensieroso ed il moderato*, in which Milton's two character sketches were joined by a third to make a three-act secular oratorio, and *Susannah*, works in which Handel adopted a pastoral vein for which he drew heavily on the example of Arne. But Arne's highest ambitions were stimulated most powerfully not by the standard English 'dramatic opera' with spoken dialogue but by the idea of genuine, 'through composed' opera with continuous music. *Comus*, in 1737, took the traditional English masque, with spoken dialogue, as its model; the four main characters do not sing, and in later editions, after 1760, movements from Handel's *L'Allegro* were printed with Arne's music, together with three songs which Handel apparently set to Milton's text to please Italian singers. *Alfred*, a highly patriotic work about the great Saxon King and his war against the Danes (1744), again has spoken dialogue. It ends with the swaggering arrogance of 'Rule, Britannia!' (for though the words simply call upon Britain to accept her divinely imposed destiny, the music is arrogant and does swagger splendidly, with a panache not characteristic of its composer, most of whose best music is pastoral and gentle). *Love in a Village* (1762), the second of Arne's settings of libretti by the Irish Isaac Bickerstaffe, is composed in continuous music and it is, in Arne's terms, entirely 'modern'. It tells the story of the simple village girl pursued by the wicked squire and saved from a fate worse than death by the timely return of her sailor boy-friend. It needs fine, smooth singing and its orchestration is rich and colourful, but the music is drawn from other works, chiefly by Arne himself. *Love in a Village* followed two other ambitious works, *Thomas and Sally* (1760), a first collaboration with Bickerstaffe in which directness and simplicity of story and music avoid the need for much spoken dialogue or recitative, and *Artaxerxes* (1762), in which Arne translated a libretto by Metastasio, the greatest poet among the librettists of *opera seria*, and set it to his own music as it stood, recitatives and all in a vocal style so elaborate and technically demanding that for a century its arias, especially those given to the heroine, Mandane, stood as the test of vocal excellence. Its vocal music, despite the exorbitant demands it made upon its singers, was delightful to the audience as well as to the company (which naturally enjoyed an opportunity to shine), and *Artaxerxes* was a success against all the odds; even the presence on the stage of *castrato* singers did not damn it although it caused some unflattering comment. It was, however, a flash in the pan; two years later Arne produced *L'Olimpiade*, another libretto by Metastasio which he did not translate but presented in Italian, but this did not repeat the success of *Artaxerxes*.

Arne, as composer to Vauxhall Gardens, where the people in general had some opportunity of listening to the liveliest and most up-to-date music, wrote a large number of songs to be heard there. He composed chamber music and occasional cantatas, all tuneful and graceful as well as beautifully written. He wrote a handful of catholic church music, though Masses traditionally ascribed to him are apparently spurious. No other composer in the theatre, until the advent of Sullivan more than a century after his death (for Sullivan's career in the theatre did not begin until the 1870s), had Arne's technical assurance. As well as his splendid melodic power, when his ambitions, were aroused he had an unusually colourful sense of the orchestra, writing for both flutes and oboes simultaneously, and even at times for clarinets, creating beautiful open-air type passages for woodwind alone; he even, at times, scored for trumpets and horns playing together. He died when the new *galant* style was beginning to dominate European music and making its way in England through the coming of J. C. Bach as composer to the opera. He is one of those English composers who should be regarded as a candidate for resurrection.

The theatre remained the single place in which a composer could earn a decent living and write as he wished to write, for though the cathedral musical establishments remained in existence, Georgian church music was a routine which inspired little vital or exciting work; it was in the theatre that something new, in style as well as in content, was always required. The rise of pantomime as an oddly eccentric, and typically belated exploitation of the Italian *commedia dell'arte*, wanted quantities of songs and dances; Burlesque was equally demanding. Dr Roger Fiske, in his authoritative and splendidly enthusiastic *English Theatre Music in the Eighteenth Century*, has shown what we miss in our ignorance of this music. Charles Dibdin (1745–1814) represents the impact of the *galant* style on this traditionally English area of music. Dibdin himself wrote a racy, if not always accurate, *Autobiography* to speak for himself.

Dibdin's scores come to us in accordance with the custom of his period, as no more than melody and bass arranged for piano and voices, so that they present a music which often seems to be undernourished to the point of semi-starvation. But they have melodies not only delightful in themselves but capable of conveying a sense of character, of embodying a situation with real dramatic quality. This was Dibdin's duty, and he had little interest in going beyond it. Like most *galant* composers, he had no particular interest in counterpoint, and his music is limited by the harmonic sense of his age; his orchestration is conventional. Modern audiences know him only as composer of the song 'Tom Bowling', his elegy for his sailor brother, which forms the cello solo in the slow section of Sir Henry Wood's *Fantasia on British Sea Songs* in the roistering conclusion of the London 'Prom' season every year, and it is hard to imagine a listener who has no curiosity about the composer of so effective and touching a melody.

William Shield (1748–1829) was a more traditionally English composer than Dibdin. The son of a singing teacher from a village near

Durham, his parents died when he was only nine years old, and he was apprenticed to a boat builder. He soon returned to music, studied with Charles Avison and gravitated to London, became a violinist in the opera orchestra but became better known, both at the opera and at concerts, as a viola player. From 1778, when he produced his first theatre piece, *The Flitch of Bacon*, to 1791 he was composer to Covent Garden, where he returned after a year's travel in Europe. He played in the King's Band, and was Master of the King's Musick from 1817 until his death. His collection of theatre music and of songs contributed to plays and the pleasure gardens is full of good, sturdy, honest tunes effectively worked out. In 1791 Shield met Haydn during the great composer's first visit to England, and his later music shows that he was receptive enough to learn a great deal from the greatest of his contemporaries.

While Shield and his music were totally and unmistakably English, Stephen Storace (1763–1796, born in London of Italian parents) was successful in Italy and Austria before he began to compose for English theatres. He was a friend of Mozart—his sister Anna Selina (known as Nancy) was the first Susanna in Mozart's *The Marriage of Figaro*, and Mozart wrote the concert aria *'Ch'io me scordi di te'*, K.505, with piano obbligato, for her in 1788. Storace composed operas which were well received in Vienna, as well as some Mozartian chamber works; in London he adapted, and to some extent recomposed, operas by Dittersdorf and Martin, composer of the opera *Una Cosa Rara*, which in 1786 had an outstanding success; in addition he composed a number of English operas of his own in a neat, melodious sub-Mozartian style, the most successful being *No Song, No Supper*, which is not yet quite forgotten. Storace, like Shield and Dibdin, deserves more attention than we give him, though Shield's song 'The Ploughboy' was given a new lease of life when Benjamin Britten included a charming arrangement of it among his folk-songs.

VIII

Concerts, Clubs and Social Classes

By this time, the musical world had changed. In a sense, the eighteenth century was the period in which music went out of social favour. The 'man of fashion', as the great but unlovable Lord Chesterfield told his son, should never demonstrate any overwhelming, unconquerable enthusiasms. Still less should he demonstrate any musical expertise. Lord Chesterfield told his son that it would do no harm for him to play the violin, but he must take care not to play so well as a professional musician. The 'man of fashion' should have taste, for that was part of his necessary social equipment, but he was not expected to have any notions about music as an interest with any intellectual pretensions, or to be worth any course of study that would demand actual work, or the pursuit of excellence. "Fiddlers, pipers and *id genus omne*," the Earl announced, "—most unedifying companions for a man of fashion". "Whenever I go to the opera, I leave my sense and my reason behind with my half-guinea, and deliver myself up to my eyes and my ears."[23] To call Lord Chesterfield a Philistine would be overstating the case against him; but he is an early example of the attitude from which English philistinism grew. To be good at anything except behaviour suggested that one had worked and made an effort; working and making efforts were not the business of the gentleman, whose concern was to demonstrate an effortless superiority. His son should not be a good violinist, for a good violinist did not demonstrate the effortless, undisturbed superiority which is a gentleman's reason for existing. Thus one must be superior not only to work, but to passions and enthusiasms; everything must be tempered, because enthusiasm is a vulgar quality, by a cool moderation; life is to be lived coolly. If Lord Chesterfield went to the opera, it was not his business to consider the structure, the art, the skill, the intellectual depth of the music he heard; his function was only to submit his ears to the possibilities of charm and coolly to approve or to disapprove. If art had any intellectual or spiritual value, that was nothing to the 'man of fashion' who attended the opera or listened to other music for no more than pleasant relaxation and because his position in society demanded that he attend.

If music had no intellectual or spiritual value, it was obviously the sort of activity that could be discarded. In Lord Chesterfield's letters of worldly-wise advice to his son, we see the first glimpse of the attitude which, in the nineteenth century, led to an almost ostentatious disregard by the upper classes for educational and intellectual values, which deadened that century and has not completely died out in the twentieth, for all classes were ready to copy the complacency and stodginess of their social superiors. It is perhaps significant that in the 1790s, whilst Beethoven was establishing himself as a pianist and composer among the aristocracy in Vienna, Haydn had returned from his two visits to England where musicians and the intelligentsia had made an enormous fuss of him but the aristocracy, attending his concerts and applauding, one supposes, as fervently as a Chesterfieldian attitude could justify, seemed to have had little personally to do with him. The sons of George III were the major exceptions to this, and Haydn's London Notebooks, as translated by H. C. Robbins Landon, preserve anecdotes about the great men of the world when such anecdotes appealed to the old composer, who mentions the musicians and the middle-class celebrities whom he meets but apparently found himself without any close contact with the nobility.

The aristocratic musical organization was the Academy of Antient Music, organized by amateurs of the highest social standing. It began operations in 1728 and made it its business to explore, if not very systematically, music from the Renaissance onwards, and found that there was a good deal of pleasure to be gained from Italian and English madrigals. In 1726, the second Earl of Sandwich, a genuine and enthusiastic amateur musician who enjoyed playing the timpani in professional orchestras, with the Earl of Exeter and a group of other notables founded the Concert of Antient Music, which attracted the attention of George III who became a regular patron, and kept his own record of the programmes he heard; as a result, the Antient Music concerts became known as the 'King's Concert'. The 'ancient' element in its constitution was that no music was to be played which was not at least twenty years old. The various gentlemen who were members took it in turn to organize a concert and choose its programme, but the actual musicians, and their conductor when a conductor became an accepted feature of London concert life, were professional musicians; the choir too was professional, its trebles being drawn from the choirs of Westminster Abbey and the Chapel Royal. Lord Chesterfield, one hopes, would have approved of the custom which separated ennobled patrons from mere executant musicians. The Concert of Antient Music continued to present programmes regularly until 1848, by which time music by Haydn and Mozart, as well as the young Beethoven, became eligible for its programmes.

The Chesterfieldian doctrine was borne out by the history of the organization which became known as the Castle Concerts. A group of gentlemen met to make music together, according to Sir John Hawkins's *History of Music*, "sometimes in private houses but not seldom at tavernes. The music was choice and exactly performed."[24] Eventually, they decided to meet regularly in the Castle Tavern, where the landlord started to invite other patrons to listen to the concert, selling seats. The gentlemen at this ceased to meet and the landlord, not to disappoint his patrons, collected professional musicians to take their place. There was a good deal of amateur and semi-amateur music of this kind available in London.

But in 1764, when Carl Friedrich Abel went into partnership with Johann Christian Bach to give regular seasons of subscription concerts, something like a genuine artistic policy was imposed upon concerts for the first time. Carl Friedrich Abel (1723–1787) had been a pupil of Johann Sebastian Bach at the *Thomasschule* in Leipzig; he settled in London and became a noted teacher, harpsichordist and player of the viola da gamba as well as composer. Johann Christian Bach, the youngest son of the great Johann Sebastian, was the family renegade; he had made his way to Italy, became a Roman Catholic and organist of Milan Cathedral. A composer of the new *galant* school, noted for the directness and elegance of his music and its rejection of the scholarly, J. C. Bach had come to London as composer to the opera, but rapidly recognizing the hazards involved in the provision of opera for England, he and Abel had begun to augment their incomes with regular concerts, first at Spring Gardens and then at Carlisle House, in Soho Square, where a certain Mrs Cornelys entertained society in every way that society wished to be entertained.

Mrs Cornelys had first been known to Europe as Theresa Immer, and deserves a footnote in English musical history. Theresa Immer, was born in Venice in 1723. By the time she was seventeen she was a notable singer and a mistress of Casanova, who, according to his *Memoirs*, succeeded a member of the Venetian senate as her lover. In 1744 she was in Vienna, married to a dancer who committed suicide. As Teresa Pompeati, that is under her married name, she sang in London in 1746, and her stage career continued until 1753 when, as mistress of the Margrave Friedrich of Bayreuth, a new lover, Prince Charles Alexander of Lorraine, gave her control of all the theatres in the Austrian Netherlands, a present which left her in flight from her creditors. In Amsterdam she may have married Cornelis de Rigebos, and in 1760 she returned to England as Mrs Cornelys—no husband accompanied her—where she bought Carlisle House and used it to give balls, masquerades and concerts. She ran her new business with considerable financial and social success until, in 1771, she was prosecuted for running a disorderly house; the indictment came almost immediately after she challenged the monopoly of the Patent Theatres by staging opera at Carlisle House. In 1772 she was made bankrupt, but invincible as ever as she began to earn her living by selling asses' milk from a stall at Hyde Park Corner; when she died, in 1791, the stall had turned into a suite of breakfast rooms.

The career of Mrs Cornelys deserves mention for its clear view of English society in the first permissive age and also as an account of the alliance between what we have come to call 'serious music' and high society. Bach and Abel were important composers of the modern, most up-to-date school, bringing to England the lightness, elegance and natural transparency of the *galant* style, and during Mozart's visit to London, when the eight-year-old boy delighted English concert-goers, Bach and he became great friends, so that Bach became an important influence on the compositions of the *wunderkind*. Bach and Abel left older music to the care of others, and there is simply no indication that they had any particular interest in it. They introduced the new Continental symphonies to England,

and brought out the pianoforte as a solo instrument in concertos. After 1776 their concerts, having used a number of auditoria, settled in the Hanover Square Rooms, in which they had invested a good deal of money; the Hanover Square Rooms held some eight hundred listeners in what the eighteenth century regarded as the height of elegance.

The leadership of taste after the end of the Bach/Abel concerts —J. C. Bach died in 1782 and Abel in 1787—was taken over by an organization which called itself the Professional Concerts, so named because the committee which managed them consisted of professional musicians, both English and foreign, active in London. Several distinguished expatriates were involved in the venture, the most active member of the committee being John Peter Salomon, a violinist and composer born in Bonn in 1745 and resident in England since 1781. Before long, however, Salomon had quarrelled with his colleagues and broken away to form his own series of subscription concerts to which, in 1791, he brought over Haydn, some of whose earlier symphonies had already proved popular at London concerts, where they and some music by Mozart had been played. The coming of Haydn led to an all-out subscription war between Salomon's organization and the Professional Concerts; the Professional Concerts were beaten into final defeat—apparently the concert audience was not large enough to support two rival series of concerts, and Salomon was so successful that he induced Haydn to return for a second series. After that, he continued to give concerts, but not in regular series, so that the need for a new organization was supplied in 1813 by the creation of the London Philharmonic Society, which we now know as the Royal Philharmonic Society.

There is a danger of regarding music as an activity that began and ended in London. Elsewhere, outside the capital, music was primarily an amateur activity, undertaken by local groups who formed a music club and made music regularly together. The Oxford Music Club, for example, was formed during the Commonwealth by the unemployed choral musicians of the various college choirs; it declined later in the seventeenth century; in 1665 its catalogue of music reached as far as music by Henry Lawes, Christopher Gibbons and John Jenkins, and, perhaps because its interests were in the music of the past, it died out until Handel's visit in 1733.

Possibly the resumption of Anglican services had left the members sufficient singing to do in their normal course of duty. After Handel's visit the club became active as an amateur orchestra. The Oxford Music Club had the music room in Holywell, described as "the oldest concert Hall in Europe", as its auditorium. Gentlemen paid a shilling, but were requested to leave their dogs outside for dogs "are a great Annoyance to the company"; ladies were admitted free of charge. For the fee he paid, a gentleman could either play or simply listen.

In the 1730s, Norwich, York, Lincoln, Lichfield and Bristol each had two music clubs. Charles Dibdin, who had been a choirboy at Winchester Cathedral, wrote in his autobiography about the weekly music meeting held there in the 1760s. When he revisited the City in 1769 with a friend, he went to the concert, paying a fee of half a crown because they were strangers to the city; each had an instrument with him, so they were invited to play with the orchestra, and at the end of the evening their subscriptions were returned to them.[25] Dr Stanley Sadie, in *Concert Life in the Eighteenth Century*, a lecture given to the Royal Musical Association in 1958, glances at the history of concerts in Salisbury, Canterbury and Winchester. A Musical and Amicable Society was founded in Birmingham, and in 1768 the first Birmingham Festival took place. The Three Choirs Festival was inaugurated in 1724; such festivals as this, run by people normally involved with the professional musicians of the choirs of Hereford, Worcester and Gloucester Cathedrals—the 'Three Choirs' of the event's name—had at their disposal not only the members of local amateur orchestras, with the help of local music teachers, but also the help of professional orchestral players of a kind rarely heard outside London except in Bath during the season. A music club was founded in Manchester in the 1740s, but it seems to have been chiefly a means whereby Jacobites could meet without arousing suspicion, for after the 1745 rebellion it died out; resurrected in 1770 as the 'Gentlemen's Concerts', it found that all the gentlemen eager to join played the flute and nothing else. Dr Sadie also uncovers a startlingly active musical life, choral and orchestral, all over East Anglia.

These societies met to play pieces, not, in normal circumstances, to rehearse and work over, in order to perfect the performance. To the music clubs, performance was a hit or miss pleasure; the standards of performance during the eighteenth century cannot be compared with those of today, when concerts are scrupulously rehearsed, and our recordings practically faultless. But those who read such biographies as those of Dittersdorf and Spohr, or the letters of Beethoven and Mozart, will notice how rarely even such exigent masters worried about performances inadequately rehearsed or even totally unrehearsed. Any local professional musicians could become members of the music clubs, adding what we can only regard as their dubious expertise to the work of the amateurs. William Gardiner, the Leicestershire hosier who was a devoted amateur musician, mentions a family of five brothers, the Valentines, in his autobiography, *Music and Friends*; the Valentines earned the bulk of their living by playing for music clubs within reach of Leicester.

The repertory, of course, was in the main old-fashioned, depending upon the baroque concerto repertory from Corelli onwards and largely upon the availability of works in print. Otto Erich Deutsch, in his *Handel: A Documentary Biography*, notes the purchase by music clubs of Handel's music—concertos, suites and overtures, as soon as they reached the public. Avison's concertos, published in his own provincial city, became available outside the north-east, and it seems that any music thus available was greeted with curiosity if not with wild enthusiasm. One of Gardiner's friends, John Valentine, published a set of *Eight Easy Symphonies . . . with solos for the different Instruments Interspersed through the whole; being an introduction to playing in Concert*. But provincial music remained anchored to old styles and to music available in published form until the nineteenth century was well under way.

Apart from the theatre and the cosy sinecures in the cathedrals, there were the Catch Clubs and Glee Clubs, in which the popularity of sociable singing among the upper classes survived in spite of the prevalence of Lord Chesterfield's doctrines of fashionable behaviour. It may be that to sit and sing a part in a concerted vocal piece is no immediate evidence of hard work, for singing can be regarded not as the result of study and effort but simply as a gift which can be exploited by its possessor without effort or lowering oneself to the level of a mere craftsman. Therefore the Glee Clubs began among the well-to-do amateurs and spread among the upper classes before it reached the masses, and the almost total obliteration of such modes of music making in the twentieth century cannot really be taken as evidence of our greater sophistication and musicality.

The glee, like the catch, was written for three or four voices, often as solo trio and chorus, or solo quartet and chorus. Unlike the catch, it moved in block harmonies and had little polyphonic or contrapuntal interest; it did not set out, as a matter of course, to be witty, and it did not, in a more genteel age, set out to enjoy high-spirited indecency. The Noblemen's and Gentlemen's Catch Club, which still survives, was founded by the second Earl of Sandwich and his parliamentary friends in 1762, holding its meetings during Parliamentary sessions; the influence of Lord Chesterfield may have had something to do with its immediate offer of Associate Membership to professional singers. It also offered annual prizes for the most effective glees and catches offered to it, and the prize winners were the most prominent English composers of an age we normally look upon as musically dead. It had, of course, immediate and attractive virtues; had a glee not been tuneful, it would not have been sung; had it not been interesting to sing, it would not have been sung; had it been impractical, nobody would have sung it, for it was meant not for work but for pleasure; and if it had offered no challenge, and no sense of achievement, it would have been left to die. The Noblemen's and Gentlemen's Catch Club set an example which was rapidly followed.

The Anacreontic Society was founded in 1766; it met in the Crown and Anchor Tavern on the Strand "for supper and the singing of catches, glees and songs." Each meeting opened with the glee by John Stafford Smith, 'To Anacreon in Heaven', which was the 'constitutional hymn' and which, not many years later, became 'The Star-Spangled Banner', the national anthem of the United States of America. The Anacreontic Society was not so socially exalted as the Catch Club, but membership was regarded as a sign of gentility. The chairman, in 1794, was Sir John Hankey, who unwisely permitted the Duchess of Devonshire, the leader of London 'Society' at that time, to attend a meeting in secret, such meetings being, of course, for men only. Hankey, as the members called for the songs they wished to hear, decided that some were unfit for a Duchess's ears and vetoed them, whereupon the members rebelled against this censorship and resigned in a mass.

By this time, however, the Glee Club itself was in operation; in 1783 it had begun to meet regularly in the houses of its founder-members; expanding, it moved to the Newcastle Coffee House and later, inevitably, to the Crown and Anchor. In 1799, Samuel Webbe the elder (1740–1816), the master among the original glee composers, had composed his 'Glorious Apollo' which was regarded by members as equivalent to the 'constitutional hymn' of the Anacreontic Society and was sung to open every subsequent meeting.

'Glorious Apollo' (Ex. 16) is a true glee, composed according to the taste and style of the inventors of the form; it is a composition of short phrases leading to a perfect cadence and then starting again, so that badly handled a glee was an extremely short-winded and choppy composition. It expanded during the period, close on a century, of its prominence, and even in time permitted some contrapuntal interest to be featured; purists would, by the turn of the eighteenth century, probably have rejected many later glees by such composers as John Callcott (1766–1821) who studied under Haydn, William Horsely (1774–1858), Samuel Webbe the younger (1770–1843), Richard Stevens (1757–1837), who had an apparent passion for setting lines by Shakespeare, and Reginald Spofforth (1770–1827) as part-songs rather than true glees—which have nothing to do with being 'gleeful' but take their name from the Anglo-Saxon word for music, *gligge*.

All these, and many other more obscure musical societies in London were largely upper-class organizations, though by the time of Dickens and Thackeray the glee had moved on into new social milieux and found new devotees. Record remains of only one 'working class' musical organization which functioned musically in the eighteenth century. The Madrigal Society was founded in 1741 by John Immyns, a lawyer who, having in some obscure way blotted his copybook, was content to work as a barrister's clerk and console himself with music. He was copyist for the Royal Academy of Antient Music, a post which was probably responsible for developing his affection for the music of the past, at that time entirely neglected; he was secretary to Johann Pepusch; he taught himself to play the lute and in 1752 became lutenist to the Chapel Royal. Apparently, according to Sir John Hawkins's *General History of the Science and Practice of Music*, Immyns found an established group of singers "who spent their lives in the practice of psalmody". They were, said Hawkins, "mostly mechanics, some weavers from Spitalfields, others of various trades and professions." They were

Ex. 16

Soli: the chorus repeats
Samuel Webbe
Glor-ious A-pol-lo from on high be-held us, Wand-'ring to
find a temple for his praise.
Soli: chorus repeats
Sent Po-ly-hym-nia hith-er to
shield us, While we ourselves such a structure might raise.
soli: chorus repeats
Thus, then com-bin-ing, hands and hearts join-ing, Sing we in har-mony A-pol-lo's
Praise. praise, A- pol-lo's Praise, A-pol-lo's Praise, A- Praise.

"not less distinguished by their love of vocal harmony than by the harmless disposition of their tempers and their friendly disposition towards each other." Immyns turned their attention towards the madrigal, and Hawkins, who became a member, said that "with a little pains and the help of ordinary solmization, which many of them were very expert in [they] became soon able to sing almost at sight an English and even an Italian madrigal."[26]

The fact that Hawkins—barrister, clubman-about-town, friend of Doctor Johnson, author, and husband of a wealthy wife (he had no fortune of his own)—became an early member of the Madrigal Society suggests that other middle-class members soon joined. Hawkins's own account of the Society is not without its little mystery; his *History* gives 1741 as the date of the foundation but the Minute Books do not begin their record of events until 1752. Michael Arne (the son of Thomas Arne) was a member; so was Joah Bates, conductor of the Concert of Antient Music, and throughout the nineteenth century until modern times many of the most eminent musicians have been members; but the Society as a home for musical artisans no longer existed after the middle-class enthusiasts began their infiltration.

The Madrigal Society, like the Academy of Antient Music and the Concert of Antient Music, was an indication of a primarily musicological (although the word did not exist before the twentieth century) interest in the music of the past, perhaps as a reaction against the passion for lightness, clarity and grace which came in with the *galant* style, the first time musicians were beginning to think of their art historically, and in 1776 Hawkins, to whom we owe our information about the Madrigal Society, published his *General History of the Science and Practice of Music*, 192 chapters in five volumes, giving a somewhat generalized account of music outside England but offering a wealth of information about the organization and performance of music in England. Hawkins's *History* is not the most elegantly organized of books, and the reader feels that, having amassed a great army of facts, its author could not drill them expertly or deploy them effectively into companies or platoons; and it seems clear that Hawkins was not interested in history as an interpretation of the past.

It was, too, a pity for Hawkins that his five volumes appeared in 1776, the year in which the first of the four volumes of Charles

Burney's *General History of Music* was published; the later volumes appeared in 1782 and 1789. Burney was an accomplished professional musician, holder of a doctorate, not without success as a theatre composer, an organist and musical organizer. He deals in his *History* more clearly with the technical development of music and toured Europe to gather materials from all the great musical centres. Burney's is what we have come to call a 'critical history' of music, voicing with complete clarity the point of view of the eighteenth-century 'Enlightenment' and regarding the music of the past as the series of often stumbling, uncertain steps by means of which music rose to the classic perfection it had reached in his own lifetime; it sees little good in the music of any earlier age and dismisses such masters as Byrd and Purcell as men deprived by their early birth of the knowledge and the style that should have brought them to real artistic splendour. His mass of material is elegantly and methodically assembled, with admirable clarity, and his prose has the coolness and order which the eighteenth century found both necessary and adorable. Burney reviewed Hawkins's book in a satirical poem whhich he called 'The Trial of Midas the Second', and his review, together with the appearance of Burney's *magnum opus*, more or less demolished Hawkins's book until the middle of the nineteenth century, when a second edition was published and made the value of the work clear.

IX
The Land Without Music

When Berlioz reflected upon his visits to England, in 1848 when he came to conduct Jullien's aborted opera season, and in 1851, as one of the judges of musical instruments shown at the Great Exhibition, he declared: "There is no town in the world where so much music is consumed as London."[27] There was music in the theatre; there was the opera; there was the Philharmonic Society; there were the chamber music concerts of the Musical Union and the Beethoven Quartet Society. And there was music in the streets. Berlioz came to the conclusion that as the average theatre player in the 1850s could hardly hope to earn more than £6 a week, he wondered why such musicians did not seize the opportunity of earning more by playing in the healthier, less tiring and more comfortable surroundings of the streets. And then, of course, there was the vast collection of amateur singing clubs, orchestras and 'Harmonic Meetings' such as that presided over in Dickens's *Bleak House* by the resident comedian, Little Swills.

For all that, England was 'the land without music', or at any rate without music of its own. England had existed through the period of Bach's sons, Haydn, Mozart and Beethoven without an outstanding composer of its own. There was ample work, in the church and the theatre, for the English composer, but neither the nature of his work nor the quality of his training was likely to challenge his creative powers nor stimulate his creative imagination. The cathedral choir schools had nurtured many great composers, from Leonel Power and Walter Frye to William Walton, but in the eighteenth-century church music had sunk into an undisturbed torpor and there was no spur in the church to the composition of effective music. Otherwise the would-be composer was trained as apprentice assistant to an established composer, just as Charles Burney was trained as assistant to Thomas Arne. The system could have worked, and did work, in other countries; in England it proved stultifying because the English opera- and concert-goers depended on foreign visitors for exciting, ambitious work and left the native composer to carry out the routine theatrical jobs which depended upon the quality and originality of the plays to which they worked, and the theatre was not offering any musician new and stimulating drama to deal with. The newest types of composition were heard in the concert halls, but England lacked the men of independent genius who needed no external compulsion to work in new ways because they had a route of their own to follow.

The career of William Crotch can, perhaps, adequately show the situation of English music. Crotch (1775–1847) was the son of a musically-minded carpenter who built himself a small organ on which, at the age of two, little Crotch could already pick out tunes; at the age of three he could provide tunes with an accurate bass. Not even Mozart and Mendelssohn, the most carefully attested as well as the most amazing prodigies in the history of music, were more phenomenally gifted than the London carpenter's son, and like Mozart, Crotch was carefully investigated by the experts. By the time he was four, Crotch was startling London society by his rare gifts; he toured the British Isles and at eleven began a two-year stay in Cambridge as organist of Trinity and King's Colleges and as assistant to the Professor of Music. At thirteen he went to Oxford, became organist of Christ Church and St John's Colleges, and he composed an oratorio, *The Captivity of Judah*, when he was fourteen. He composed several ceremonial works for the university and was given his Doctorate of Music in 1799. When he betook himself to London, he lectured to the Royal Society and composed his oratorio *Palestine* in 1812. In 1822 he became the first Principal of the Royal Academy of Music. Musically, however, he seems hardly to have developed at all after his childhood and while his music is never less than pleasant and well-written, it seems to have little to say to us.

In 1820, the Philharmonic Society brought Ludwig Spohr, composer, violin virtuoso and conductor, to London. In 1829 Mendelssohn and England began the impassioned love affair which made Mendelssohn a frequent visitor until his death in 1847. In 1848

Berlioz was invited to conduct the opera season projected by Louis-Antoine Jullien, the conductor of Promenade Concerts, and in 1852 he spent a season in London as conductor of the New Philharmonic Society. By that time, Michael Costa, the Italian conductor, was already firmly settled in England as conductor at the opera; he had made his home in England in 1830. Berlioz was succeeded at the New Philharmonic Society by Peter Joseph Lindpainter, who came from Koblenz via Munich.

In 1855, Wagner spent an unhappy season as conductor of the Philharmonic Concerts but failed to impress either the orchestra or London audiences with his qualities; the players could not understand his beat, designed to control minute freedoms of rhythmic give-and-take within a firm tempo, and he hated the length of London concerts, especially as they were presented with what he regarded as the barest minimum of rehearsal. Gounod became an English hero in 1870, when he began a five-year stay in this country. Dvořák visited England in 1883 and conducted his *Hussite* Overture, which was commissioned by the Philharmonic Society, as was his D minor Symphony a year later; his popularity in London was an obvious help to his career on the Continent. Saint-Saëns first came to England in 1871 and was a regular visitor for the rest of his life. In 1860 the New Philharmonic Society came to an end, and its concerts became 'Mr William Ganz's Concerts', taken over by a German violinist who came to this country in 1850. Such visits by the great musical eminences did not stop at London; the great visitors were in demand at the important provincial festivals.

During the nineteenth century, as before and since, every celebrated instrumentalist and singer was heard in London; London audiences were appreciative and London engagements profitable. John Ella, a music critic who founded and ran the Concerts of the Musical Union, which gave concerts of chamber music, found it necessary in an article to explain his attitude to foreign artists. There was an English lady whose ambition was to play for the Musical Union, and Ella explained why he could not give her an engagement: "My expenses are considerable, the subscription low, and without attracting visitors by the engagement of new and eminent professors from the Continent, I could not afford to pay my artists."[28] Summing up thirty-two years of activity by the Musical Union, Ella wrote that seventy-four pianists, a hundred and two string players and twenty-seven wind players had been heard at its concerts; of these, forty-eight had been English and the foreigners had included all the greatest names of the period except that of Liszt, whose more or less new fashion of appearing alone on the platform to give what he called a 'recital' made it unnecessary to share a platform with anyone else. Berlioz, in *Evenings in the Orchestra*, remembered Balzac's story of an Italian singer who explained that Italy had lost all her singers to France and England: *"Paris les juge,"* she explained, *"et Londres les paye."*

The formation of the London Philharmonic Society in 1813 owed a good deal to the colony of foreign musicians who worked in London. Since the Professional Concerts had unwisely crossed swords with John Peter Salomon and his concerts with Haydn, and since Salomon no longer promoted regular seasons of subscription concerts in London, there was a gap in the capital's musical life. The Immigrants who helped to found the Philharmonic Society included the pianist J. B. Cramer, who was already established as a publisher in London; his brother Franz, the violinist-conductor who ended his life as Master of the Queen's Music; Salomon; Clementi, the pianist-composer whose headquarters as a maker of pianos was in London; Moralt, the violinist; Viotti, the violinist-composer, and others. They were joined by quite authoritative English musicians—William Dance, William Shield, Sir Henry Bishop, Charles Neate, who claimed to be Beethoven's only English pupil, Vincent Novello, the publisher, Attwood, Horsely and Webbe the younger, both composers of glees, and Sir George Smart. The names themselves demonstrate the seriousness and the go-ahead nature of the enterprise.

From the start, the Philharmonic Society was go-ahead, and its patron saint was Beethoven, from whom the Society commissioned the Ninth Symphony and to whom it sent a gift of £100 to aid him in his last illness. However, Beethoven's dealings with his London admirers were not the most straightforward and scrupulous; when the Society commissioned three new overtures from him, he sent works already heard in Vienna and elsewhere, and he sent the score of the Ninth Symphony to Berlin and arranged its first performance in Vienna. But in the first seasons, three of his symphonies were played, one of them being the *Eroica*; the other two cannot be identified from the accounts of the events of which they were part.

The Society's ideas were severe; no solo music, vocal or instrumental, was to be heard, but chamber music and choral works could be included; the embargo on solo instrumental works was lifted in the 1820s, to allow Charles Neate to play the Beethoven piano concertos, and solo singers—including the legendary Malibran, sang in the 1829 season. At the same time, English music was to be encouraged; manuscript works submitted to the committee would be rehearsed and, if satisfactory, included in a concert programme; significantly, none of the works submitted reached a public performance.

The Philharmonic Society did not create its own orchestra or appoint its own regular conductor. At first it gave its concerts on Tuesday evenings, when there was no performance at the Opera, and took over the players from the pit there. These instrumentalists were not offered a season's contract but were offered separate individual engagements concert by concert, so that as London's musical life developed through the multiplication of musical events, the Philharmonic Concerts became a prey to the 'deputy system', through which a player offered two engagements on one evening considered himself to be at liberty to accept the more lucrative so long as he sent a deputy to the one he missed, even though the deputy had attended no rehearsals and might well be left to play part of the programme at sight. This system continued until 1904, when Sir Henry Wood refused to accept deputies in the Queen's Hall Orchestra. The first conductor to be appointed by the Philharmonic Society was Sir Henry Bishop. At the beginning of its career the Philharmonic Concerts had been directed by the leader and a musician who sat at the otherwise redundant piano with the orchestral score; it was Ludwig Spohr who, according to his own account of the event, first startled the Philharmonic Society by conducting with a baton. Bishop was appointed in 1844 and conducted only three concerts before his health broke down, so that in the following year Michael Costa, Italian by birth, was imported from the Opera. Costa was not an inspired interpreter of symphonic music, but he was a splendid orchestral disciplinarian. Bernard Shaw, writing as 'Corno di Bassetto' in 1889, described Costa as the only man feared by the orchestra which was "killing Covent Garden by its slovenliness and killing the Philharmonic by its perfunctoriness."[29]

The financial troubles of the Philharmonic Society, and the conviction of its committee that nothing of any note had happened in the musical world since the death of Beethoven, except the advent of Mendelssohn, led to the challenge of a new organization.

In 1851, Henry Wylde, organist, composer and conductor, founded the New Philharmonic Society in direct rivalry to the established Philharmonic Society. He gathered a committee of wealthy music lovers and issued his prospectus: it said, "The growing taste for the arts, more especially for music, in this country, demands a new institution where the greatest works by the greatest masters of all the ages may be heard by the public at large. . . . Exclusiveness, the baneful hindrance of all progress in art, will not be tolerated in this society." Exclusiveness, however, was inevitable for the old Philharmonic Society itself, as its concerts were given in the Hanover Square Rooms which held audiences of no more than eight hundred; either seats were to be expensive or the Society, at a time when it was feeling the financial pinch, was bound to face economic disaster.

Not only was Berlioz the first conductor of the New Philharmonic Society—he had won the allegiance of London musicians as conductor of an abortive opera season projected by the conductor Jullien at the Drury Lane Theatre in 1848. Berlioz's exact and detailed knowledge of every score he conducted, the precision of his beat and the courtesy of his manner to his players set the venture off with impressive *élan.* The New Philharmonic Society's concert hall was the Exeter Hall, in the Strand. Exeter Hall was the headquarters of English Methodism, which, holding audiences of three thousand as well as a large orchestra and choir, could afford to reduce prices in the cheaper parts of the hall until they were within reach of the artisan class.

The authorities in charge of the Exeter Hall, however, were uncomfortable at the use of their premises as a concert hall; their statutes allowed the hall to be used only for religious, charitable or scientific purposes, and in 1854 withdrew the New Philharmonic Society's permission to use it, so that the concerts moved to the Hanover Square Rooms, and inevitable, unwilling exclusiveness; it was forced, until the opening of the St James's Hall in Piccadilly, into a social strait-jacket identical with that worn by the old Philharmonic Society. The rest of Wylde's prospectus held good.

"The New Philharmonic Society," he had declared, "does not entertain the opinion, acted on by an older institution, that no schools except those which can be called classical are to be considered as capable of affording pleasure, and that such schools can only be enjoyed by a select few amateurs and artists." When Wylde retired in 1879, and Wilhelm Ganz took over the concerts, Ganz adopted Wylde's liberal musical policy.

London was the world's most populous city. Its huge population was catered for, so far as concert music was concerned, by a small concert hall regarded as the home of serious music. Hence the exclusiveness of musical life in England. When William Sterndale Bennett, the most original and accomplished of early Victorian composers in England, went to Leipzig in 1838 to play his First Piano Concerto with Mendelssohn (who thought very highly of him) and the *Gewandhaus* Orchestra he was, according to his son J. R. Sterndale Bennett, "prepared to find music more widely cultivated than in England. He also observed that in Germany a love for [music's] more advanced forms was to be found in all classes. On the evening when he made his début at Leipzig, he espied the man who blacked the boots at his lodgings sitting in the gallery of the *Gewandhaus*."[30]

Obviously there were social and financial reasons why music had no such popular appeal in England, and anyone attempting to win a less restricted audience would need to educate its audience and make no stringent demands on their concentration. The model for concerts which attempted to do this seemed to be given in Paris by Philippe Musard, who during the 1830s won enormous success as a conductor of light music and masked balls; by 1837 he had recruited a chorus and added 'classical' music to his repertory. In 1838 a series of 'Promenade Concerts *à la Musard*' was given at Drury Lane Theatre, each consisting of four overtures, four quadrilles and a piece for a solo wind instrument. In a month, a rival series had begun at the Crown and Anchor Tavern, where such concerts survived for a season with considerable musical ambition, introducing symphonies to the programmes; they continued throughout Lent, when the theatres were closed. The conductor was Edward Eliason, a member of the Philharmonic Society who had played Beethoven's Violin Concerto at its first performance in England.

In 1846, Eliason took charge of another season of Promenade Concerts at the Lyceum Theatre, with an almost unknown French assistant conductor, Louis-Antoine Jullien; in the winter, Musard himself was brought to England, and it seems that while the Philharmonic Society was struggling to survive under financial pressure, there was a reliable audience for concerts of a less formal and less demanding kind; admission to Eliason's concerts was particularly cheap—no more than a shilling—and Eliason's seasons were all rivalled by similar concerts under different management. In 1841, Jullien took over Drury Lane Theatre for his own Promenade Concerts, and the future of such events was immediately put beyond doubt. Jullien, more than anyone else, was responsible for the idea of the conductor as a sort of magical personality, a hypnotist with powers far beyond those of Svengali, exerting dominating power over every orchestra.

Jullien was a brilliant showman, eccentrically elegant, with elaborate moustaches; his gestures were imperial. He conducted from inside the orchestra, not standing in front of it, so that the audience was able to study his activities from all angles. On the rostrum, like a throne, was a large, gilded chair; he liked to sink into this when he had acknowledged the applause at the end of a work, to recoup his energies before the next item. He recruited a large orchestra but added as many as six military bands to it to take part in the quadrilles, to which he gave topical titles, and which were the sensations of his concerts. Jullien added as much factitious drama as he could to each event, taking care that the drama was visual as well as merely auditory. Somehow or other, he decided that the symphonies of Beethoven, properly 'produced', so to speak, and with effective orchestral additions such as a thunder machine in the 'Pastoral' Symphony, would appeal to his audience; he conducted Beethoven's music with a jewelled baton and a pair of clean white gloves, all carried to him on a silver salver; in climaxes his military bands joined in, and while the storm in the 'Pastoral' Symphony became not so much a musical evocation as a titanic natural convulsion, the jubilations at the end of the Fifth Symphony, with bands as well as orchestra playing a tremendous fortissimo, were a mighty celebration.

Jullien's taste was obviously faulty and his treatment of great music unspeakably vulgar, but as well as being an inspired showman he was obviously a fine musician; even the spectacular elements of his performances were carefully rehearsed and drilled, and from this point of view it seems quite possible that his adulterated Beethoven performances were rather better played than devoutly serious performances at the Philharmonic Concerts, and we cannot know how many of those who went to listen to 'monster quadrilles' and to relish the uproar became converts through Jullien to symphonic music. His attempt to mount an opera season at Drury Lane Theatre, with Berlioz as conductor but with no repertory and no clear idea of what an opera repertory should be, but with a potentially splendid orchestra and choir, ended in failure and bankruptcy. (Berlioz is sardonically funny about Jullien and his schemes in his *Memoirs*.[31] In 1849 he returned to action with an orchestra of four hundred, three separate choirs and three military bands, but his *Concert monstre et Congrès musical* was not a success, and his opera *Pietro il Grande*, mounted lavishly at his own expense in 1852, lived for only five performances. A tour of the United States set him on his feet again, and in 1853 he returned to England, only to lose his entire library of music, including all his unpublished but spectacularly successful quadrilles, in the fire that destroyed Drury Lane Theatre in 1856. He invested heavily in the Royal Surrey Gardens Company, and its collapse in 1857 cost him something like seven thousand pounds; a year later he returned to France, imprisonment for debt, and death in a French lunatic asylum.

Jullien was not simply a charlatan. He seems to have lived upon applause and adulation; he adulterated the best music he played but he gave efficient, effective performances of his dubious versions and played important music to people who would have been afraid to set foot in the Opera House, the Hanover Square Rooms or the St James's Hall. And he vanquished all his rivals. Michael William Balfe (1808–1874), a singer-violinist-composer who had made a name for himself in Italy with his operas (which were very successful in England—one of them, *The Bohemian Girl*, is the only English opera of the period to survive) began a series of National Concerts in Her Majesty's Theatre, building his programmes on Promenade Concert lines, with a large orchestra, an effective choir and illustrious soloists. After Jullien's retirement from London, Promenade Concerts continued for audiences who seem to have regarded them as the next best thing to Jullien's sensational performances. Alfred Mellon, Arditi (the composer of songs), and Arthur Sullivan were among the conductors who from time to time took charge of the Promenade Concerts before they lapsed. In 1895, a summer season of Promenade Concerts was given at the then new Queen's Hall under a newcomer to English music, Henry J. Wood, whose exploits belong to a slightly later period of English music. The point about the early history of Promenade Concerts is that they demonstrated the existence of a popular audience for concert music if it could be encouraged to find its way to the concert hall without the antics of a Jullien to entice it.

While the regular provincial festivals recruited orchestras year by year, calling on London musicians as well as local players, the Liverpool Festival Choral Society had ambitiously established its own semi-professional orchestra when, in 1840, a group of businessmen founded the Liverpool Philharmonic Society. Its orchestra remained semi-professional; its first conductors were local organists and its early programmes included chamber music and madrigals. In 1843 it appointed a permanent conductor, a Swiss violinist, Jacob Zeugher Hermann, who had been trained in Munich and who settled in the north of England as conductor of the Gentlemen's Concerts in Manchester. By 1849 the Society had outgrown the available accommodation in Liverpool and it opened its own hall, in which it played to audiences of up to 2,100, and there was room on the platform for an orchestra and choir of 250.

Concert manners in Liverpool were designed to ape those of the metropolis in social exclusiveness at a time when social exclusiveness was no longer sought in London. It was possible to become a 'proprietor' of a stall or box instead of a mere subscriber in need of a seat; 'proprietors' could bequeath their seats in their wills, but could not casually lend or sublet them. A list of the gentlemen having the '*entrée*' was displayed in the hall, and all others were banished to one of two side galleries unless they were officers in the army or navy or ministers of religion. These rules continued to be applied, with greater or less strictness, until 1909.

While the Liverpool Philharmonic Society was endeavouring to impose rather outmoded social conventions on its concert life, such conventions were effectively discarded by Charles Hallé in Manchester. Hallé was an outstanding pianist, born in Germany in 1819, the friend of Liszt, Chopin and Berlioz. He had settled in Paris in 1836 and lived there until the Revolution of 1848 destroyed his teaching practice and put a temporary end to concert life. Making his way to London, he quickly established himself as a player and teacher—he was the first pianist to play a sonata by Beethoven in public in London, in spite of the anxiety of John Ella, at whose Musical Union he did so. At the invitation of a friend, Hermann Leo, Hallé left London for Manchester on the guarantee of enough pupils to provide him with an adequate living. The considerable and wealthy colony of German businessmen in Manchester made him welcome, as did the Gentlemen's Concerts, at which he played in spite of an orchestra which made him wonder if he would not be wise to abandon Manchester to its fate, although his friend Chopin played with the orchestra, and he himself had accompanied the great singers Grisi, Mario and Tagliafico in a Manchester concert. In 1849, with three Manchester string players, he began a series of chamber concerts, undaunted by tiny audiences because he had decided that it was his duty to educate Manchester.

In 1849, too, he became conductor of the Gentlemen's Concerts, accepting the invitation to do so on conditions that gave him complete charge of the repertory, more public concerts, more adequate facilities for rehearsal and the right to replace inefficient players. In 1852 he recruited a choral society to work with the orchestra; in three years he had become the centre of Manchester's musical life, such as it was.

In 1856, an International Exhibition of Art Treasures was arranged in Manchester, and the authorities gave Hallé the task of organizing an orchestra of international status to play at and in connection with the Exhibition. The orchestra, fifty-two strong, was recruited from the orchestra of the Gentlemen's Concerts, from the Liverpool Philharmonic, from London and from the Continent, where Hallé's reputation was still remembered. Reluctant to disband his orchestra when the Exhibition closed, Hallé decided to use it, for as long as possible, to give concerts under his own management; he did not form a committee of well-wishers or subscribers but kept control entirely in his own hands and made all his orchestra's activities public. The players were all professional musicians engaged for the complete season year by year and not, like London musicians, separately for each individual concert, the deputy system, which prevailed in and bedevilled London concerts, did not arise and Hallé's orchestra rapidly set standards of performance previously unreached by English orchestras. A profit of two shillings and sixpence on his first season of ten concerts—equivalent to a profit of threepence of the old pre-decimal style on each concert—

was enough to encourage him to continue for a second season; by 1862 his profits were £1,228, and in 1866 they were over £2,000.

Hallé kept admission prices as low as he could, with a handful of seats costing no more than a shilling saved at the back of the hall for the poorer classes. According to his son and daughter, who completed the *Autobiography* Hallé left unfinished, the letters of appreciation he received from mill workers and factory hands were among his greatest treasures, for such people did find their way to Hallé Concerts. In 1882 he became regular conductor of the Liverpool Philharmonic Concerts; in the 1880s, the Hallé began to play regularly in London, but it was only in Manchester, where the entire enterprise was under his control, that his policy of encouraging working-class listeners was implemented.

Hallé, without any training as a conductor, must have been, as the years gave him experience, exceptionally good. His tastes were liberal. He was devoted to the music of Berlioz, who described him as the pianist *sans peur et sans reproche*; he had a higher opinion of Mozart than was usual among nineteenth-century musicians; and both Verdi and Wagner made themselves heard. Hallé loved the music of Rossini, and works by Donizetti found their way into his programmes. He wanted to encourage English music; Sterndale Bennett's Second Piano Concerto was heard in an English programme in his first season, with the overtures to Balfe's *The Bohemian Girl* and Wallace's *Maritana*; possibly his eagerness to play English music was often frustrated by the difficulty of finding English music to play.

To the majority of Englishmen, opera and concert music were unknown. If the average English working man came into contact with music, he did so either through Methodism and the spread of Noncomformist religion, or as the result of the social ideals which English employers and workers had learned, either directly or indirectly, from the Methodists.

John Wesley, the reformer of religion, seems to have been the least musical member of a remarkably musical family; to him music was a blessing when it became an adjunct of religion, a means by which simple, uninstructed, probably illiterate people could learn and remember the truths of their faith. He encouraged singing in religious services, the use of hymns to convey religious truths in simple terms set to easily assimilable tunes. Music which made any greater demands than this on its hearers' minds and its singers' attention was dangerous because it distracted attention from the thought of God and necessary doctrine. John Wesley's nephews, the sons of his hymn-writing brother Charles, were among the most important English musicians of their period. Charles the younger (1757–1734) was a well-known organist of the day and a successful composer. Samuel (1766–1837) was the most celebrated organist of his period, conductor of the Birmingham Festival, an authority on the music of Bach and a noted lecturer. He became a Roman Catholic in 1784 and sustained a serious head injury in 1787; for the rest of his life he suffered from fits of depression during which he abandoned music. He composed symphonies and concertos, chamber music, glees, part-songs and piano music as well as church music for the Anglican and Catholic Churches. One of his Latin motets, *In exitu Israel*, a massively powerful work for double choir, remains in the English cathedral repertory, and his orchestral works have more than a merely historical influence.

Samuel's natural son, Samuel Sebastian (1810–1876), was the most outstanding church composer of his period, organist of Leeds Parish Church and then, from 1849, of Winchester Cathedral, Professor of Organ at the Royal Academy of Music, and conductor of the Three Choirs Festival. He left a handful of songs, part-songs and piano works as well as church music which remains in the cathedral repertory. He added a rather sentimental lyrical appeal to the English tradition which he served.

The Wesley family, however, in spite of their musical gifts, had less influence than their unmusical uncle on the development of music in England; the encouragement of singing as a religious pleasure which was also a duty had more effect. Nonconformity spread among the new industrial workers for whom the Church of England had little appeal and who were, in reality, neglected by the Established Church which did not understand either them or their way of life. Singing is a communal activity, and this seems to have been a large part of its appeal to the workers lost in the urban slums to which industrialism had transplanted them, Singing was good for those who sang; with a minimal training it gave them a rewarding discipline; it was a harmless occupation which induced good manners and the habits of civilization.

It would be unjustly exaggerated to suggest that employers in the areas where industry spread encouraged singing from any cynical motive; many of them were themselves nonconformists. But involvement in musical activity, as it was organized inside or outside a place of worship, tended to keep employees honest and sober. The industrial workers, a new and deprived poor, crowded into areas where there was no provision for leisure and very little leisure to enjoy. The first generations of industrial workers did not move into established communities as they moved from the countryside into the new industrial towns. If they were to have any social life, the workers must make it for themselves.

The nonconformist chapels encouraged singing, and so did many of the employers, who were very often men who, by virtue of greater energy, greater determination and greater ingenuity had struggled out of the class which they employed. It did not take long for the more far-sighted of them to realize that the employment of children in mills, mines and factories was evil, and to see that unless something more than harsh, unremitting and badly paid work were given to the large numbers of young and youngish workers in the towns, the results of industrialization, already appalling, could become catastrophic beyond the most lurid imaginings. "Iron masters and the owners of collieries and mines," writes A. E. Dobbs, "are found building chapels, opening pleasure gardens and supporting schools."[32] It was not long before workers themselves saw a way out of their intolerable existence through education and began to join evening classes in working-men's institutes, lyceums and similar organizations, looking for ways of escape.

One of the most popular studies at such institutes, though their original ideal had been to offer the most strictly practical training in the 'three Rs', was music, so that in addition to the singing classes of the chapels was added the less doctrinaire music of the organizations for educational self-help. They filled a pitiful gap in the lives of the industrial workers. Methodism encouraged the working-man's desire for education, and was therefore doubly responsible for the growth of a type of musical activity which had no direct contact with the life of concert halls, opera houses and theatres. In 1833, the French and Latin teacher at the Mechanics' Institution in Lincoln was a young man of twenty-eight, Thomas Cooper. Originally a cobbler in Leicester, Cooper had become a Methodist and a chartist, and taught himself languages. At Lincoln, he found himself not only teaching languages but organizing and singing in a choral society formed at their own request by young members of the Institution, and forming an amateur orchestra in the city to support its performances of music by Handel, Haydn's *The Creation*, Mozart's *Requiem* and Beethoven's *The Mount of Olives*.

Such outbursts of spontaneous musical enthusiasm had little or nothing to do with the established musical centres and the normal musical life of the country. Employers encouraged them. When Robert Owen, in 1797, had set up his model industrial community in New Lanark, he had refused to countenance child labour but had opened schools in which music was a subject to be learned, and he encouraged choral music as an activity for the workers' leisure. William Gardiner, the Leicester hosier (who, incidentally, sent Haydn a present of a pair of hose with the notes of the Emperor's Hymn woven into them) was sufficient of a musician to arrange a collection of hymn tunes made out of melodies by Haydn, Mozart and Beethoven. In his *Music and Friends*, he writes with admiration of those employers who cared for the social and intellectual well-being of their workers; among these were George, William and Joseph Strutt, "men of great wealth and acquirements, [who] employ nearly the whole population of Belper." "To give a higher taste to the work people, Mr John Strutt [the son of George] has formed a musical society . . . making a band of instrumental performers and a choir of singers. These persons are regularly taught to play and sing in the best manner. Whatever time is consumed by their studies is reckoned into their working hours."[33] So, too, were the normal rehearsals of the musical society. John Strutt made it his practice to combine business trips to London with interesting events at the opera or the concert hall to which he took members of the musical society at his, or the firm's expense.

The works' band, subsidized by the employer, who often provided the instruments, became a common feature of life in industrial areas, so that the possession of some instrumental skill was a valuable qualification for a job-hunting artisan, and steps had to be taken by employers like the Strutts to hold on to valuable members of their band. The same employers rarely formed a works' choir; instead, they supported local choral societies which, not infrequently, they helped to set up. The Apollo Glee Club, the Cecilian Society, and Liverpool organizations, like the St Cecilia's Society which

Hallé formed in Manchester in 1850, were middle-class organizations; the choral societies of the smaller industrial towns where there was little middle-class population to depend on, grew from the working class, its allegiance to Methodism and its eagerness to improve its situation. It maintained, without really knowing that it did so, the old English tradition of music in a massive style, reinforced by a genuine mass of voices. The Sacred Harmonic Society, which could at one time crowd seven hundred singers on to its platform, was the largest of the London choral societies. It was founded in 1832 and first established itself in the chapel in Gate Street, Lincoln's Inn. It moved to Exeter Hall where its allegiance to nonconformity made it acceptable, for it seems that the authorities of the Society persuaded the Methodist authorities that their activities constituted the practice of a science as well as a religious exercise; they were allowed to use Exeter Hall so long as only religious music was played and applause was forbidden. As well as oratorios, the Society gave occasional concerts of anthems and church service music in programmes arranged historically, or chronologically. In 1855, Wagner attended some of its concerts and, in *Mein Leben,* wrote of them with more approval than he usually gave to whatever he saw in England.

> *The oratorios given there* [in Exeter Hall] *nearly every week have, it must be admitted, the advantage of the great confidence to be gained from frequent repetition. Neither should I refuse to recognize the great precision of the chorus of seven hundred voices. . . . It was here I came to recognize the true spirit of English musical culture, which is bound up with the spirit of English protestantism. An evening spent listening to an oratorio may be regarded as a sort of service and almost as good as going to church.*[34]

The Sacred Harmonic Society continued its work until 1882, after which it staggered on for a year and then disappeared. It was, however, in the provinces that the choral societies cut the deepest furrow. Working-class choirs and singers provided the motivation for the various simplification of musical notation which culminated in the Tonic Sol-fa system developed by John Curwen, a Methodist minister, in his book *Singing for Schools and Congregations,* published in 1843. Large-scale singing classes for the poorer classes were instituted by Joseph Mainzer, a German who began his career as a teacher of singing to large bodies in Paris and transferred his operations to England in 1841; most of his later work was done in Manchester. His example was followed by John Hullah, who had won some success as a composer of light opera (he was the composer who set Charles Dickens's libretto, *The Village Coquettes*, in 1836). Hullah concentrated his efforts on London, and in 1841 began a series of classes intended primarily for teachers but found them crowded with the general public, who signalled their gratitude to him by subscribing to the building of the St Martin's Hall, the foundation stone of which was laid in 1847. The St Martin's Hall became the venue of all Hullah's later classes and concerts. The Huddersfield Choral Society, maintaining the primacy of the north in this field, was founded in 1836, refusing membership to anyone who had attended the rationalist, radical Halls of Science formed in honour of Robert Owen.

It was not very long before such choirs had their impact on concert music. When, in 1825, the London Philharmonic Society mounted the first English performance of Beethoven's Ninth Symphony, Schiller's 'Ode to Joy', the words of the choral movement, had to be translated into Italian to make it intelligible to the professional chorus, the members of which were largely Italian and who were used to singing nothing but Italian opera. (When Wagner was presented to Queen Victoria during his 1855 stay in London, she talked to him about his *Tannhäuser* and suggested that he had the libretto translated into Italian so that the work could be played at the Opera, which at that time was officially known as the Royal Italian Opera.) This rather ludicrous situation was gradually remedied as such works began to attract the attention of the many expert amateur choralists who were to be found in this country.

John Ella was a violinist in the orchestra of the Concert of Antient Music from 1832 until 1848. He noted their impact:

> *In the early part of my engagement in the orchestra of the King's Concert of Antient Music, the principal female choristers were brought from Lancashire. These ladies were supposed to have finer voices and a more intimate acquaintance with the* chefs d'œuvre *of the sacred composers than the theatrical choristers in London, were adequately remunerated to remain the whole season in town and sing exclusively in twelve concerts.*[35]

In 1881, the Philharmonic Society gave two performances of Berlioz's *Romeo and Juliet* with an amateur choir; an amateur Philharmonic Choir was formed to capitalize on this innovation but was disbanded, for no recorded reason, after a year.

The longer-living Royal Choral Society, which began its career in 1873 with a performance of Bach's *St Matthew Passion*, grew from a body called the The Royal Albert Hall Choral Society, formed to sing, with Gounod as its conductor, at the opening of the Albert Hall in 1871. Its members were reluctant to disband after the event for which they had assembled; the members amalgamated with Barnby's Choir, an organization established by the music publishers, Novello and Co., to give oratorio concerts under Joseph Barnby, organist of St Anne's Church, Soho, and a prolific composer of services, anthems, songs, part-songs and hymns. In 1888 Queen Victoria approved of the change of its name to 'Royal Choral Society'. Barnby, not a very interesting composer, was an interesting conductor; before the amalgamation, his choir had been responsible for the first performance in England of Verdi's *Requiem*, which the composer had conducted, and he gave an annual performance, with orchestra, of Bach's *St John Passion*.

To consider in detail the work of English composers through these years would be a labour unlikely to spread much light among listeners and music lovers a century later. The spread of choral singing provided composers with a ready market for music which was edifying by virtue of its religious themes rather than by the quality of composition. More important, probably, is the development of other musical institutions. The Royal Academy of Music began operations in 1822, with George IV as patron and its management vested in a committee of noble, titled amateurs. The actual musical administration was to be in the hands of a Principal and four eminent professors. At first, admission was limited to forty boys and forty girls, all admitted at what modern educationalists concerned with the general education of the young would regard as a dangerously early age; William Sterndale Bennett, the most interesting English composer of the age, became a student at the Royal Academy before he was ten. The first Principal was Crotch, and among the professors were Attwood, Shield, Sir George Smart, Cipriani Potter, Clementi and the German J. B. Cramer and his brother F. Cramer. The Royal College of Music was inspired chiefly by the men who inspired the Philharmonic Society, and like the Philharmonic Society, it tended to remain in the age in which it first saw the light, unaware of the passing of time or the development of styles. By 1883 it had become so thoroughly conservative that a rival institution, the Royal College of Music, was felt to be necessary and opened its doors under the patronage of the Prince of Wales, who eventually became Edward VII; Sir George Grove (an engineer who became a major power in English music as a writer and administrator), was its first Director, and Sir Hubert Parry and Sir Charles Stanford were among its original professors. In 1893 Hallé was able to open the Royal Manchester College of Music with a staff as impressive as that of either of the London institutions and Hallé's own cosmopolitan attitude to music. Brodzky came from Russia to be Professor of Violin and Carl Fuchs, a young cellist who became a devoted Mancunian, came from Germany to become Professor of Cello and a noted concerto and chamber music player.

X
Popular Music in the Nineteenth Century

The professional musicians of the eighteenth century had worked almost entirely in London. Elsewhere, professional musicians were teachers and joined in the amateur music-making of their localities, where music was simply what the people sang or played. Even in London, where professional music occupied the theatres, the opera and the socially exclusive world of concerts, many concerts remained the business of amateurs making music for pleasure. The change to professional music, in the nineteenth century, affected music of all styles, heights of brow and weights.

In *Pendennis* (1850) and *The Newcomes* (1854), Thackeray immortalized the 'Song and Supper Rooms' which, in the 1830s, had marked some of this transformation into professionalism. At one time the patrons of drinking and eating places had made whatever music they had wanted, but now the audience was entertained while it ate and drank in a mood quite different from that which prevailed at the Opera or in a concert hall. The mood was quite different, too, from that of the various Glee Clubs at which the eaters and drinkers made their own entertainment. Up to midnight the audience listened to madrigals, glees and part-songs, not taking part; choirboys from St Paul's, Westminster Abbey, and any other church which had a regular professional choir with adult male singers, provided the music. Then the atmosphere had loosened up, so that Colonel Newcome was shocked by the comic songs his young son had to listen to—the choirboys were sent home at midnight—and these comic songs compelled the half-attentive audience to pay more attention to what was going on and helped to ease its members into the mood of rather raffish conviviality for which the Song and Supper Rooms became either famous or notorious. At Evans's in

Covent Garden (the proprietor had bought it from a man named Joy, so that the sign outside read 'Evans Late Joys'), the principal comic singer was Charles Sloman, who became a great attraction. His voice, apparently, was not specially attractive, so that what must have counted was his ability to 'put a song across'. Sloman was an *improvisatore*, singing extemporary verses, mere jog-trot doggerel so far as they have been preserved, about members of the audience who attracted his attention.

Evans's, patronized by Dickens, Thackeray, George Augustus Sala, Lord Landseer and all the other notables, was the best remembered of these places, but the idea of the Song and Supper Rooms spread. Charles Sloman set an example for successful entertainers by appearing in similar halls in Central London and the East End, travelling from one to the other and staying simply to perform his act. By 1836, in *Sketches by Boz*, Dickens was noting very similar entertainments in a milieu rather remote from the deliberate bohemianism of Evans's in Covent Garden:

> *"Gen'l'men," says the little pompous man, accompanying the word with a knock of the president's hammer on the table—"Gen'l'men, allow me to claim your attention—our friend, Mr. Smuggins, will oblige."—"Bravo!" shout the company; and Smuggins, after a considerable quantity of coughing by way of symphony, and a most facetious sniff or two, which afford general delight, sings a comic song, with a fal-de-ral—tol-de-ral chorus at the end of every verse, much longer than the verse itself. It is received with unbounded applause, and after some aspiring genius has volunteered a recitation, and failed dismally therein, the little pompous man gives another knock, and says "Gen'l'men, we will attempt a glee, if you please."*[36]

Bleak House, which began to appear in monthly instalments in March 1852, describes a similar entertainment lower down the social scale, at the 'Sol's Arms' where the resident comic singer, Little Swills, finds his material in the inquest which has just taken place on the broken-down gentleman-law-clerk whose suicide is the cause of calamity. The 'Sol's Arms' is a poor tavern tucked away into the backwaters between Chancery Lane and Holborn, and the inquest was held in the "first floor room at the 'Sol's Arms', where the Harmonic Meeting takes place twice a week."

"In the zenith of the evening, Little Swills says, Gentlemen, if you'll permit me, I'll attempt a short description of a scene of real life that came off here today. Is much applauded and encouraged; goes out of the room as Swills; comes in as the Coroner (not the least in the world like him); describes the Inquest, with recreative intervals of pianoforte accompaniment to the refrain— —With his (the Coroner's) tippy tol li doll, tippy tol lo doll, tippy tol li doll, Dee!"[37]

It seems as though little had influenced the world of popular music since the retirement of Grimaldi in 1823; the change had come, however, little as it affected the 'Sol's Arms' and its Harmonic Meeting, when the Eagle Tavern in the City Road (where the weasel, and probably other things, could be popped) grew into the Royal Eagle Coronation Pleasure Ground and Grecian Saloon. The Saloon, which could seat seven hundred people and had an organ as well as self-acting pianoforte, set out to combine entertainment with uplift; it presented ballet, and it recruited an orchestra with which operas—by Rossini, Bellini and Donizetti, by Adam, Auber, Boieldieu and Balfe—were produced.

The example was worth following. The Britannia Tavern, Hoxton, was backed by waste ground on which sprang up another, less high-minded saloon-theatre, where opera and ballet, with vaudeville and 'laughable farces', were offered to patrons paying sixpence or a shilling by artists some of whom earned as much as £150 per week. It was Charles Morton who added the Canterbury Music Hall, with an art gallery as an annex, to the Canterbury Arms near Lambeth Palace. Prices of admission were low, because the profits of the entertainment came from the food and drink sold there. The seven-hundred-strong audience at the Canterbury saw a cut (and legally doubtful) production of *The Tempest* and heard Gounod's *Faust* in its first English performance, presented without action and settings, in oratorio style; the *confrères* and successors of Little Swills performed there, but the men who established the early music halls wanted to uplift and educate as well as entertain. Even in the twentieth century, Dorothy Moulton, the soprano who sang the first English performance of Stravinsky's *Pribaoutki* and pioneered Schoenberg's Second String Quartet, appeared from time to time in the fading music hall and in pantomime, learning that brilliant coloratura arias would delight audiences who would never dream of attending the operas from which the arias were taken. (She was the wife of Sir Robert Mayer and, in 1922, joined him in establishing the highly successful Children's Concerts.) The early efforts to combine entertainment with enlightenment did not succeed. The music hall gradually expanded into more fashionable areas—the Oxford Music Hall, situated where Oxford Street meets Tottenham Court Road, was opened in 1861—and created its own stars who did most to establish music hall among the upper classes. They did so by making the upper classes recognize their kinship with the poor. 'Burlington Bertie' came from Bow; it was self-satisfied derelicts who lived in Trafalgar Square with four lions to guard them; the audience discovered what was likely to happen when, in the course of a midnight flit, you dilly-dallied on the way although your old man had told you to follow the van; and the audience learned what it was like, after forty years of marriage, to be separated at the workhouse from your old Dutch. The music hall in its great days was the creation not of managers and *entrepreneurs* but of artists who could weld an audience into a community. Many of the songs survive because they are simply good tunes from composers who worked effectively within the music hall style; the great stars made plain the universality of the style, but the material they used expresses the thoughts, aspirations, joys and tragedies of the industrial working class.

The music hall was a nation-wide delight; there were stars from every part of the country, many of whom came to London where they could do as much work as they wanted once London had accepted them. A good number of the songs had local London references and would have to be jettisoned or changed should the artist decide to leave London. Cockney songs were effective anywhere, and some local accents—usually those of the north-country—were always funny to London audiences; a Liverpool accent amused everybody, a Birmingham accent was always ugly, and a Tyneside accent had to be moderated to be intelligible to the outside world; a west-countryman was always slow, bucolic and dangerously shrewd. Tyneside was almost a world of its own, with its own composers and singers who wrote lively songs in many moods, and an honourable folk-song tradition, but the strange language of the north-east prevented these songs from travelling far outside their birthplace. The words of J. B. Priestley perhaps better than any other convey the power of the 'halls':

> *Looking back soberly at those music hall shows . . . I can see now that in those noisy smoky halls, with their brassy orchestras, and their plush and tarnished gilt, their crudely coloured spotlights raying down from the gallery, we were basking in the brilliant India summer of a popular art, a unique folk art that sprang out of the gusto and irony, the sense of pathos and the illimitable humour of the English industrial people.*[38]

Older customs survived until the music hall overtook them in the provincial backwaters. Edwin Clayhanger, the hero of Arnold Bennett's trilogy, left school in July 1872. On the following Monday he went to work for his father, in whose absence he had to call that night at The Dragon to discuss the order for a wedding announcement; his father was a printer. He visited The Dragon with his father's 'jobbing compositor', James Yarlett, who was due to sing at a 'free and easy' there. All the members of the Bursley Glee Party, of which James Yarlett was bass, shared "a certain elasticity of religious opinion. Big James, for example, had varied from Wesleyan, through Old Church, to Roman Catholic. It all depended on niceties in the treatment accorded to him, and on the choice of anthems."

On the way to The Dragon, the orchestra and company of Snagg's, more usually known as 'The Blood Tub' (the theatre), were performing on a platform outside the doors, hoping to entice a larger audience to enter, but what Edwin and the Glee Party might have found in The Dragon might easily have been found fifty years before at Evans's in Covent Garden, or in the Coal Hole on the Strand, except that such places were middle-class Bohemian and The Dragon plebeian respectable. The Glee Party sang 'Loud Ocean's Roar'; the Bursley Prize Handbell Ringers played "a selection of Scotch and Irish airs"; a young man played an ophicleide solo; and Miss Florence Simcox (in private life the wife of Mr Offlow, who had recited 'The Patent Hair-brushing Machine'), "champion clog-dancer of the Midlands" and the star of the show, "obliged".[39]

That was in 1872. Sixteen years later Edward Elgar played in the orchestra of the Hanley Festival, grumbling about accommodation for the orchestra in the New Victoria Hall, for by that time Arnold

Bennett's 'Five Towns' had coalesced into Stoke-on-Trent; much of their social obscurantism had been swept away, and their people were among the first to accept the compositions of the comparatively young Elgar.

Of course, the songs of the music hall were among those that sat in the piano stool of most English homes or lay on top of the piano. At the beginning of the nineteenth century a piano cost twenty-five guineas. The development of the upright piano, first made in England in 1800, had brought the instrument within the means of all but the poorest classes. At the end of the eighteenth century there were some thirty pianoforte makers in London, and Broadwood, who had provided Beethoven with a piano, was using steam power and primitive methods of mass production to keep down prices. By the middle of the century, Broadwood was making about 2,300 pianos each year, and Collard, the firm originally started by Muzio Clementi, was making about 1,500. Each new development in piano manufacture during the first half of the nineteenth century meant an increase in the power and brilliancy of the instrument's tone and, consequently, a replacement by the rich of the instrument they owned for the sake of an improved model, so that second-hand pianos slid down the social scale from the wealthy homes in which they had started as cheaper new models were made.

Therefore a vast number of homes, almost all except the very poor, gave house-room to a piano, and a vast number of girls learned to plav the instrument to some extent. What they played, apart from the accompaniment to popular songs and ballads, were often meretricious arrangements of popular songs, and show pieces specially written to allow even mediocre players with a limited technique to give a spurious impression of brilliance. Such works were not provided specially by English composers, for the popularity of the piano was a European and not specially an English phenomenon; in the 1830s Mendelssohn had written a letter in which he complained about the habit of young Viennese ladies to waste their time on showy but worthless piano music.

The essential music of the Victorian age in England, however, was the 'ballad', usually sentimental, usually derivative. Some of them are still current in the late twentieth century because, whatever their faults, they are supremely singable and flatter the voices of their performers while appealing to beliefs that the average Englishman and woman held dear. They appeared in their hundreds every year. In 1877 Sullivan composed 'The Lost Chord', words by Adelaide Anne Proctor; in twenty-five years it sold five hundred thousand copies, although a sheet music copy of a song, voice and piano set out together, cost four shillings and was not a great deal of use to anybody except singers and pianists.

The exemplary sentiments of such songs—their insistence on the importance of love and fidelity, on the innocent beauty of childhood, on the nobility of self-sacrifice, on the splendour of patriotism—expressed to a great extent the feelings of the English people; if perhaps the songs were generally superficial, so too were the sentiments they expressed. But they were the work of practical musicians who understood the voice and the singer, and who knew how to create the effects they wished to make, so that their revival by admired concert singers in the 1970s is quite comprehensible; few composers offer the singers new songs that can give an equivalent effect. But so far as commercial interests were concerned, publishers were rarely content to rely on popular feeling to bring them success. Popular singers were paid a royalty on the sale of copies of any recent ballad they took into the repertories. Ivor Newton, who was her accompanist in the early years of his career, wrote of the great Dame Clara Butt:

> *Her mastery of ballads was doubly profitable to her. Her audience loved them as she did, and she contracted with their publishers to sing them, receiving a royalty on the sales of those she made popular. I believe that every copy sold of 'Abide with me' brought her threepence. When I asked her why she had dropped one highly popular song from her programmes, she explained that she had made a contract with its publishers for a royalty on sales which had continued for seven years; the contract had expired, and she was not prepared to go on advertising the song.*[40]

Music, of course, remained omnipresent, and the hotels and restaurants employed musicians to entertain their customers with what has come to be known as 'Palm Court Music'. This, however, although it was an English taste, was rarely English music; indeed, there is a sense in which a foreign name won a good opinion from the listener at a time when an English name secured the composer nothing but distrust. It was only in the music hall and the ballad concert that an English name was not a sign that something unimportant was going to be heard because the players were suffering from a misplaced outburst of patriotic feeling.

XI
Victorian Composers

So, far from being 'a land without music', England in the nineteenth century was an island 'full of noises' coming from churches, chapels, theatres, music halls, opera houses, concert halls, public houses and streets thronged by buskers, German Bands, isolated instrumentalists and the begging hymn-singers whom W. H. Davies, in *The Autobiography of a Super-Tramp* called 'Grinders'. There were, too, barrel-organ and barrel-piano grinders whose instruments powerfully taught the urban English the melodies of Verdi. The difference between England and other countries was that England was not even *Das Land ohne Komponisten*, simply that English composers meant little or nothing to the people for whom they wrote. It was not that their music was bad, or badly written; once they stepped outside the music hall, most of it was simply irrelevant. There was no talent about big enough to make it relevant.

At the same time, the growth of the amateur choral societies and their apparently indissoluble alliance with nonconformity meant that cantatas and oratorios were the English composer's road to success. Most of the English composers shared the religious beliefs of their fellow-countrymen with complete sincerity, but, sadly enough, sincerity is never a satisfactory substitute for talent. Of the mass of Victorian music which appeared from a considerable number of composers, little is remembered. There is the case of Sir Henry Rowley Bishop, for example. For thirty years or so before his death, Bishop was extremely busy as a composer for the theatre and an adapter of other composers' scores for the theatre. He was, too, busy as a conductor. But of the music he left—more than twenty-one arrangements of foreign operas, nine musical versions of novels by Scott, five ballets, incidental music to twenty-three plays, and a number of masques, cantatas and odes as well as thirty operas of his own—one melody is remembered, that of the song 'Home Sweet Home', from his opera *Clari,* or *The Maid of Milan.* This is a song beloved of sopranos who know that a smooth, simple and graceful melody, sentimental but delivered with complete sureness of breath control and simple elegance, can have as much effect upon an audience as the most extravagant coloratura pyrotechnics, especially after the listener has been excited by such sensationalisms. Probably, if the Law of Averages applies to such things, there are other equally affecting melodies to be found among Bishop's enormous *oeuvre,* but no one finds it necessary to look for them. Bishop was established as a composer of opera by the time that he was twenty; in 1845 he became, for less than a season, the first appointed regular conductor of the Philharmonic concerts in London though he was not a gifted conductor of symphonic music. He arrived before the great days of the choral societies and his career was fixed along lines that prevented him from encountering them.

It would be unfair to think of Bishop as no more than the composer who adapted other composers' scores. He was, however, responsible for a number of strange perversions of other men's music; he decided what needed to be done to make *Don Giovanni, The Marriage of Figaro, Der Freischütz* and *William Tell* suitable to English taste with what seems to be a blind disregard for the composer's intention. *William Tell,* composed by Rossini in 1829 to suit the French taste for spectacular grandiloquence, is an awkwardly lengthy, unwieldly work which triumphs over its defects; in Bishop's hands it became *Ninette* in 1830, but this revision was itself revised in 1838, when it became *Hofer, the Tell of the Tyrol* and the *ranz des vaches* (the oboe's cowherd tune which follows the storm in the overture) became a contralto aria later in the work. Bishop's own operas were relatively innocuous, never straying far from the direct simplicities of the ballad-opera tradition.

Ballad opera and well-meaning church music, together with the unaltered conviction that Beethoven was the supreme musician who had led the way to the more manageable but equally adorable music of Mendelssohn, produced rebels. Richard Lucan Pearsall (1795–1856) reverted, so to speak, to the Elizabethan period; his best work consists of madrigals written with real skill and charm. Henry Hugo Pierson (1815–1873) was educated at Harrow and Cambridge but went on to study in Germany where he met Mendelssohn and Schumann, associating himself with the modern movement. Although he became Reid Professor of Music in Edinburgh in 1844, he held the appointment for only a short time and spent most of his adult life in Germany. He wrote two oratorios, for the Norwich Festivals of 1852 and 1869, and his songs were reviewed generously by Schumann. His incidental music for a production of Part Two of Goethe's *Faust* and his operas *Leila* and *Contarini*, produced in Hamburg, were highly regarded in Germany. Pierson's death meant nothing to the English Press, but his life and work were discussed with respectful enthusiasm by the German newspapers.

Michael William Balfe (1808–1870) was born in Dublin and won attention as a child prodigy. He played the violin and composed a *polacca* when he was seven; he published ballads which gained public attention in Ireland before 1823, when he went to London as a pupil of Charles Edward Horn, played the violin in the orchestra at Drury Lane and was taken up by an Italian patron, Count Mazzara, who took Balfe to Italy, where he studied composition and singing. Rossini engaged him to sing at the Théâtre Italien in Paris, and he sang in *The Barber of Seville*, appeared in Palermo, Milan and Bergamo and, in 1833, returned to London. His first opera, *The Maid of Artois*, was produced in 1833 with the legendary soprano Malibran in the title role; twenty-eight more operas followed, their librettos either Italian or English—among them *The Bohemian Girl* (1843), which was enormously successful and has not yet been totally forgotten.

Balfe wrote fluent, singable melodies that clung to the listener's memory, and he presented his tunes with considerable elegance and neatness. The subject matter of his operas is at best superficial and sentimental. *The Bohemian Girl*, however, was the most effective of the three operas which became known in late nineteenth-century England as 'The English Ring' by virtue of their popularity and the frequency which which they were played by the touring opera companies; the implied comparison with Wagner is not in any sense valid and must not be taken seriously. The second contributor to 'The English Ring' was Sir Julius Benedict (1804–1885). Benedict was born in Stuttgart and studied under Rummel, who passed him on to Weber in 1821. Weber, Benedict said, was as good as a second father to him; in 1823 Weber was able to secure the post of conductor at the Karntnerthor Theatre in Vienna for his protégé, who abandoned Vienna for Naples in 1825, where his first operas were produced at the San Carlo Theatre.

Benedict arrived in London in 1836 to conduct the orchestra of the Opera Buffa at the Lyceum Theatre. A year later his Naples opera, *Un Anno ed un Giorno*, was produced in London; in 1859 he produced *The Gypsy's Warning*. As conductor at Drury Lane he dealt with several of Balfe's biggest successes and brought out two operas of his own, *The Bride of Venice* (1844) and *The Crusader* (1846). The librettos of both were by Alfred Bunn, the manager of Drury Lane Theatre and librettist of some of Balfe's operas. The Birmingham Festival took Benedict into the world of oratorio, so that in 1852 he combined the conductorship of Her Majesty's Theatre with that of the Harmonic Union, an organization which specialized in bringing out works by living composers. He also composed two symphonies and two concertos, but it was his operas, especially *The Lily of Killarney*, which made him famous. *The Lily of Killarney*, based on Dion Boucicault's play *The Colleen Bawn*, was produced in Germany, the United States and Australia and is, in all respects but one, a better and more polished work than *The Bohemian Girl*, more inventively orchestrated and more resourceful; its only weakness when it is weighed against Balfe's masterpiece is that its melodies do not remain in the memory even when the memory does not particularly welcome them. Benedict, despite his long experience and craftsmanship, was not by nature a dramatic composer.

Vincent Wallace (1812–1865) completed the so-called 'English Ring' with *Maritana* (1845), a work which, like *The Bohemian Girl*, survived into the twentieth century, beloved of amateur companies. At its Vienna production, it seemed equally successful, though *Matilda of Hungary*, which followed in 1847, hardly came to life at all. *Lurline*, in 1860, made a fortune for the English Opera Company at Covent Garden, but did not survive for long.

Wallace, the son of an army band sergeant, was born in Ireland; his first compositions were for his father's band. At sixteen he was occasionally leader of the orchestra at the Theatre Royal, Dublin. His life was, to say the least, romantic. He became a Catholic in order to marry; inspired by Paganini's example, he toured as a violin virtuoso and travelled the world. In Australia he took up sheep farming and tried his hand at whale fishing. He had a great success in South America, fraternized with cannibals, hunted tigers and both wrote and told remarkable stories of his adventures. In *Evenings in the Orchestra*, Berlioz assured his readers that all Wallace's stories were true because Wallace was far too indolent to invent anything. Wallace's character and adventures are, on the whole, more rewarding than his music, for *Maritana* is a parade of melodramatic nineteenth-century attitudes, with self-sacrifice, recompense, love, patriotism and so on inextricably involved together. The music is efficiently set down but completely undistinguished.

In 1837 William Sterndale Bennett (1816–1875) made his début at the *Gewandhaus* in Leipzig, playing his Third Piano Concerto, having met Mendelssohn in London and been taken under the great man's wing. English critics saw Sterndale Bennett as a great composer, and so, too, did Schumann in an excited article in his magazine *Der Neue Zeitschrift für Musik*. Bennett's father, once a choirman at King's College, Cambridge, had been organist of Leeds Parish Church; he died in 1819. The boy had been taken into King's College Choir in 1823 and became a student at the Royal Academy of Music before he was ten. Attwood, Mozart's boyhood friend and organist of St Paul's Cathedral, allowed Bennett to sing there, and he appeared as Cherubino in a student's production of *The Marriage of Figaro*. Crotch taught him to write double chants, but even as a small boy he wrote string quartets, using those of Mozart as models, so that in 1832, when Cipriani Potter became his teacher and encouraged Bennett's ambition, the boy developed quickly. Bennett's First Piano Concerto was played at an Academy Concert and given public performances in Cambridge and at the Hanover Square Rooms, where Mendelssohn heard it and invited the seventeen-year-old composer to Leipzig.

Bennett seems to have been one of those musicians who flower early; as a student he wrote four symphonies and a quantity of piano music. Possibly his early close contacts with the Continent kept him away from choral music and the type of song which wins easy popularity in England. His compositions have taste, elegance, wit, grace and, quite often, infectious gaiety and a real originality. His great qualities are, of course, those that we call 'Mendelssohnian', but his boyhood music had them before Mendelssohn's works became known in England; Mendelssohnism was something in the nineteenth-century air and came as naturally to Sterndale Bennett as it did to Mendelssohn himself, so that Mendelssohn often seems a rather tough, unduly forceful composer to those who have been concerned with Sterndale Bennett. His one oratorio, *The Woman of Samaria* avoids the sentimental religiosity which Victorian choirs, and Victorian audiences, loved; it is clean, direct music, as is all his small collection of anthems.

But almost all Bennett's best music was composed in the first half of his life, for he was forced into the position of a spare-time composer. A poor man, he had to earn his living by teaching, conducting and eventually by administration; the types of composition —opera and songs, oratorio and cantata—which might have become extremely popular, seem to have meant little to him. *The May* Queen, a 'pastoral' for chorus and orchestra, does not exploit the great choral masses or sentimental pathos. He composed two big odes which were heard and slid away as occasional works are apt to do. So to support wife and family he taught as many pupils as possible as often as possible, conducted the Philharmonic concerts for ten years after 1856, resigning from the conductorship when he was appointed Principal of the Royal Academy of Music in 1866. Without the ruthlessness through which many other men might have forced their own works into the repertory, he allowed his gifts to be smothered by the everyday tasks through which he earned his living.

Sterndale Bennett might, had he been a different type of man or had he been born and lived elsewhere, have dominated English music throughout the nineteenth century. His contemporaries—Sir Alexander Macfarren (1813–1887), John Bacchus Dykes (1823–1876) and John Stainer (1840–1901)—had a more restricted range and less active musical minds. Macfarren's work as a teacher was influential; he was responsible for the policy of teaching modal constructions and modal counterpint at the Royal Academy of Music; his compositions were correct and grammatical and admired in their day, but never more than mildly interesting. We remember little or nothing of Macfarren's music, but his influence persisted through his pupils at the Royal Academy and was carried to the Royal College of Music.

Dykes composed little apart from hymn tunes—'Abide with me', 'Nearer my God to thee' and others equally well known; they seem to communicate the Victorian religious spirit with complete clarity;

they are patently sincere, sentimental and possessed by a sort of strange passive religiosity which many people in the twentieth century would find unappealing were their melodies not among the earliest treasured memories of those who still remember their regular church-going days.

John Stainer is remembered by Anglican and nonconformist choirs as composer of *The Crucifixion,* a work part-narrative and part-reflective still dear to many as a Passiontide meditation. Those who consider it more coolly and in the context of European religious music find it no more than musically inoffensive, decently grammatical and always in good taste. As a scholar, Stainer was a pioneer in the attempts to recover a great deal of music from the late Middle Ages and the early Renaissance. *The Crucifixion*, however, is carefully constructed, singable, and has enough intellectual energy to respond year by year to artificial respiration.

The whole complex of Victorian religious music demands some thought. The great Continental masterpieces—the *Requiems* and *Te Deums* of Verdi and Berlioz, the *Te Deum* and masses of Bruckner, the *Stabat Maters* of Rossini and Dvořák—nothing composed in nineteenth-century England can be considered in the same thought as these works. The Englishmen were devout, or at least practising Christians; Berlioz was an agnostic and Verdi a rather doubtful case; neither Bruckner nor Dvořák were half so musically learned as either Macfarren or Stainer. It is musical ability and imaginative power, not religious devotion or academic knowledge, which creates great music.

At the same time, none of the composers of the Continent were directed by the impulse towards religious music which motivated the English composers. A Continental composer who wanted fame and fortune, or at least recognition, an audience and some financial security, tried to find a foothold in the opera house or to work out a *modus vivendi* with a publisher; an English composer wrote for amateur choirs who preferred religious subjects to all others. The question of sincerity is not an issue to be raised here, for nothing in the religious music of the nineteenth century suggests that its composer had experienced any vision of heavenly peace or joy, become possessed with any sense of divine glory, or any awareness of the terrors of judgement and hell; what the English composers wrote was reduced to terms of simple humanity. At the same time, the idea of music for music's sake seemed to be rather trivial to audiences and to composers who felt that music must carry some important spiritual, or at least generally religious message; the sense of the importance of a composition could best be justified through the notion of its service to religion even though the religion had lost all sense of the spiritual or the transcendental. When Bernard Shaw heard Hubert Parry's *Job* in May 1893, he exploded into what can be taken as the real objection to Victorian religious music.

> *I take* Job *to be, on the whole, the most utter failure ever achieved by a thoroughly respectable musician. There is not one bar in it which comes within fifty thousand miles of the tamest line in the poem . . .* [Shaw wrote] *Here, on the one hand, is an ancient poem which has lived from civilization to civilization, and has been translated into an English version of haunting beauty and nobility of style, offering to a musician a subject which would have taxed to the utmost the highest powers of Bach, Handel, Mozart, Beethoven or Wagner. Here, on the other hand, is . . . not even Mendelssohn or Schmann, but Dr Parry, an enthusiastic and popular professor, forty-five years old, and therefore of ascertained powers.*[41]

So long as English musicians in general believed that music was justified by its subject matter and that musical quality subsisted in exact obedience to grammatical rules deduced from the practice of earlier composers, the possibility of a broader and livelier musical attitude seemed remote. It came, unexpectedly, in the 1860s and 1870s from a composer whose background and training seemed to fate him to become a pillar of the Victorian musical establishment. Arthur Sullivan (1842–1900) was a choirboy in the Chapel Royal, a student at the Royal Academy of Music and from the first a fluent composer whose music from his teens had an un-Victorian neatness, elegance and wit. At the age of thirteen he had composed and had published an anthem, reaching fame in one bound. In 1856 he became the first winner of the Mendelssohn Scholarship instituted at the Royal Academy of Music, which made it possible for him to study at the Leipzig Conservatoire, where he composed incidental music to Shakespeare's *The Tempest* which was played at a Crystal Palace concert in 1862, repeated a week later and brought out in Manchester not long after. In 1864 his 'Irish' Symphony was a success, and in terms of the academic dullness of most orchestral music by British composers in the 1860s more than merited the favour it gained. He became Professor of Composition at the Royal Academy in 1866, the year in which his overture *In Memoriam* was first performed.

Sullivan, a popular and active organist, was thus at the age of twenty-four, not only a composer of considerable range and skill but also a major musical personality. A cello concerto, an overture (*Marmion*), songs, hymns, a handful of the piano music and some religious music (though religious music never bulked large in his output) if they proved nothing else, proved that his interests were not circumscribed by the Victorian inferiority complex which had convinced English composers that there were forms which English composers could not handle and the conviction that English music is never other than earnest. What Sullivan wrote is never portentous and never inflated; it is beautifully scored, with instruments used neatly and idiomatically, closer to the style of Sterndale Bennett than to the unrelieved seriousness of Sullivan's immediate contemporaries. Generally speaking, it is conservative in harmony and in the symmetry of its construction. Whether or not it was a major contribution to the repertoire (in the sense that a composer after Beethoven had, to prove his worth, to wrestle with his fate, defying a hostile destiny) it is hard to say. What Sullivan wrote is skilful, inventive, stylish and natural; he was a craftsman who knew how to do whatever he found necessary. If his society imposed upon him tasks not necessary or natural to his gifts, the fault cannot be laid at his door.

Therefore when, in 1867, the farce *Cox and Box* was turned into an operetta with a libretto by F. C. Burnand, Sullivan's music immediately found the style—neat, singable and theatrical—that it demanded. Sullivan had, apparently by accident, found his unique gift. His operettas to texts by W. S. Gilbert were, he felt, an interruption to his career as a serious composer which he would find it hard to justify upon the day of judgement, but they are an irreplaceable contribution to English music. Between *Trial by Jury* in 1875 and *The Gondoliers* in 1889 he wrote eight 'Savoy Operas' in which his touch was faultless, his tendency to Victorian sentimentality restrained and his wit as lively as his librettist's. Unfortunately, Sullivan's full scores remain unpublished and the piano scores by which the Savoy Operas are represented in print do his impeccable orchestration little justice; they omit, for example, little musical jokes like the quotation of a Bach fugue (in G minor) relevant to the Mikado's song about the proper punishment of music hall singers. Two more Gilbert and Sullivan works followed *The Gondoliers*, as well as operettas with other librettists, but they lack the sparkle of the original series.

In 1873, Sullivan's oratorio *The Light of the World* reminded the world of Sullivan's claim to be regarded as a serious composer whose ambitions soared far beyond operetta and even his 'Irish' Symphony and his Cello Concerto. The mawkish 'The Lost Chord' (1877) was, like *The Light of the World*, a work which he took seriously. The operettas, beautifully made and beautifully worked, were always things of which he felt ashamed although they showed him to have a wider range and greater resourcefulness than, say Offenbach, and less sentimentality, as well as greater rhythmical variety, than the younger Johann Strauss.

Sullivan's melodies are beautifully moulded and infallibly memorable. His ensembles become lively pieces to which individual characters can contribute without losing their individuality. Gilbert (whose contribution to the operettas seems now to be inferior to that of his partner) was a first-rate theatrical craftsman with an almost adorable gift for verbal fun; when sentiment is called for, however, Gilbert tends to fall into conventional rhythms, and at such points (the second-act song, 'The sun whose rays are all ablaze' in *The Mikado* is a case in point) Sullivan seems always able to find and impose a more characteristic, less conventional movement. Musical climaxes are always built with an exact knowledge of how to achieve precisely the degree of power that they need, and power in Sullivan's scores never means mere noise.

At the same time, Sullivan was on inspired parodist, capable of subtle, and usually witty, references to all manner of other music, and also of convincingly parodying a general style. That Captain Corcoran should address the crew of H.M.S. *Pinafore* in almost *secco* recitative is simply an example of a composer being funny for the sake of fitting in a pleasant joke regardless of its limited relevance to the situation, but that the first act of *The Gondoliers* should apply the mannerisms and general style of Italian opera before *Aida* to comic purposes entirely the composer's own is something quite different; the situation of two newly-married brothers taken from home to find which of them was not a gondolier but a prince in disguise would not be startling in an Italian opera, after all. In spite of the vast popularity of opera in nineteenth-century England, there is no indication that any other composer in 1889 could have found the stylistic knowledge, apart from the inventiveness and elegance, to do so. Probably, too, none of them was capable of such irreverence. Sullivan's dramatic counterpoint of contrasted themes, as when, in *The Pirates of Penzance*, policemen, pirates and the daughters of Major-General Stanley musically combine is extremely funny, delightful to listen to and, dramatically, exactly right.

Sullivan, who by the age of twenty was the Golden Boy of English music, suffered from two things. The first is the fault that made him so many times deal perfunctorily with overtures and orchestral interludes. He was never perfunctory in his treatment of words, and patter songs, for example, show him rejecting the obvious temptations to cheap, easy jocularity while looking for opportunities for real wit. His other misfortune was that his operettas became the favourite music of the average unmusical Englishman and the preserve for many years of a company more interested in preserving an often spurious comic tradition than in doing justice to his impeccable workmanship and his remarkable melodic gifts. 'Serious' musicians, of course, faulted him for his lack of any elevated operatic aim; they felt that a composer should be more interested in Love, Fate, Destiny and Death than in the social attitudes of the English peerage and the agonies of a too susceptible Lord Chancellor. Sullivan's one serious opera, *Ivanhoe*, has his immaculate craftsmanship, his fine sense of an effective melodic line and his precision of effect; like his serious music in *The Light of the World* and *The Golden Legend* (1886) it rarely comes to life, suggesting that the composer needed Gilbert's sharpness and skill as a juggler with words and ideas to get the best out of him. It was, perhaps, the fault of his age that Sullivan mistook his masterpieces for hackwork and his sometimes inflated hackwork for masterpieces, so that he overestimated everything he did that had a serious, religious or quasi-religious, subject.

XII
The Renaissance

Only nine years separate the birth of Charles Hubert Parry (1848–1918) from that of Edward Elgar (1857–1934); only five years separate the birth of Elgar from that of Charles Villiers Stanford (1852–1924). Parry was only a year younger than Alexander Mackenzie (1847–1935). Mackenzie, born in Edinburgh, was one of a family of musicians and went to Germany when he was ten to study the violin under a member of the orchestra of the Duke of Schwarzburg-Sonderhausen, in which he himself played among the second violins. In this way he grew up not on the normally restricted diet which had to satisfy English musicians, and on the precedents which were taught at the Royal Academy of Music, but on the music of Liszt, Berlioz and the Wagner of *Lohengrin* and *Tannhäuser*. He entered the Royal Academy, after his German training, with the King's Scholarship, and kept himself by playing in theatre orchestras. A crowded professional life, practical experience as a violinist in orchestral and chamber music and an energetic career as a conductor in London and Edinburgh did not prevent him from composing seven operas, an oratorio *The Rose of Sharon*, a number of cantatas, concertos for violin and piano, other orchestral works, and numerous part-songs, songs, piano pieces and chamber works. Much of his music is deliberately national; his piano concerto is known as the 'Scottish' Concerto, he wrote a *Pibroch Suite* and a *Highland Ballad* for violin and orchestra, and three *Scottish Rhapsodies* for orchestra; there are numerous Scottish pieces on a smaller scale. He remained aware, all through his career, of continental movements. As conductor of the Philharmonic Society Concerts from 1893 to 1900 he was responsible for the first English performances of Tchaikovsky's 'Pathetic' Symphony and Borodin's B minor Symphony. For thirty-six years, from 1888 to 1924, Mackenzie was Principal of the Royal Academy of Music, arriving at a time when its extreme conservatism was under attack, and his undogmatic practicality and liberalism moved that aged institution firmly into the twentieth century.

Hubert Parry, however, had a more profound and lasting influence on his age. A country gentleman's son—his father was a skilled amateur painter some of whose frescos can be seen in Ely and Gloucester Cathedrals—Parry was educated at Eton and Oxford. He was a games player (with a passion for cricket) and horseman, devoted to country pursuits, and passionately interested in religion and politics though his views were not always those expected from the members of his class. At Eton he was a schoolboy pianist, organist, violinist, baritone and composer; he became Bachelor of Music at Oxford in 1867, before he had left Eton. More than that, he was throughout his life a man of lively humour and great charm, so that Bernard Shaw, launching into his attack on Parry's *Job* in 1893, wrote that he was glad that he had never met Parry because the composer's personality always disarmed those who should have been his critics. In himself, coming from the landed gentry, Parry seemed to exorcize the influence of Lord Chesterfield; he made music not only a suitable pleasure for ladies and gentlemen but also an art at which they could, without shame, aim to excel.

He worked in every form except opera although he was, from his schooldays, a passionate admirer of Wagner and even as late as *Job* some critics objected to his Wagnerism. Much of his music is choral and vocal, and he sets words, in English and the classic languages, with a natural sense of their own rhythmic life. His orchestral works include four symphonies, a 'Symphonic Fantasy', a piano concerto and an impressive set of Symphonic Variations, though he was never so much at home with instruments as with voices. Critics have often suggested that his orchestration is less than expert, but Vaughan Williams, a student who came under Parry's spell, suggested that criticism of Parry's orchestration was usually a reaction against Parry's "almost moral abhorrence of luscious sound".[42]

Two of Parry's works, a setting of the Psalm 'I was glad when they said unto me', written for the coronation of Edward VII in 1902, and the unison song 'Jerusalem' (to Blake's lyric "And did those feet in ancient time", its accompaniment orchestrated by

Elgar in 1922, six years after its composition) have become part of English life. Parry's music has an unstrained, unself-conscious nobility of utterance, and his big melodies never disappoint because they are naturally big.

From 1900 until 1908 Parry was Professor of Music at Oxford, but pressure of work compelled him to resign. When Sir George Grove died in 1908, Parry became his successor as Director of the Royal College of Music. He was a skilled administrator who combined devastating common sense with geniality and humour. He taught composition with a great liberalism of outlook as well as unswerving integrity, looking always, Vaughan Williams said, for the signs of personality in a composition, so that his students adored him. Shaw, who adored the music of Elgar and became Elgar's friend, taught himself to believe that Parry was part of an academic establishment which had deliberately stood in the way of the unschooled, lower-middle-class Elgar, and it was Elgar himself who made clear the indebtedness he felt to Parry for generous help and encouragement.

The pupils of the Royal College of Music who worked under Stanford were often less than adoring. Stanford could be harsh and dismissive, but those who could survive his harshness found him a richly lovable, humorous personality. The son of an eminent Irish lawyer, Stanford was as early a beginner as Parry, something of a prodigy as a pianist. He went to Queen's College, Cambridge, in 1870 as a choral scholar, became organist of Trinity College in 1873 and spent vacations studying in Germany, discovering that his allegiance went to Brahms and the classic tradition rather than to Wagner. He was one of the founders of the Cambridge Musical Society, which grew from the amalgamation of two smaller university organizations, and became an effective, precise conductor in Cambridge and London, where he conducted the Bach Choir. He conducted the Leeds Festival from 1901 to 1910. From 1883 onwards he was Professor of Composition at the Royal College of Music, a post in which his ferociously unsparing integrity gave him enormous influence on the young musicians of more than two generations. In his *Musical Autobiography*, Vaughan Williams writes:

Stanford was a great teacher, but I believe I was unteachable. I made the great mistake of trying to fight my teacher. . . . Stanford never displayed any great enthusiasm for my work. I once showed him a movement of a quartet which had cost me hours of agony, and I thought that I was going to move mountains this time. "All rot, my boy," was his only comment. But his deeds were better than his words—later he introduced my work to the Leeds Festival, thus giving me my first opportunity of a performance under these imposing conditions. . . . With Stanford I always felt that I was in the presence of a lovable, powerful and enthralling mind. This helped me more than any amount of technical instruction.[43]

Stanford was a ferocious worker, adhering strictly to a timetable in which the period allotted for every task was strictly observed; he was, too, a startlingly rapid worker who, once he had clearly seen the nature of a task, carried it through with dazzling rapidity. His greatest ambition was to succeed with opera, and of his seven operas which reached the stage—another four have never been produced—*Shamus O'Brien* won international success, and occasional revivals of *The Travelling Companion* and *Much Ado About Nothing* have shown them to be works of real value, with dramatic power as well as musical skill and wit. The England of Stanford's day was simply not ready to pay attention to opera in English by a British composer.

The only works by Stanford that the listener can be sure of hearing half a century after his death are his settings of the Anglican Services, which carry the tradition of Anglican church music into the twentieth century, and the *Songs of the Fleet*, op. 117, to poems by Henry Newbolt, for baritone, chorus and orchestra. But his *opus* numbers extend beyond 170 and include seven symphonies, two concertos each for violin and for piano, eight string quartets and other chamber music, piano and organ pieces, part-songs and solo songs. All are the work of an impeccable craftsman. His orchestration has a bite and sparkle foreign to Parry's, and though his symphonic works tend to fall apart into fascinating episodes rather than to cohere into cumulative experiences, a great deal of the music he left is too valuable to deserve the oblivion into which it has fallen.

Mackenzie, Parry and Stanford were the glow of a new dawn; they helped English music to escape from its inhibitions and look at what the rest of the world was doing, finding great stimulation in the new view. Edward Elgar, born in Worcester in 1857, was in every respect unlike them. Parry was born into the landed gentry, Stanford into the successful professional class, and Mackenzie into a successful musical family. Parry and Stanford were the products of public school and university; neither was a poor man. Elgar's father owned a small music shop, was a piano-tuner and small-time church organist in a Roman Catholic Church, though he himself a Protestant until after 1853. His wife had become a Roman Catholic a year earlier. He was also a violinist regularly engaged for the Three Choirs Festival when it met in Worcester. William Elgar seems to have been a colourful personality who went to piano-tuning engagements on a thoroughbred horse and slipped out of Mass on a Sunday morning for a drink during the sermon. He was musician enough to be called into consultation about the make-up of the Three Choirs Festival programmes.

In later life, Edward Elgar adopted the dress, manner and moustache of a retired army officer who had taken to the life of a country gentleman, professing interests in chemistry and horse-racing, pretending to be disdainful of music, especially of his own music. He seems to have varied unaccountably from moods of riotous high-spirits with a love of puns and verbal horseplay to fits of hardly endurable depression. Neither the history of social conditions, training or the lack of it, or any external facet of a man's life can explain the eruption of genius, and Elgar's genius burst fiercely into flame when he was in his forties; before that, he had composed effective and interesting works but not the masterpieces which were to explode during his middle age. He had received some violin lessons as a small boy, from a local player, but was largely self-taught until, in his twenties, he travelled to London every week for the lessons which, he hoped, would enable him to become a virtuoso. He had piano lessons as a small boy, and somebody, probably his father, taught him to play the organ; he also played the bassoon in a serenade group formed by one of his friends. His father's shop provided a few text books and the scores of standard works, but in most respects he was self-taught in composition, and he found his way to a personal style which was an eclectic amalgam of late nineteenth-century compositional practice. Wagner, Brahms, Schumann, Berlioz and César Franck all contributed to what we now know as quintessentially Elgarian; his models did not give him idioms and expressions which he could quote or to which he could refer, but stimulation and the knowledge of what actually were the problems that he had to solve. His music never presents itself as an act of homage to the masters who inspired him, but declares his authorship at a first hearing.

Until 1899 Elgar was a local musician—organist, violinist, conductor, involved in the music-making of Worcester and a slowly expanding area around his home town. Efforts to move into a wider and more rewarding world had no success. He composed prolifically; salon pieces, church music, songs, part-songs and, in the 1890s, big, colourful dramatic cantatas—*The Black Knight* (1892), *King Olaf* (1896), *The Banner of St George* (1897) and *Caractacus* (1898), patriotic works with pseudo-historical themes, and an oratorio, *The Light of Life* (1896). Much of the colour and vitality of these early works comes from their orchestration, which is as expert and idiomatic as anyone would expect the scoring of an active conductor of amateur orchestras to be. Indeed, in all these works, none of which is negligible, there are frequent premonitions of the composer Elgar was to become, and they all won considerable popularity among the amateur choirs and orchestras of the Midlands while their composer slowly edged into the notice of London conductors, players and orchestras. The *Serenade for Strings* (1892), with a slow movement that combines richness with a sense of heartbreak, is the work of a musician still developing and refining an extremely personal vision.

In 1899 the *Enigma Variations* had its first performance, with Hans Richter conducting, and Elgar was immediately accepted as a great master. The *Variations*—there are fourteen, each one a character sketch depicting his friends, his wife and finally himself—have a wide emotional range, from orchestral horseplay to playful delicacy and deep, noble serenity. In 1900 *The Dream of Gerontius* had a disastrous first performance at the Birmingham Festival. A year later the work was hailed by Richard Strauss, at the Lower Rhine Festival, as the first masterpiece of a new, modern English School. A year later still, the work triumphed in England. There were several reasons for the original difficulties of *Gerontius*; its fervently emotional Catholicism—the work deals dramatically with the death of a believing Christian and the passage of his soul to judgement and to purgatory—did not immediately arouse the sympathy of English audiences, or even their immediate response. Furthermore, its musical idiom was new and entirely personal. Elgar's masterful dealings with Cardinal Newman's text—a richly expressive *arioso* for the soloists—was puzzling perhaps because it was at once both completely naturally and immediately musical, but the music of the chorus (who are at times prone assistants round the death bed, angels and demons) asked a variety of responses from the singers: the music is austere but, at times sumptuous, exhaustingly passionate in expression. It demands total surrender from everyone involved. One musician said that the work "stinks of incense"; George Moore, the novelist, noticing its Wagnerian construction—Elgar uses characteristic themes in the style of Wagner's *leit-motive*—described it as "Holy Water in a German beer barrel". Hans Richter, who conducted the first performance of *The Dream of Gerontius*, was possibly less sure of Elgar's choral writing, which treats its English words with unsurpassed sensitivity, than he had been of the orchestral splendours of the *Enigma Variations*.

Elgar's later masterpieces—two symphonies, a handful of orchestral overtures, the first four *Pomp and Circumstance* marches, the Violin and Cello Concertos, the oratorios *The Apostles* and *The Kingdom*, the *Introduction and Allegro for Strings* and the symphonic poem *Falstaff* were all written in the twenty years that followed the *Enigma Variations*. With the valedictory Cello Concerto came a Violin Sonata, a String Quartet and a String Quintet, all in a similar mood. He lived until 1934 remembering that he was Master of the King's Musick and had therefore a social duty to produce works for official occasions, and was punctilious in doing so. It became customary, in the 1920s, to regard Elgar as a permanent Edwardian, luxurious, extravagant, powerful and grandiloquent. Now it is possible to see a broader and more complex Elgar, who found his deepest content in moods of reminiscence and whose thoughts, though not often his style, often move quite close to those of Mahler. Elgar, like Mahler, found a not always ebullient expression in marches; their music shares the sense of drawing trains of thought to their conclusions, and in *Sospiri*, a piece for strings and organ which he wrote in 1914, it is almost as though Elgar has settled in the mood of the *Adagietto* of Mahler's Fifth Symphony although Mahler's strings aspire upwards, longing for illimitable heights, while Elgar's sink downwards, looking for a place of rest.

Elgar's music does not explore the possibility of new harmonies. It does not investigate new forms or new methods of organization.

To this extent it is firmly and unashamedly conservative. The two symphonies are cyclic constructions, carrying themes or varied restatements of themes from one movement to another; each has a motto theme which opens proceedings and returns in a glorious apotheosis at the conclusion, and the theme of the *Adagio* in the First Symphony is restated and varied to become the theme of its scherzo. Elgar developed no new harmonies or harmonic techniques. The blazing originality of his achievement is its synthesis of an intensely personal vision with a late nineteenth-century technique in which a variety of diverse European influences are united. The result is intensely English, not in any allusion to folk-song or the music of the English past but in its qualities of emotion. E. J. Dent, in an essay once thought to be highly controversial, accused Elgar's music of an un-English surrender to extremes of emotion; it would be easy to point out that neither in the sonnets nor the plays does Shakespeare show an upperlip properly stiffened by Victorianism. Constant Lambert (1905–1951), composer, conductor, critic and one of the founders of modern English ballet (he was musical director of the Sadler's Wells Ballet in its exploratory, adventurous and formative years) wrote of Elgar in his book *Music Ho!* "Elgar was the last serious composer to be in touch with the great public."[44]

It was a commonplace of English criticism, in the 1920s, '30s and '40s to see Elgar as an essentially old-fashioned figure who had taken English music into a musical world that, in all other places, belonged to the past. The expansiveness of Elgar's style, his swift emotional responses to experience and his extra-musical attitudes—conservatism, Catholicism and his preference for a life lived outside metropolitan influences—all seemed to belong to the past. He was, critics assured us, a less adventurous contemporary of Richard Strauss (1864–1949). The English discovery of the music of Mahler (1860–1911)—which has been followed by a slower international discovery of Elgar—perhaps more than anything else revealed to us Elgar's affinity with Mahler's 'progressive' strains of Central European music. Like Mahler, Elgar had a passion for strong marching rhythms, a gift for expressing intensities of nostalgic reflection. He did not, like Mahler, ever find it necessary to his purposes to strip his orchestra down to its skeleton and subject tonality to almost catastrophic assaults in order to discover the techniques which vindicate it. Tonality, in Elgar's music, is often made vague and uncertain by the sense of the chromatic possibilities of almost every chord through and by means of which he moved, and when he eventually finds his way to its ultimate vindication, he does so, as in the first movement of his Second Symphony, as though, having exhausted all the possible alternatives, he had found no other resting place but the tonic key which had earlier seemed to be nothing but one of a multitude of possibilities. The criticism which, for too long, saw Elgar as the complacent mouthpiece of an outmoded imperialism seems, now to have come from writers incapable of hearing, let alone understanding, not only the terror of dying Gerontius but also the wild passion which overtakes the scherzo of his Second Symphony and the heart-broken reconciliations of the Cello Concerto which, in 1919, proved to be his last major work.

Five years younger than Elgar, Frederick Delius was born in Bradford in 1862. Elgar died in February 1934, Delius a few months later in June 1934. Delius's father, a wool merchant, planned a commercial career for his violin-playing son, but in 1882, the twenty-year-old Frederick settled in Florida as a orange grower but, apparently, devoted himself to music rather than to oranges. A few text books, scores and a local organist were the only available sources of instruction; negro workers on his own and other plantations, sang, and their melodic and harmonic styles influenced him; in 1886 he took himself to the Leipzig Conservatory where Jadassohn and Reinecke were his teachers. Grieg, living in Leipzig at the time, was a stronger influence. From 1890 onwards, Delius's home was in France, and slowly he established himself as an entirely individual musician. His works are numerous—six operas; several large works for soloists, chorus and orchestra; concertos for piano, violin and cello; a double concerto for violin and cello; various works for orchestra; songs, some with orchestral accompaniment; and a handful of chamber and pianoforte works.

Delius totally rejected the classical tradition and traditional notions of form, which he dismissed as mere repetition and the result of poverty of invention and imagination. Several of his smaller works remain cherished in the repertoire, and most of his important works are available on record. Many of his compositions seem to follow the same psychological pattern; they begin in longing, achieve some sort of triumphant glory, but then die away into heart-broken nostalgia. His English Rhapsody, *Brigg Fair*, composed in 1907 and dedicated to Percy Grainger (who discovered and notated the Lincolnshire melody on which it is based), is untypical of his music in using a folk-song as its basis, but it is typical of his works in its rapturous evocation of a summer morning, of the countryside, of love and ecstasy; few works achieve a more glorious triumph. But *Brigg Fair* ends without lovers, the countryside is deserted and the sense of transcience and loss in which it closes is close to heartbreak. Untypical, too, is *A Mass of Life*, in which several of Zarathustra's great rhapsodies, from Nietzsche's *Also Sprach Zarathustra*, are set to music of great power, interposed with lyrical passages of great beauty; the work ends with a setting of Zarathustra's 'Midnight Song' in which Delius's lay-out and general style seems for some minutes to draw near to the final overwhelming ecstasy of Mahler's Eighth Symphony. Nietzsche provided, too, the text of a bitter, anti-religious *Requiem* which was the composer's reaction to the First World War.

Delius seems to have made comparatively little effort to popularize his work but to have explored his own emotions and found himself always aware of the transcience of all human emotion. Sir Thomas Beecham, who did more than any other conductor to popularize Delius's work, described him as totally inept as a conductor, and strangely casual about the accuracy of the copies from which orchestras played; but more than that, according to Beecham, Delius was "a supreme and conscious egotist". It may be that such an egotist, finding the meaning and purpose of life in his own thoughts and experiences, is of all men most likely to sense the tragedies of transcience. For the last ten years of his life Delius was blind and totally paralysed from syphilis, but in 1928, a Yorkshireman named Eric Fenby offered the composer his services as amanuensis and evolved a way of working which enabled him to put on to paper several complex works which showed Delius, despite pain and physical ruin, to be unchanged in style, outlook and technique.

The larger works of Delius are not very frequently heard these days. All his music has great sensuous beauty and a personality which is unmistakable, presenting complex and extremely chromatic harmonies which seem themselves to evolve into passionately memorable melodic lines. His passion for Scandinavia and the north, like his admiration for Grieg, seems hardly to have affected the richness of his scores; a poor performance can leave the listener feeling that Delius's work has little muscular power, but conductors who, like Beecham, can find and deploy his melodic lines, show it to be strong and powerful.

For one who achieved so many fine choral works and usually found fine texts for them, Delius treated words and sometimes voices with completely cavalier disregard as though the singers were simply instruments. His songs are often attractive minor works, but their fluent tunefulness suggests little of the complexity or strength of the major works. *A Mass of Life* begins and ends with powerful vocal statements which remain in the listener's mind as vocal melody; beautiful as is the lyrical sweep of *A Mass of Life*, *Sea Drift* and *The Song of the High Hills*, the singers and their words in the first and second only set the mood, just as the wordless chorus of the third is only another colour to be used in the sweep and mass of tone deployed orchestrally. Delius's music is difficult for performers because it is a music of beautiful, elegant line which tends to be lost in the scoring and needs to be rediscovered by the player and conductor.

Granville Bantock (1868–1946) was, in a sense, a more surprising phenomenon than Elgar or Delius. Without the unique genius of either, Bantock seemed to do nothing that is not marked by a massive competence. His operas indicate the range of his interests and thought. Their subjects are Celtic history and mythology, Eastern mythology and literature, English mythology and literature. Bantock was fascinated by the East, sometimes with the result that that his music in all forms picks up rather commonplace idioms to suggest their oriental provenance. His huge, and mostly impressive setting of Fitzgerald's version of the *Rubiayat*, which he called *Omar Khayyam*, handles a large orchestra and choir with great authority and glowing colour but is broken by an orchestral interlude, 'The Caravan Passes', which slips from a level of exalted thought and emotion to a splash of conventional orientalism of a sort which finds its way into some of his Biblical settings. Bantock's sense of practical possibilities and his sense of colour and the picturesque lead to music that, if not consistent in depth and intellectual power, is never dull.

By the time Elgar reached his Second Symphony, in 1911, the revival of folk-song and the rebirth of interest in Tudor music, movements not directly concerned with composition, had begun to exert their influence. Cecil Sharpe (1859–1924) was Associate to the Chief Justice of Southern Australia at twenty-four, organist of Adelaide Cathedral and founder of a music school there when he was thirty. Returning to London in 1893, he became a preparatory school music master and began to feel that the German musical tradition in which he, like almost all English musicians of his period, had been brought up, was not the natural music of the boys he taught, and, discovering English folk-song, devoted the rest of his life to its collection and preservation. In 1903 he noted his first folk-song. 'The Seeds of Love'. He was not the first scholar in this field: John Broadwood, an Anglican clergyman, had noted down the songs sung at Harvest Homes in Surrey and Sussex, publishing a collection of them in 1843. His daughter, Lucy, took up the task of collecting English songs, and was the driving force in the formation of the English Folk-Song Society; she published two extremely important collections, *English Country Songs* (1893) and *English Traditional Songs and Carols* (1893). The journals of the *English Folk-Song Society* fed the enthusiasm which grew from her work.

Sharpe found in folk-song and folk-dance more than an indigenous music of extreme interest and often of great beauty. To him, it suggested ways of escape from the drab and dehumanizing effects of industrial life. Folk-song, he discovered, suggested that there is in the people themselves a rich vein of musical creativity. Round him, in the early years of the century, he gathered an impressive group of collectors and musicians, young men looking for a way forward from the impasse that seemed to block the way of the young musician as the last energies of nineteenth-century romanticism came to an end. For Harley Granville-Barker, the dramatist and theatre director, he assembled music and dances for Barker's trail-blazing production of Shakespeare's *A Midsummer-Night's Dream* in 1914, and spent a year during the First World War in the United States, finding fine and authentic versions of songs taken across the Atlantic by early settlers: these he published in 1932 as two volumes which he called *English Folk-Songs from The Southern Appalachian Mountains.*

Edmund H. Fellowes (1870–1951) spent the years in which Sharpe collected folk-songs performing a not dissimiliar service for the music of the Tudor composers. Fellowes, educated at Winchester and Oxford, had been a passionate musician from his schooldays;

a gifted violinist, he took part in whatever musical activity was going on round him. Ordained in 1894, he became a minor canon at Bristol Cathedral and a member of madrigal societies at Bristol and Windsor, where he became a minor canon of St George's Chapel in 1900. The whole corpus of Tudor vocal and choral music was anything but available to singers, and Fellowes decided that authentic and trustworthy editions should be produced and made available. He edited the thirty-six volumes of *The English Madrigal School*, which occupied him for eleven years from 1913 onwards; to these he added *English Madrigal Verse* (1920) and *English Madrigal Composers* (1921), *The English School of Lutenist Song Writers* (early 1920s), a study of Orlando Gibbons (1925), and an exhaustive study of the life and music of William Byrd in 1936 replacing an earlier and slighter study. He was one of the editorial committee which produced *Tudor Church Music*, a monumental critical edition of the works of the great English masters from Taverner to Tomkins, completed in 1948. Fellowes edited the complete edition of Byrd's works, having tracked down parts missing from Byrd's *Great Service*, the twenty volumes of which were completed in 1950. From a vantage point at the end of the 1970s, it seems incredible that so much superlative and well-loved music should have been more or less unknown at the beginning of the twentieth century, but Fellowes's editing, painstaking, accurate and utterly scrupulous in in search for and use of authorities, as well as his enthusiastic propaganda, provided escape from the post-romantic impasse.

Ralph Vaughan Williams (1872–1958) came from a well-to-do family related to the Darwins and the Wedgewoods. Educated at Charterhouse and Cambridge, he made his way with a B.Mus. degree to the Royal College of Music, where he was taught by both Parry and Stanford. He was one of the pupils not intimidated by Stanford's caustic tongue, just as, when in 1907 he went to Paris for lessons from Ravel eager to study Ravel's economy and precision, he did not allow Ravel's example to deflect him from aims that were already clear in his own mind; he had gone simply to study ways in which they might be achieved. He spent some time as organist of St Barnabas Church in Lambeth, and in 1910 completed his first symphony, the *Sea Symphony*, a bulky, powerful but rather sprawling work for soprano and baritone soloists, chorus and orchestra with words by Walt Whitman.

By this time, however, he had discovered English folk-song. Coming from an educated, cultured family he had grown up aware of opera and concert music and had been composing since he had been a small boy. He had surrendered wholeheartedly to the power of Wagner, but he had discovered that surrender to Wagner would make it impossible for him ever to find a voice of his own. English folk-song came to him as a revelation, directing his attention to modal melodies and the possibility of modal constructions within the forms and the harmonic grammar worked out for tonal music; it established in him a sense of Englishness which remained with him for the rest of his life. Although his religious attitudes seem to have been agnostic, his absorption by English traditions both musical and literary led him to write for the English liturgy, to find music for Biblical texts, for hymns, for the devotional poetry of George Herbert and, perhaps above all, for Bunyan's *Pilgrim's Progress*. All these, as part of the English tradition were, like English landscape but not English history, a source of inspiration.

Vaughan Williams often set out to write strong, rough-hewn music and seems very often to aim at revelations of great strength and power. The sea on which he meditates in the *Sea Symphony* is a revelation of strength that has few playful moods; London, in the *London Symphony* (1914) is peopled in its scherzo by mouth-organ-playing cockney roisterers but the city has a personality of its own which, perhaps, is the collective power of its multitudinous inhabitants; its use of the Westminster chimes thus becomes anything but an almost trivial splash of local colour—it is a series of notes implicit in the work's personality and purposes. The *Pastoral Symphony* (1922) suggests the landscape and the cloudscape of England as felt by a composer some of whose roots stretch to the Cotswolds, and when people appear in it, again in the scherzo, they seem to be the people of T. S. Eliot's 'East Coker': "Earth feet, loam feet, lifted in country mirth. . . ."

Vaughan Williams's sense of himself as an English composer was not restricted to an awareness of himself as a composer who loved and was influenced by English folk-song, although folk-song and its idioms became integral to his style. Most of his admirers would agree that the true, distinctive voice of Vaughan Williams was first heard in *Towards the Unknown Region* composed in 1905, a setting for chorus and orchestra of a text by Walt Whitman which begins with words that might almost be their composer's motto, "Darest thou, O soul, go forth towards the Unknown Region"; it was performed in the Leeds Festival two years later by Stanford, who had never shown any partiality for the music Vaughan Williams had written as his pupil. Round about the same time he wrote his setting of William Barnes's 'Linden Lea' which comes close to folk-song. In 1907 Vaughan Williams went to study under Ravel, choosing a teacher whose habits and style were in most ways antithetical to his own, because he felt that Ravel's economy and precision of style could help him to cure what he felt to be clumsy diffuseness in his own work. The result was *On Wenlock Edge,* a setting for tenor, string quartet and piano of six poems by A. E. Housman which in its fourth song ("Oh, when I was in love with you") achieves a complete recreation of the folk-song idiom in a work which has learnt economy in suggesting and implying complexities which the earlier Vaughan Williams would have worked out in comparatively forceful detail.

At about this time he worked on his one-act opera *The Shepherds of the Delectable Mountains,* an episode in Bunyan's *Pilgrim's Progress* which, nearly forty years later, was taken into his full-scale operatic treatment of Bunyan's allegory. Between 1911 and 1914 he was busy with *Hugh the Drover*, a ballad opera which could easily be heard as a celebration of English life and character in songs that are recreations of the traditional popular idiom. The year of 1910 saw the first performance of the *Fantasia on a Theme by Thomas Tallis,* for string quartet and string orchestra, music mystical, luminous and intense which soon marked considerable popularity; in 1911, the *Five Mystical Songs,* for baritone chorus and orchestra; in 1922, the *Pastoral Symphony* and, in 1923, the *Mass in G Minor* a setting of the Latin text for double choir first sung at Westminster Cathedral. Just as much of the early work had found ways of applying the folk-song tradition to modern themes and an urgently modern consciousness, in the Mass he applied modality and the Tudor style; it is a work which is as direct an expression of religious feeling as anything written by the Tudor composers who were its inspiration.

In this way, work by work, Vaughan Williams's emotional range and technical abilities gradually developed and expanded. *Flos Campi,* for solo viola, small chorus and small orchestra, was first performed, in 1925. There are six movements, each prefaced by a quotation from *The Song of Solomon.* The music is ecstatic, with a sort of rich puritan ecstasy. *Sancta Civitas* (1926), with tenor and baritone soloists, brought another (if not new) strain to Vaughan Williams's work into the foreground; its mood is one of prophecy. A new opera, *Sir John in Love,* in 1927, takes its words from Shakespeare's *Merry Wives of Windsor* and its music from folk-songs: it is the source of the *Fantasia on 'Greensleeves'* which became the most universally popular of all Vaughan Williams's music.

In 1930 came *Job,* which the composer called "a masque for dancing"; it is the music for a ballet based on the drawings by William Blake for the *Book of Job.* The work's dramatic climax is reached in a passage in which Satan sits on God's throne—an apparent triumph of evil which is characterized in a passage of fourths and chords made up of fourths which, from this time onwards, seem to have been the composer's symbol for active evil. The pastoral Vaughan Williams eventually ends the work in a mood of moving serenity. In the Fourth Symphony in F minor of 1934, a harshly dissonant, painfully grating work in which distressing harmonic implications are unsparingly worked out, the investigations of harmonies based on fourths continues with a fierceness and energy which startled and shocked those who had accepted Vaughan Williams as a withdrawn, catholic personality in search of comfortable routes by which he could retreat into the past. "If that's modern music, I don't like it," the composer is reported as having said after the Fourth Symphony's first performance. "I don't know whether I like it, but it's what I meant" is another of his *dicta.* He always disclaimed the programme suggested for the work by those who saw in it a vision of war clouds gathering and a denunciation of Nazi wickedness in Germany. It is, however its emotional burden be felt, a work of precise logic and organization.

The Fifth Symphony (1943) is quite different. It is a work which grows from the complex of ideas and emotions that were gathering in Vaughan Williams's mind round the *Pilgrim's Progress* as Bunyan's allegory took operatic shape in Vaughan Williams's mind, and it stands as the richest application to symphonic and orchestral thought of Vaughan Williams's exploration of the recreated Tudor, modal style, as though the subdued horn call with which it opens begins a train of thought that penetrates to modern concerns in the light of attitudes that belong to no period either Tudor or modern but are relevant to both.

The Vaughan Williams style is adventurous and original; neither his attitudes nor his technique were conventional, and his aims were not those of any of the accepted schools ancient or English or foreign or modern. Envying Gustav Holst's experience as an orchestral player, he involved himself in practical music-making in every way a freelance composer could, and was always ready to provide music where it was needed and for whoever needed it. His work on the *English Hymnal*, as its music editor, was typical of him; to do the work to his own satisfaction involved far more work than its literary editors and its publishers anticipated, or than its buyer provided for. In the 1940s, film music came his way as a technical and expressive challenge which he accepted almost gleefully. It was clear that his work was, to him, not only a deep personal satisfaction but a necessary social duty.

The discovery of English folk-song provided Vaughan Williams with a base from which he could expand in all directions and which a vigorously adventurous mind could explore. To him, English music was meant to be England's contribution to the international language of music. Gustav Holst, too, recognized the beauty and value of English folk-song, but Holst had no private income to subsidize the work of folk-song collection, and anyhow, folk-song to him was only one possible road ahead. Despite their Swedish name, Holst's great grandfather settled in England in 1807, bringing with him an eight-year-old son who married an Englishwoman, as did his son, who was to marry an English pianist. At the age of nineteen, Gustav Holst entered the Royal College of Music; he suffered from neuritis and was therefore prevented from developing into a concert pianist, and so concentrated on composition as a pupil of Stanford. Unlike Vaughan Williams, with whom he shared an enquiring, adventurous mind, Holst never gave the impression that he had found a fixed musical area which he could expand. Holst, fascinated by techniques, found himself stimulated to write by external influences and idioms to which his technique could be applied. Compared to Vaughan Williams's music, Holst's can sound austere, cold and uncommunicative, pattern designed for the sake of no more than its own intricacies.

For five years Holst was a trombonist in the orchestra of the Carl Rosa Opera and the Scottish Orchestra. His intimate knowledge of the orchestra was of the greatest value to him for the rest of his life. From 1903 onwards, whatever time was not given to composition was given to teaching; as well as a professorship at the Royal College of Music and another at Reading University, he was Director of Music at Morley College, and he taught at James Allen's Girls' School and St Paul's Girls' School. As a teacher he was demanding but encouraging, not only stimulating and broadening the minds of his pupils but also mustering their ambitions enough to give them the desire to work hard at what they might have felt to be beyond them. Folk-songs, old traditional music, the works of the Renaissance masters and of the eighteenth century as well as new music were all material for his amateur musicians.

Much of his work in the 1890s was influenced by his discovery of folk-song, and English folk-song remained a powerful influence on his work. In the first decade of the twentieth century Indian poetry and legend attracted his attention; it motivated an unpublished opera *Sita* and a chamber opera, *Savitri*, composed in 1908 but not staged until 1916. *Savitri* is a sparse, taut masterpiece, almost uncomfortably economical and creating an atmosphere that belongs only to Holst. These works and the four groups of hymns with texts from the *Rig-Veda* (three for mixed voices unaccompanied, the other for female voices and harp) have no particular interest in orientalism but treat their subjects as moving and important verse, as though Indian thought demands no special and possible meretricious colour of its own.

There was no big concert work to create a sensation in all this, and Holst was not the composer to look for a sensational subject in order to attract an audience. *The Planets*, composed between 1914 and 1916, was heard in 1918 and proved to be a powerful, popular work—the one work by a composer whose mind was by nature both powerful and emotive which the concert-goer is sure to know. *The Planets* is not comfortable music; it is a suite of seven movements which contains, in 'Jupiter', one superbly irresistible tune (subsequently used as a hymn tune for the words by Cecil Spring Rice, "I vow to thee, my country") and in 'Mars' what still sounds like a terrifying vision of mechanical warfare and its destructive power. 'Saturn, the Bringer of Old Age' is music of cold dread, and

'Neptune, the Mystic' seems to come from a world terrifying in its cool serenity, fading away on an unresolved dissonance. Throughout *The Planets*, Holst makes his way through unfamiliar worlds with absolute certainty of touch, and it is music which seems not only to speak prophetically about man's condition but also about several of the future directions of music.

Holst wrote a great deal of music for his students to sing and to play, and big works came as he cleared away the time necessary to answer these compulsions. His interests ranged from Eastern legend and poetry and astrology, to medieval and modern poetry, and this liveliness of mind presupposed an ability to find the effective technique to convey his ideas. His opera *The Perfect Fool* (1921) looks back to the period dominated by Wagner; however, Holst created a work which cannot be set down seriously as a Wagner parody because it is powerful and effective music to those who do not know their Wagner well enough to recognize the parody. Before *The Perfect Fool* had been staged, *The Hymn of Jesus* had been performed with effect almost comparable to that of *The Planets*. The text comes from *The Acts of St John* included in the collection of early Christian writings known as the Apocryphal New Testament, and its main substance is a ritual dance of Christ and his disciples. This is introduced by a passage of exhortation after the presentation of two eloquent and effectively scored plainsong hymns; the music asks for double chorus and a large orchestra, but it remains clear, hard and uncluttered. Two more operas, *At the Boar's Head*, drawn from Shakespeare's *Henry IV*, and *The Tale of the Wandering Scholar*, are on the surface smaller-scale works, the first made out of folk-song melodies, both brightly coloured and lively. *Egdon Heath* (1927), the prelude and scherzo *Hammersmith* (1930), the usually bitonal Concerto for Two Violins (1929) and the Choral Fantasia (1930) show him, in his sixties, as a composer with an unmistakable personal style but a readiness to work out the technique appropriate to a task he had considered so clearly that his aim could be achieved. The bareness and austerity of his music, perhaps, preclude its popularity, but the greatness of its achievement is clear.

Josef Holbrooke (1878–1958) was in his young manhood and middle age a far more prominent figure in English music than either Vaughan Williams or Holst. Holbrooke seemed to be born into the modern movement, to be an heir of Richard Strauss born to carry on Strauss's work. A pianist never less than effective, he gave innumerable recitals of modern English music by the young composers of the day. Enormously prolific, he first attracted attention as a composer through a series of what can best be called post-Straussian symphonic poems even larger than those of Strauss but handled with complete certainty; the writings of E. A. Poe and Longfellow provided him with subject matter. A set of Variations, again for a large orchestra, on 'Three Blind Mice', was for a time a popular Promenade Concert work.

After 1909, Holbrooke turned to opera, with a trilogy of related works on Welsh legends: the first, *The Children of Don*, was produced in 1912; the second, *Dylan*, followed in 1913; the third, *Bronwen*, was not seen until 1929. *The Children of Don* was produced in Vienna and Salzburg in 1923. Before the First World War, Holbrooke's music won a great deal of attention; after the war, though he was younger than either Vaughan Williams or Holst, his previous admirers seem to decide that time had left him behind, but it seems to be time for a really conscientious re-examination of his work.

XIII
The Time of Expansion

In the summer of 1895, Robert Newman, the manager of the Queen's Hall, opened eighteen months before, established a summer series of Promenade Concerts there; the Queen's Hall Orchestra was conducted by a twenty-six-year-old musician, Henry J. Wood (1869–1944), an organist and singing teacher who had already gained experience as a conductor of opera. Wood was, history has shown us, the right man in the right place, and he continued to conduct six-week seasons of Promenade Concerts every summer until 1944. In addition, Wood conducted innumerable other concerts in London and the provinces, but his name is indissolubly linked to London's Promenade Concerts. In 1895, the first half of each concert was standard, accepted 'serious' music, the second half light and popular. The first of Wood's Promenade Concerts included songs, solos for flute, cornet (Schubert's "Serenade") and bassoon. The songs were operatic excerpts and ballads. A lot of the music was unknown to London and two of the items in the first programme were first English performances. "How many of my young Promenaders could stand and listen to it if I repeated it nowadays I leave to their judgement," Wood wrote in 1938. "I doubt whether I could tolerate it myself, but both they and I must remember the conditions ruling then. This was a new venture, and as such *it had to be popular*."[45]

Wood was a passionate musical educator. In the first season Wood conducted a Beethoven concert, a Schubert programme, Lalo's *Symphonie Espagnole*, as well as music by Rimsky-Korsakov and Tchaikovsky. Towards the end of the season, Wood found it possible to put English music into the programmes. In a comparatively short time Wood found that the concerts could hold their audience—which rapidly became marked by its growth—through a second half as ambitious as the first. The amount of new music, or music new to London, played season by season at the 'Proms' is hardly credible, and there was always a considerable amount of English music; this was a policy which he followed for the rest of his life; Elgar, Bantock, Josef Holbrooke, Cyril Scott, Balfour Gardiner, Vaughan Williams, Delius, Roger Quilter, Eugene Goossens and Frank Bridge provided novelties to join novelties by Tchaikovsky, Rimsky-Korsakov, Richard Strauss, Mahler and Schoenberg. Wood's promenade seasons explored English music and invited its composers to conduct it, producing not only important new works but new conductors. Wood's programmes for fifty years provided regular Wagner, Bach and Beethoven as well as programmes devoted to other composers. As well as that, in a way rare in London, Wood welded his audience into a community which, at the end of the season, turned the last concert into a roistering party.

In 1904, Wood's irritation with the deputy system led to a remodelling of the Queen's Hall Orchestra; a considerable number of Wood's players left the orchestra rather than surrender the old system, and formed the London Symphony Orchestra, controlled by an elected committee of its own members. The residue of players, and a number of new recruits to bring the team up to strength, formed the New Queen's Hall Orchestra, working under seasonal contracts. The deserters, inviting conductors of the stature of Richter and Nikisch to work with them, found that Wood's action had indirectly limited their freedom because it led to a raising of orchestral standards with which the new organization had to keep up.

Wood's Promenade Concerts, however, involved him and the New Queen's Hall Orchestra in six concerts a week for an extended season and thus precluded careful and exhaustive rehearsal. Accepting the duty of performing new and often extremely difficult music —Wood declared that his duty was in part to perform new music, not to enjoy it, and that his own greatest pleasure came from the music of Mozart—Wood's rehearsals had to be devoted to new music and to the recognized danger points in well-known works, and by these methods, with a great deal of hard work, he maintained a standard of performance that rarely fell below the convincing. England's debt to this work remains incalculable and, to his audiences, especially to the young people who filled the Promenade in the body of the hall from which the seats had been removed, he was a hero.

Thomas Beecham (1879–1961) brought a huge family fortune, wit, elegance of style and wide personal tastes to music. His tastes were both wide and unorthodox, for he professed no particular enthusiasm for the music of Beethoven and Wagner, though he gave splendid performances of music by both, rejected Bach and professed a huge enthusiasm for French music. Beecham's conducting technique was even more unorthodox than his views; he conducted phrases and not bars, and the eloquence of his phrasing created performances of a vitality and delicacy (qualities which he declared to be the essence of musical performance) that were usually startling, though these qualities were not often associated at the beginning of the century with English orchestras. His own fortune was at the service of musical organizations (like the Royal Philharmonic Society) when they needed it and as an impresario he presented opera in seasons which, both in London and Manchester, went far beyond the customary English repertory. Though he conducted little music that did not appeal to his own taste, and though he could at times perpetrate forcefully insensitive performances of works which he did not find sympathetic, his repertoire was remarkably wide and he had a rare ability to make a great deal of relatively unimportant music sound great. Throughout a career that lasted for more than sixty years, Beecham brought an exciting virtuosity into English music, and a glorious high-spiritedness.

While Elgar, Delius and Bantock—Elgar desultorily after 1918, Delius in the almost miraculous Indian Summer granted him by the devoted work of Eric Fenby—continued to stand until the 1930s as dominating figures, in the early twentieth century they were joined by younger men with new attitudes. Elgar, by his eclectic genius, had united English music to the European mainstream, but the European mainstream had lost its sense of direction since Wagner had explored intense chromatic harmonies in *Tristan und Isolde* and *Parsifal*, and we could justifiably argue that Mahler's music is the work which manages to re-establish tonality after the work of Wagner had tended to dissolve it. The example of Wagner, and the power of Wagner's musical imagination were so strong, that the young composer at the beginning of the century had either to submit his personality to it or to rebel.

The coming of the cinema and silent films provided another boost to musicians—the most humble cinema in a poor neighbourhood needed a pianist to accompany whatever occupied the screen with appropriate music. Larger cinemas even in quite poor areas could accommodate some sort of small orchestra, while important cinemas in city centres had, if only for the sake of prestige, to employ large orchestras though the music they played was often unimpressive. In 1929, the critic Edwin Evans estimated that up to four-fifths of the "paid musical employment" in Britain was provided by the cinemas. These golden days, of course, ended with the coming of the 'talkies' in the late 1920s, after which even the most opulent cinemas were satisfied with an organist and a Wurlitzer organ usually described as 'mighty'. It was not for some time that the English film-makers, following examples from the United States and Russia, began to commission music from English composers. Sir William Walton's first film score, for *Escape Me Never*, appeared in 1934.

By the outbreak of the First World War, it was becoming possible for those with the eye of faith to see gramophone recording as a new feature of life which musicians might take seriously. The great singers—Melba, Caruso, Chaliapin, John McCormack and others—were making records which treated their voices not unfavourably, although it was not until the late 1920s that electrical recording began to do justice to any sort of instrumental or orchestral music. The gramophone was, of course, limited to the amount of music that could be performed on a single ten-inch or twelve-inch side, providing four or five minutes' worth of music.

The coming of broadcasting in 1922, when the British Broadcasting Company was founded, had a more profound influence on musical tastes and habits. From the start, broadcasting was regarded, particularly by the broadcasters, as an important public service, and in 1927 the Company was transformed into the British Broadcasting Corporation, independent of government control or commercial pressure. It saw its function as the provision of information, education and entertainment, and music has always played an important part in its provisions. In 1927, the BBC took over the management of the Promenade Concerts, leaving their policy and repertory in the hands of Henry Wood. In 1930, Adrian Boult moved to the BBC as the Corporation's Musical Director. His international reputation had been steadily growing and he had conducted London orchestras in concerts of unusual enterprise, introducing a great deal of English music; he had also spent six years as conductor of the Birmingham Symphony Orchestra. Boult had conducted the first performance of a number of important English works—Holst's *The Planets*, Vaughan Williams's *Pastoral Symphony* and the *Colour Symphony* by Arthur Bliss (1891–1973) amongst others—and had introduced a number of important European works to England; he was not concerned, though his greatest achievements were in English music, to propagate any single style of music or advance the claims of any particular school.

The style of entertainment music loosely called 'Jazz' came to England, and to the rest of Europe, round about the turn of the century. However, the music most frequently taken up by white musicians in America and Europe was a dilution of the improvisatory Negro style of music, with its own harmonic rules and its rich vitality of rhythm; its energy and freedom of style rapidly became popular and slowly helped to kill off the tiring music hall style. Until the 1920s and '30s it had little influence on trained, 'classically' orientated musicians, but by the 1920s it was virtually impossible for anybody whose ears were receptive to grow up without the effects, idioms and rhythmic formulae created by popular musicians from an Afro-American style which is always weakened by formulation.

When the BBC, with Boult in charge, decided to form its own orchestra, it did so under conditions which guaranteed security no other English orchestra had ever experienced. Its members' contracts were genuinely permanent, so that their salaries covered holidays; their terms of service precluded them from making music under any other auspices. It took only a short space of time, during which Boult became the BBC Symphony Orchestra's Chief Conductor as well as the Corporation's Musical Director, for the orchestra to grow into an extremely reliable ensemble capable of great performances.

Not every musician was equally enthusiastic about the possibilities of broadcasting. Both Hamilton Harty, leading the Hallé Orchestra in Manchester through a period of splendid musical achievement and financial stringency, and Beecham felt that the availability of music in the home would empty concert halls. Beecham, however, had been pondering the necessity for a new London orchestra which would set and maintain a standard of musical excellence and had discussed possibilities with the BBC before the Corporation created its own orchestra. By 1932 he had gathered guarantees of sufficient work to ensure the new orchestra's future and had electrified London with the first concert of the London Philharmonic.

Musically, as in every other way, England suffered losses in the First World War. George Butterworth (1885–1916) was killed in action in France leaving behind him two volumes of settings of poems by A. E. Housman and two beautifully written small orchestral works—*A Shropshire Lad Rhapsody* and *The Banks of Green Willow*—which exploit a similar style, taut, lyrical and aware of the work of Cecil Sharpe and Sharpe's disciples. Ivor Gurney (1890–1937), an entirely lyrical composer and a moving lyrical poet from whom music came with something like the apparent spontaneity of Schubert or Dowland, was gassed, shell-shocked and left to live on for twenty years a mental and physical ruin. His few published songs all influenced by the poetry of Housman, and are beautiful in a style which from the first seemed to have nothing to do with the twentieth century. If the war had apparently little influence on the often remote, exploratory outlook of Holst, it deepened the tendency to prophetic denunciation in Vaughan Williams without removing either his innate geniality or his sense of fun. The war, and the sense that it had ended the world to which he belonged, seemed to have a great deal to do with the almost complete silence of Elgar in the later years of his life.

Arnold Bax (1883–1953) belonged emotionally if not technically to the period of Elgar and Bantock. A product of the Royal Academy of Music, he emerged with a technique which seemed capable of mastering every compositional difficulty that could be encountered in pre-Schoenbergian music, and an apparently unprecedented ability for playing complex orchestral scores at sight on the piano. The Celtic revival in Ireland was perhaps the biggest influence on his work, which exploits Irish rhythms and turns of melodic phrase—though he had no Irish blood. He developed a powerful style of piano writing, ranging from massiveness in the piano sonatas in F sharp minor and G major, both published in 1919, to an inventively decorative style turning harmonies into ornamental arabesques. In the carol for unaccompanied double choir, *Mater Ora Filium*, he achieved a masterpiece in a style he never again attempted in any of his other choral music, and three of his symphonic poems, *The Garden of Fand*, *Tintagel* and *November Woods* (1916, 1917 and 1917) are rich and colourful. His First Symphony, completed in 1922, has an almost brusque, forceful masculinity; the later six symphonies, the Seventh composed in 1939, all have colour, richness of emotion and a tender care for beauty of sound even when they are displaying power and eloquence; but they all seem to follow a similar pattern, working their way through complexities of tonality and presentation to an epilogue (though the term is used only in the Third and the Sixth) in which Bax looks back with a sort of nostalgic contentment to the course of the work he has accomplished. He described himself as "a brazen romantic", and it seems that for all the beauty with which he stated, his romanticism lacked qualities that imposed it on a world from which he was apparently eager to withdraw into beautiful scenery and legends.

In a period when most composers found it natural to work for large orchestras in large-scale music, John Ireland (1879–1963) remained most concerned with the solo piano, songs and the smaller chamber music forms. Two sonatas for violin and piano, and one for clarinet and piano are accomplished and remarkably imaginative works, the composer's natural lyricism moulded without strain or clumsiness into satisfying extended forms. His songs, often choosing unconventional lyrics but always prompted by poetry of real value, share the qualities of grace and integrity shown by his sonatas. Starting his professional career as organist of St Luke's Church, Chelsea, he naturally wrote some church music, effective and grateful to sing, but apparently inhibiting to his rarer natural gifts. A handful of larger works—an effective virtuoso Piano Concerto, a setting for baritone, choir and orchestra of a poem by John Addington Symonds called *These Things Shall Be*, the *London* and *Satyricon* Overtures, and a remarkably atmospheric, brooding and original orchestral fantasy, *Mai-Dun* (finding in the Dorset earthwork Maiden Castle a strange, disturbing sense of timeless awe and menace)—show that his avoidance of larger forms had nothing to do with uncertainties and inabilities. It is, however, his piano music, evocative, imaginative and quite often strangely sinister that is entirely personal and unique. Ireland's music leads nowhere; it is not, at present, a starting point for new developments; those, perhaps, come through his students and the Royal College of Music.

At the RCM, Ireland taught Benjamin Britten, originally taught as a schoolboy by Frank Bridge (1879–1941). Bridge was, unlike Ireland, an orchestral and chamber music violinist and a good conductor. He entered the Royal College of Music as a violin student, won a composition scholarship and studied under Stanford. Bridge became well-known through his chamber music, which delighted players for the pleasure they found in playing it. His orchestral works, slower to win an audience, had the same qualities of consideration for his players and a rich, lyrical mode of expression which, in the late nineteen twenties, moved towards a more modern, more toughly intellectual style. In everything he did, however, he showed a scrupulous, precise technique which gave all his work a finely smooth, attractive surface.

Arthur Bliss went in the other direction. Before the First World War he studied composition and conducting at the Royal College of Music. Two of his early works, a String Quartet and a Piano Quartet, he later suppressed. In 1918 Bliss completed *Madam Noy*, which stands as the first of his compositions; it is a song, with words by E. H. W. Meyerstein, for soprano, accompanied by flute, clarinet, bassoon, viola, harp and double-bass. It was first performed in 1920. In 1919 came *Rout*, a work for soprano and chamber orchestra, the soprano singing not words but vowel sounds. A 'concerto' for soprano, tenor, piano, strings and percussion composed in 1920 turned into a concerto for two pianos, strings and percussion; it had previously been a Rhapsody for the same vocal soloists and eight instruments. *Mélée Fantasque* (1921) was his first full orchestral work, and by this time Bliss had made it obvious that he was a composer with an experimental mind and a decisive style. The *Colour Symphony* (1922) is a big, muscular work, each movement representing a colour and its connotation in human life; the first movement is purple, 'the colour of amethysts, pageantry, royalty and death'. The second is red, 'the colour of rubies, wine, revelry, furnaces, courage and magic'. The symphony continues with blue, 'the colour of sapphires, deep water, skies, loyalty and melancholy'. and its last movement is green, 'the colour of emeralds, hope, joy, youth, spring and victory'. In the *Colour Symphony,* Bliss came into contact with the generality of concert-goers and made it clear that for all the novelty of his style and daring of his early experiments his music stood firmly in the English tradition, and from the *Colour Symphony* onwards the two elements in his musical personality grew together though he never again worked with the oddly assorted instrumental groups of his early works. *Lie Strewn the White Flocks*, a composition for mezzo-soprano, flute, drums and strings in which Bliss used an anthology of poems from Theocritus to Robert Nichole, showed again that Bliss could make traditional styles live in the modern world. Two years later *Morning Heroes*, a 'symphony' for orchestra and choir with poems spoken by an orator, both honoured the courage of fighting men and bemoaned the suffering of war; because Bliss's style is decisive, masculine and forceful, some listeners did not succeed in hearing its protest against war, but it remains a powerful, strong and moving work. *Music for Strings* (1935) has the characteristic energetic stride of Bliss's music and stands with Elgar's *Introduction and Allegro* and Vaughan Williams's *Tallis Fantasia* in its eloquent use of a string orchestra. The music for the film *Things to Come* (1935) proved to be one of the rare film scores which could survive in the concert hall—it ends with an excellently optimistic march—and *Checkmate* (1937), the first of three ballets written for the Sadler's Wells Company, matched colourfully original music to original choreography and a romantic theme. *Miracle in the Gorbals* (1944), a second ballet, has a similar romantic theme—redemption coming to debased, devitalized slum dwellers—and similarly romantic music to *The Olympians* (1949), Bliss's only full-scale opera, the libretto of which (by J. B. Priestley) is equally romantic and optimistic. *Variations on a Theme by John Blow* (1955) shows the composer as eloquently powerful, and as lyrical, as in any of his early works.

The twentieth century, however, promptly provided a group of rich talents. Alan Bush (b. 1900), Edmund Rubbra (b. 1901), William Walton (b. 1902) and Constant Lambert (1905–1951) were an unusually rich, impressive, and startingly diverse group of talents. Walton was the first to arrive as a shocking young iconoclast. Walton, son of a music teacher in Oldham, became a choirboy at Christ Church Cathedral, Oxford; Christ Church encouraged his early work, most of which he destroyed though a few choral pieces —notably *A Litany* (words by Phineas Fletcher), *The Winds* (words by Swinburne) and *Tritons* (words by William Drummond) have survived. The relative emptiness of wartime Oxford (where Walton had great encouragement from musical and academic authorities) permitted him to enter Christ Church as an undergraduate at the age of sixteen, and from this time onward Walton was almost totally self-taught. A piano quartet (1918–1919) was already a personal work, with something of the rhythmic drive and the sweeping romanticism that were to become his unmistakable finger-print. A string quartet (1922) was one of the three British works played at the Inaugural Festival of the International Society of Contemporary Music in Salzburg a year later. To musicians, Walton had arrived and was a vividly gifted, ruthless modernist. A year later the world at large heard his name.

As an undergraduate he had become a friend of Osbert, Edith and Sacheverell Sitwell, and in 1923, *Façade*, his 'entertainment' for speaker and six instruments to poems by Edith Sitwell, had its first public performance at the Aeolian Hall in London. The three Sitwells, brilliant, witty and irreverent about conventions, had already won some inveterate enemies in the Press, and the idea of poems spoken through a megaphone from behind a screen, the poems being in the tradition of witty nonsense poetry devised as a poet's technical studies, to music scored for flute and piccolo, clarinet and bass clarinet, saxophone, trumpet, cello and percussion, was an obvious proof to such enemies of its creators' effete silliness. The music critics who attended, however, saluted the wit, the brilliant parodies of popular dance forms, the aptly irreverent quotations and misquotations, and the elegant grace and beautiful workmanship of the work; it took more than a first hearing to reveal the precision with which the music reflects a poem if not word by word at least image by image. The economy of Walton's writing is dazzling, and the two ballet suites from *Façade*, scored for standard orchestra, have become extremely popular.

The flippancy and wit of *Façade* was, however only one element in Walton's musical constitution and each successive work revealed others. *Portsmouth Point* (1925), a recreation in musical terms of a drawing by Thomas Rowlandson, made lively use of the jazzy, popular idioms that he had used in *Façade*, exploiting them to give briskness and nervous vitality to a traditionally English view of seafaring and dockside scenes, while the unjustly neglected *Sinfonia Concertante* for piano and orchestra (1927) suggested that the English Handelian tradition, seen through the eyes of an entirely twentieth-century sensibility, was still valid. To these qualities, the Viola Concerto (1928–1929) added wistfulness, nostalgia and a sense of the possibility of tragedy. Two large symphonic works in three years was a swifter rate of production than Walton was ever to achieve again, and it became clear that the enormous rhythmic vitality of his music, and its impeccably finished and polished craftsmanship were both products of a sternly self-critical, scrupulously perfectionist view of the composer's task.

In 1931 came *Belshazzar's Feast*, written for the Leeds Festival and entirely disconcerting to those who expected something in the nature of a traditional oratorio or sacred cantata. Walton himself has said that he thinks of it as a choral symphony. After a slow homophonic introduction for brass and men's voices, it moves into a long, tragic polyphonic setting of Psalm 137—"By the Waters of Babylon"—which screws itself up to an outburst of rage. A baritone soloist launches into a free, unaccompanied recitative about the baleful splendour of Babylon, and then there is a splendid, brassy ceremonial march in which Belshazzar and his court sing in praise of their false Gods and sacrilegiously drink from the sacred vessels looted from Jerusalem. This is a glory cut off in mid-stream by the writing on the wall, the baritone's account accompanied by grating, rasping and squeaking sounds from flute, double-basses and percussion, taken up by the men's voices. The last movement is a wild hymn of exultation from the enslaved Israelites, halted only for a few moments when they remember the glory that had been Babylon's. This was not a Bible story told in traditional oratorio style but an account of fanatical nationalism and race hatred retold with a savagery unique in music.

The rage and savagery of *Belshazzar's Feast* are matters of precise calculation. The work unleashes devastating power, but the power, despite a large orchestra with extensive percussion and two *ad libitum* brass bands in emulation of Berlioz's *Requiem*, is firmly under control and the invention of effective gestures apt and vivid. It was followed, in 1932, by three movements of the First Symphony, the finale of which was not completed until 1935. Though Walton has uncharacteristically avowed a private and personal motivation for the symphony, with its bone-shaking rhythms and its grating clashes with the tonality of B flat minor, the work's official key, it seemed natural to regard it as a reflection of an England and a world sinking deeper into the troubles that led to the Second World War. The extreme tension of the first movement is screwed up to even greater intensity by the scherzo, which is marked *Presto con malizio*, and the promise of relaxation offered by its *Adagio* is belied by a development that returns to the stresses of the earlier movement. The last movement, a series of linked *fugato* passages, leads to a jubilant conclusion perhaps distantly related to the ecstatic 'alleluia' that closes *Belshazzar's Feast*; this was the first part of the symphony to be written down and it poses problems; without care and extreme control by performers, it cannot sound like the solution to the tragic questions raised within earlier movements.

There are suggestions in the first movement that Walton was moving into the world of Sibelius, to most English musicians in the 1920s and 1930s the greatest living composer, but the coronation of King George VI in 1937 prompted a march, *Crown Imperial*, which has a combination of glitter and gusto which suggests that Walton is an intensely romantic composer for all his originally shocking modernism. It would be obtuse to the point of musical illiteracy to say that Walton abandoned his modernism; his later music moves on to a state of mind in which disruptive violence, agonized intensity and desperation would have been out of place. The savagery of *Belshazzar's Feast*, once said, could not be repeated validly. In a sense, his Violin Concerto (1938), written for Jascha Heifetz and demanding enormous virtuosity, the Cello Concerto (1956), written for Gregor Piatigorsky, and the Partita, like the *Johannesburg Festival* overture, are more objective, less concerned with Walton's own mind than with the creation of good music for its own sake. The same is true of the relatively mellow Second Symphony (1962); all this music is scrupulously composed, precise in its effects and enjoyable. After all, in a mood of some objectivity Walton composed music for *The First of the Few* (1942), the wartime film about the invention, testing and manufacture of the Spitfire fighter plane, and accompanied factory scenes with what is now known as the *Spitfire Prelude and Fugue*, fierce music of crackling, controlled and determined energy. Critics who accused Walton of falling off from the savagery and violence of his earlier works really wished him to stay in middle age where he had been in early manhood.

Troilus and Cressida, produced in 1954, the first of Walton's two operas, is a work in which his essential romanticism is coupled with a lively sense of character; its harmonic vocabulary is no more conservative than that of his earlier works, but the opera's full-blooded melodic gestures and wide-spanned melodies persuaded some critics that it marked a regression in its composer's style, so that after twenty-five years the work is still awaiting adequate critical consideration. A one-act opera, *The Bear*, to a story by Chekhov and first produced at the Aldeburgh Festival, had a success both with critics and the public. A light, comic work with leading roles flamboyant enough both in music and in acting to attract fine singers, it shows Walton in a mood of sly, witty parody.

Constant Lambert, at first seemed destined for every possible success. The most unalloyed of golden boys, Byronically handsome, with a Byronic limp, a fine conductor, a brilliant, apparently omniscient, witty critic, a brilliant, witty conversationalist, Lambert was only twenty when Diaghilev commissioned him to write a ballet, and in 1926 *Romeo and Juliet* was produced in London and Monte Carlo; later it turned into *Adam and Eve*, with other, earlier compositions added. A set of *Eight Poems of Li Po*, for voice with flute, oboe, clarinet, double-bass and piano was composed between 1926 and 1930, *Music for Orchestra* in 1927, and *Elegiac Blues*, for piano, two flutes, oboe, two clarinets, bassoon, two horns, two trumpets, trombone, percussion and strings, arrived in 1927.

There was no symphony and instrumental sonata among these early works. Instead there was a composer who had come to maturity in the 1920s writing music, often brilliant, sometimes melancholy, in entirely modern forms, not only aware of jazz but at home in its harmonic language and melodic idioms. In 1929, Lambert's *The Rio Grande*, a setting of a poem by Sacheverell Sitwell for contralto, choir, piano and orchestra was heard, Lambert conducting, at a Hallé Concert in Manchester and promptly repeated in London; an earlier radio performance had made little impact. *The Rio Grande*, a work which glitters spectacularly but is touchingly nostalgic, which augments the symphony orchestra with jazz percussion which uses jazz idioms, particularly those of South American jazz, is high-spiritedly and effectively written; its choral writing, though it sets a large choir to sing in rhythms unfamiliar to choralists, is splendidly effective.

A piano sonata followed in 1929, and a piano concerto, its

orchestra consisting of flute, three clarinets, trumpets, trombone, percussion, cello and double-bass, in 1931; it is dedicated to the memory of Philip Heseltine (Peter Warlock) and is perhaps the most purely melancholy of all Lambert's work. By this time, he was deeply involved in work as musical director of the Sadler's Wells Ballet, conducting its orchestra, administering to its musical needs, composing and, more often, finding and arranging suitable music for its use. Composition had to become a spare-time activity. His ballet *Horoscope* (1937) has been both published and recorded, but its successor, *Tiresias* (1951) has not been revived. One of his rare orchestral works, *Aubade Heroique*, won same attention (it was a salute to the seventieth birthday of Vaughan Williams); and he was responsible for some film and theatre incidental music. Of all his work, Lambert seems to have valued most highly *Summer's Last Will and Testament* (1937), a composition for baritone, choir and orchestra with words by Thomas Nashe; it is witty, colourful, tuneful, at times both desperate and frightening and is still waiting for attention. For some years, Lambert was a regular music critic for the *Sunday Referee*, and in 1934 he published his book *Music Ho! A Study of Music in Decline*; in it he finds more merit in the work of Duke Ellington than in those of Schoenberg and Stravinsky, praised the then-unfashionable Elgar and the possibly over-praised Sibelius, deplored the universal availability of music through the radio and the gramophone and achieved one of the few serious statements about music which can be read for sheer fun and irreverence.

Alan Bush is a different matter. A product of the Royal Academy of Music and a private pupil of Ireland, he also studied the piano under Moiseivich and Schnabel and musicology at the University of Berlin. His early works, a string quartet in A minor (1924) and *Dialectic*, also for string quartet, immediately established him as a composer whose thought processes were intricate because they were concerned with intricacies, but who expressed them in genuinely worked-out music. His Piano Concerto won a great success in 1938, his Symphony in C had an equal effect at a Promenade Concert in 1942. In 1949, both his Nottingham Symphony and his Violin Concerto maintained his stature. In 1951, his opera *Wat Tyler* was one of the four prize-winning entries in the Festival of Britain opera competition, but it had its first performance in Leipzig and was heard over East German radio. Its successor, *Men of Blackdown*, has had no English performance.

Bush is a convinced Marxist, one-time conductor of the London Labour Choral Union and founder and President of the Workers' Music Association. During the Second World War, he seems to have rethought his musical principles and simplified his style in accordance with the doctrines of Socialist Realism, but his music remains vivid, completely thought-out and vigorous. His *Byron Symphony* (1965) is colourful, eloquent and original in its sense of orchestral presentation.

Edmund Rubbra, too, is a composer who has so far been given less than his due by listeners and by what one may call the musical 'establishment'; although much of his work is unusually original it is rarely sensational. The son of working-class parents, he won a composition scholarship at Reading University and eventually reached the Royal College of Music where he studied under Holst who seems to have been a great personal influence as well as a great musical influence on Rubbra's mind. He has written in almost every form, always convincingly. The Royal College of Music, and Holst, seem to have sent him in the direction of the Tudor madrigal and church music in a way that has affected everything he has written. His seven symphonies are among the few works that convincingly combine the idea of symphonic thought with fundamentally polyphonic writing, so that his symphonies do not oppose first subjects with contrasting second subjects but evolve their second subject through the polyphonic treatment of the first. This style made the first three symphonies, composed in 1936, 1937, and 1939 difficult to assimilate at a first hearing, but from the Fourth Symphony (1941) onwards, Rubbra has admitted passages of homophony and taken greater care of orchestral colour, so that the music has grown increasingly luminous and rich with no dilution of its precise and often profound qualities of thought.

The years between the two world wars saw the emergence of other composers. Philip Heseltine (1894–1930) was educated at Eton and Oxford but was won for music by the work of Delius. A conscientious objector found unfit for National Service, he developed a great devotion to Elizabethan music, provided a number of first-rate, practical editions of hardly-known work and in *The Sackbut*, which he founded in 1920 and edited, published a number of important studies of the work of the Elizabethan composers and their European contemporaries; he wrote a valuable book, critical but appreciative, on Delius, and with his friend Cecil Gray, another on Carlo Gesualdo.

Heseltine's songs were at first beautifully written songs of almost crippling melancholy, but round about 1918 he began to publish his music under the name Peter Warlock; 'Peter Warlock' published songs in all moods: rollicking, amorous, meditative, sociable and occasionally grim; he also wrote settings to traditional carols often mystical in mood as well as very beautiful, and he seemed to have had an inexhaustible power of invention, finding melodies that, in Byrd's phrase, are "framed to the life of the words".

Alan Rawsthorne (1905–1971) was a late starter who did not begin serious musical study until 1926. From 1935 onwards he devoted his time entirely to composition. *A Theme and Variations for Two Violins* (1938) and *Symphonic Studies* (1939) were heard at successive festivals of the International Society for Contemporary Music, and established his international reputation. His music is always taut, energetic and intelligent, never wears its heart on its sleeve but is always concerned to present musical thought clearly, concisely and intelligently.

By 1939 and the coming of the Second World War, England was no longer without music. International opera filled the Covent Garden Royal Opera House during the traditional London social season, and at Sadler's Wells a genuine *Volksoper* company was producing opera throughout the year with considerable success, even succeeding in winning a hearing for various English works. The BBC Symphony Orchestra, apart from its reliable routine work, had an international reputation and Beecham's London Philharmonic was praised everywhere. English composers were accepted and listened to; less than fifty years had changed the whole attitude of English music.

XIV
Consolidation?

The First World War had made little difference to our musical tastes and attitudes, but the Second World War revolutionized them. Opera performances and concerts were crowded. Shortly before the war, Beecham had left England to fulfil engagements in Australia and the United States; the London Philharmonic turned itself into a self-governing body and played concerts almost everywhere within reach of London despite the difficulties of travel. Dame Myra Hess, most beloved of British pianists, instituted daily lunchtime concerts in the National Gallery; they were thronged with office workers and servicemen and women.

The new enthusiasm for music was not restricted to London. In Manchester, the Hallé offered its permanent conductorship to John Barbirolli, a vivid and indefatigable Anglo-Italian who had spent several years in New York as Toscanini's successor; faced with only the nucleus of an orchestra, Barbirolli recreated the Hallé. Its committee of management, undertaking concerts in towns all round Manchester, raised the amount of local government support the orchestra received to a point at which the worst of its financial worries would be over so long as its members and conductor were ready to undertake a crushing load of work. The Liverpool Philharmonic—for many years virtually the same players wearing different hats—had reorganized itself on the same lines and with more generous local government support.

The creation of the Arts Council to disburse government funds to all the Arts was in accordance with the new attitude which crowded the majority of concerts and most opera performances. A new opera company was formed at Covent Garden aiming at the highest standards of performance. The Bournemouth Symphony

Orchestra, a hard-working and reliable ensemble founded in 1893, followed the example of Liverpool and Manchester to broaden its base. A new, smaller orchestra, the Northern Sinfonia, was set up with its base in Newcastle-upon-Tyne. In London, Beecham found himself without a regular orchestra and created the Royal Philharmonic Orchestra, and such was his reputation that in a short time he had collected a team of players, some established and some unknown, capable of his own perfectionist standards, while Walter Legge, a great power in the world of recording, created the Philharmonia Orchestra to make gramophone records with great conductors; inevitably it became a concert orchestra as well and, when Legge decided to end his association with it, it organized itself into a self-governing orchestra and it continued on its own account to carry out the policy for which it had been designed.

The presence of five concert orchestras in competition for London audiences led for a time to a policy of safety first which meant that the popular symphonies of Beethoven and Tchaikovsky, and the popular concertos, by Beethoven, Tchaikovsky and Rachmaninov, were repeated interminably until the London Orchestral Concert Board was set up to rationalize programmes, so that London programmes quite rapidly became adventurous. In the 1950s and 1960s first Mahler and then Bruckner, composers previously neglected in England, became extremely popular. Music which English audiences had previously rejected—by Schoenberg, Berg and Webern, and young composers like Boulez, Stockhausen, Berio, Maderna—was heard. Younger English composers were ready to work in the same way and explore the same techniques.

The BBC, however, became more exploratory and liberalizing than any other agency in the country. In 1946 it inaugurated its Third Programme to make space and time for such plays and music as would not fit into normal programmes, with their fixed landmarks of news services and invariable series. The Third Programme explored Mahler and Bruckner, was ready to make listeners aware not only of the music of Schoenberg and 'the second Viennese School' but also to pay attention to younger composers writing in unusual styles. Moving into areas where critical awareness was not a guide, the Third Programme tried to be musically inclusive and was ready to take risks; after all, its failures could soon be forgotten and would do no lasting harm.

It seemed, by the end of the Second World War, that periods were overlapping in a rather vertiginous sort of way. Vaughan Williams, still adventurous, untamed by time, had four more symphonies to write. Walton, reserved, carefully perfectionist, issued works slowly. For the film *Henry V*, the first and most powerful of Laurence Olivier's Shakespeare films, he wrote a score that satisfied him enough to be allowed to appear as a concert suite. Rubbra, increasingly a master of his own personal style, worked on. But in 1941, Michael Tippett's *A Child of Our Time* created something of a sensation, appealing from its own days to the music of tradition though not to the harmonic language of style in which the tradition had originally expressed itself.

A Child of Our Time is a secular oratorio and a Passion; it concerns a Jewish boy who assassinated a Nazi diplomat and thus precipitated a savage pogrom. Tippett himself wrote its libretto, finding a literary style which can be faulted in many ways but which seemed admirably to evoke the mood of the music. To create the sense of participation, so that audience as well as performers are involved in the action, Tippett used negro spirituals at the crucial points of his work, as Bach used the Lutheran chorales in his Passions, but Tippett's arrangements would not encourage the audience to sing even if the spirituals were far more familiar to the average audience. Tippett has an unusually complex mind, seeing, or sensing, often unusual, rarely apprehended connections between thoughts, events, moods and emotions, a quality which often makes his libretti, which he writes himself, obscure until the music arrives as a clarification.

Tippett was a pupil at the Royal College of Music. Composition came slowly to him; he suppressed one of his earliest works, his Symphony in B flat. He taught, notably at Morley College, where his students found him invigorating, lively, and inspiring, as though he were following in the spirit as well as the footsteps of Gustav Holst. His first string quartet, in 1935, is music of great rhythmic complexity, but *A Song of Liberty*, for choir and orchestra to a poem by Blake, indicated that he could be musically concerned with matters which carried music into the outside world. The Concerto for Double String Orchestra (1939) is direct, vigorous and full-blooded music which seems to grow out of the instruments and the textures they make it ensemble; it has, too, a radiance which is unlike almost anything else in twentieth-century music.

At the beginning of the Second World War, Tippett declared himself a pacifist, and his almost casual refusal to acknowledge wartime regulations saw him briefly imprisoned. His early music won the attention of critics and musicians. *A Child of Our Time* had a much broader effect; it was addressed, so to speak, to the world and it has pages of traditional massiveness like its powerful setting of the spiritual 'Deep River', while other pages have a total simplicity, orchestrally bare but beautifully expressive. The natural complexity of Tippett's mind took control of his First Symphony, originally subtitled *1945*. It is busy, rhythmically and orchestrally complex, heard in its early days without sufficient rehearsal to accustom players and conductors with its composer's general style. Something of the same was originally true of his first (and possibly finest) opera *The Midsummer Marriage*, completed in 1952 and produced at Covent Garden in 1955. Tippett did not, perhaps, assist comprehension by a series of newspaper articles which explained the aims and aesthetics of the opera in terms comprehensible to few beside himself, obviously the product of deep reading in disciplines in which few musicians and not many opera-goers were capable of following his thought. In an odd way, Tippett's music came to clarify his explanatory writing, and to do so principally through the sense of exaltation in which the opera reaches its culmination.

Tippett's concern with traditional values led him to use other men's music as starting points for tense personal explorations; the classical strength of Handel and Corelli and the passionate human values of Beethoven, for example, resulted in compositions which do not sound in any way like the works which prompted them. Tippett's music often seems to set out to test the validity of such statements by setting them free in the twentieth century and confronting them with alien styles and techniques. The 1941 *Fantasy on a Theme by Handel*, for piano, and the 1953 *Variations on a Theme by Corelli*, for string orchestra—not so glowing and luminous a work as the earlier concerto, but worked out with great power and compelling energy—both take a brief text from earlier music and find that it leads into a variety of modern crises, rhythmic and harmonic. The sense that technical crises are expressions of crises in actual life, that life and music are linked manifestations of certain stresses in the nature of things, is made plain by Tippett's choice of subject matter—his hatred of war, which is the subject matter of his second opera, *King Priam*; identity, sexuality and the nature of reality are the subject of the third, *The Knot Garden*; and race, tolerance, brotherhood and nature occupy the fourth, *The Ice Break*. The Beethoven of the Fifth and Ninth Symphonies, the possibilities of freedom, brotherhood and triumph are the concern of his Fourth Symphony. But to simplify Tippett's mind into statements of specific subject matter is to disregard the fact that Tippett's subjects are complexes, and in this respect his works overlap as though each carries one of his major preoccupations further.

The justification of Tippett's many-sided traditionalism seems to be its power to induce ecstasy, or to enable the composer to find his way to ecstatic music; the musical materials seem always to push technique—both the composer's own technique and the technique of whatever performers he involves—to the limits of possibility and effectiveness. The three string quartets all tease or torment their players with problems of rhythm and phrasing. The Fourth Symphony takes it for granted that orchestral players both can and will succeed in expressing themselves in the idioms of the 'blues'. But what results from, and what justifies the operation is the intensity of emotion it generates, the radiance that can at times, as in the oratorio *The Vision of St Augustine*, become almost frightening. The intensity is sometimes hardly bearable.

Tippett's music generates its power and incandescence, often without needing to deploy itself over great lengths of time or demanding large forces, for the power is in the music itself and not in its presentation. It is present in the 1937 Fantasy Sonata for piano as well as in the 1956 Piano Concerto and it makes the part-song 'Dance, Clarion Air' as memorable as anything he has written on a large scale. *Boyhood's End*, for tenor and piano, and the cycle to poems by Sidney Keyes and Alun Lewis, *The Heart's Assurance* (1951) are as powerful, as capable of transforming normal life, as the larger, more crowded works.

Tippett was not, so to speak, a master born; he was over thirty before he began to write the music that has become part of our consciousness, and it seems that his mastery was won by extreme hard work and effort, so that it is sometimes natural to wish that he had spent some of the years he devoted to teaching working in and with professional musical organizations which might have led him to more direct ways of conveying his meaning. But for all that, Tippett's complexities, the intense activity of his music, in which every voice and every instrument is always active, are part of an extreme originality of outlook and a passionate concern for aspects of life that do not reveal themselves to others. Benjamin Britten (1913–1976), on the other hand, seems to have been born with the power to solve every problem that presented itself to him; the problems that he did not solve, the listener feels, were those with which he was not confronted because they were irrelevant to his purposes.

This aspect of easy mastery, of course, is part of a musical mind which engaged itself from Britten's teens onwards in processes of simplification; Britten's music never gives the impression that the composer is struggling to find the right mode of expression because the composer's task as the work formed in his mind was that of discovering the simplest terms in which it could be expressed. Until the 1950s, and perhaps even later in some quarters, conventional criticism said that the apparently facile fertility of Britten's music made it unnecessary for him to strive after profundity—he allowed himself only easy satisfactions. As work succeeded work, it seemed that Britten worked at his music until it achieved the naturalness and appearance of ease that he wished it to have, allowing no external problems to interpose between him and the performers and listeners whom he regarded as his community.

Britten, at the Royal College of Music, studied briefly under John Ireland; his principal teacher was Frank Bridge. Before he became a student at the Royal College, he had already written *A Hymn to the Virgin*, a setting of an anonymous medieval poem for unaccompanied choir—a setting that has become justly popular—and the earliest of his surviving songs, a setting of Hilaire Belloc's poem 'The Birds'. In 1933 came the choral variations *A Boy Was Born* which, like many later works, chooses a number of texts from poems that were mostly little known. *A Boy Was Born* anticipates other devices of which Britten was to make use in later works. Voices—the work is for unaccompanied choir—imitate instruments and there is a startling passage at the end in which the choir, divided into eight parts, all settle in unison on the note D (above Middle C), spacing their entries out widely to repetitions of the word "glory". Boys' voices, as distinct from the sopranos, appear for the first time as a distinct musical colour with an effect of its own. The words often seem not to complement each other but deliberately to clash; Christine Rossetti's poem 'In the bleak mid-winter' is bleak and disconsolate, moving slowly in dissonant suspensions and common time when the boys break in, in six-eight time, with a bright setting of the Corpus Christi carol. The binding force which unites these apparent incongruities is the overall rhythm which both settings are made to propel. A composer, some critics said, could not be as clever as that and exploit his cleverness while saying anything serious at the same time.

In 1934, Britten was employed by the GPO Film Unit, providing music for documentary films made with the minimum of expense. Film music is naturally a matter of taut discipline, demanding specific effects at precise moments, and denying its composer any opportunities for self-indulgence. Arranging and composing film scores for the GPO Film Unit encouraged Britten's resourcefulness, for the music had to make its effect with few instruments. *Coal Face* and *Night Mail* have become classics of this genre. *Coal Face* uses voices and percussion, the voices engaged in unusual effects which never ask them to betray their own nature, to hum and to whistle as well as to sing. *Night Mail*, which has a poem by W. H. Auden as its commentary, is scored for flute (doubling piccolo), clarinet and strings, with which it reflects the incidents of the journey from London to Edinburgh. There is, of course, no concert suite drawn from any of these scores; they set out to be no more than effective musical commentaries on their films. The characteristic Britten cleverness is shown by the way in which he does all that is necessary with the minimum of instruments, and by the colour his scores create with such limited forces, as well as by the lively handling of often minuscule films.

To these years belong a set of children's songs with piano accompaniment in which Britten sidesteps the tradition of the preternaturally sweet and angelic choir-school treble voice and suggests that boys might at times enjoy shouting and making a din. The songs have great rhythmic vitality and take it for granted that boys with unbroken voices, if offered attractive, appealing melodies, will face any number of musical challenges to sing them successfully.

In 1936, the Norwich Festival commissioned a work from him and Britten responded with a 'symphonic' song-cycle, *Our Hunting*

Fathers, the text of its three songs arranged by Auden (who provided a prologue and an epilogue). Its theme is man's treatment of animals, and it was not what its original audience expected; it is hard-edged, satirical and only the central song is allowed to make conventionally beautiful sounds. The orchestra, too, found it disconcerting at the first rehearsals, for the scoring is lean almost to the extent of being skeletal, and it ends with a funeral march on which the xylophone is the most prominent influence. English audiences in 1936 knew little of the music of Mahler; had the Austrian composer's music been accepted, Britten's first hearers would have seen the point more rapidly. A sympathy with Mahler was not something they could recognize or approve of.

Another expansion of Britten's style appeared in *On This Island* (op. 11), a song-cycle to poems by W. H. Auden. Britten approaches the poems as a contemporary of Purcell's might have done, as words needing music to present and point them. Since the word 'rhetoric' has become devalued in modern usage and is now taken to involve implications of insincerity, to say that Britten, in *On This Island*, began to rediscover an effective musical rhetoric may mislead the reader. Britten's aim was to find the music which would deliver words and their meaning within musical forms and expressions completely satisfying as music. The first Auden poem invites the composer to indulge in an elaborate vocal cadenza; there are Freudian allusions in 'Nocturne', the penultimate song, and a facetious jazziness in the satirical final song. Britten never carried a banner saying "Back to Purcell", although he was responsible for some exciting realizations of Purcell songs, and it seems unlikely that he would ever have instructed us to go "back to" anybody. But *Our Hunting Fathers* and *On This Island* show a young composer in the twentieth century naturally approaching words in the way that, close on three hundred years before, Purcell had approached them. Academic teaching at the time was, incidentally, doubtful about the value of songs which set too many notes (or even more than one note) to any word.

The Variations on a Theme by Frank Bridge (op. 10) was written for the Boyd Neel String Orchestra to play at a concert in the Salzburg Festival of 1937. The concert was to include the first performance of a new English work, and given the commission, Britten sketched it in ten days and completed the scoring in another month. Its novelty and freshness—it involves nothing in its performance that does not belong to the legitimate nature of string instruments, but it is full of new sounds—with its beauty and brilliance created a sensation in Salzburg and was the first of Britten's works to become widely popular. It contains a good deal of parody, a scintillating *Aria Italiano*, a kindly but satirical look at the comic potentialities of the Viennese Waltz, and a Mahlerian funeral march which is very moving as well as marvellously scored to create the impression that its chamber orchestra has suddenly received a powerful influx of muffled percussion.

In 1939, shortly after playing the solo part in his Piano Concerto in a Promenade Concert Britten, a convinced pacifist, sailed to America, following in the footsteps of Auden; his partner and lifelong friend the tenor Peter Pears joined him. In the United States, he composed the Violin Concerto, the song-cycle *Les Illuminations* to words by Rimbaud, the *Sinfonia da Requiem* (in memory of his parents), the *Diversions on a Theme* for piano (left-hand) and orchestra, the *Seven Sonnets of Michelangelo* for voice and piano, and the first String Quartet as well as a variety of other, smaller works. With Auden he wrote *Paul Bunyan*, an American opera about the archetypal lumberjack who cleared America of forests and prepared the continent for civilization. Britten suppressed *Paul Bunyan* after its first production until shortly before his death. There is a sense in which *Paul Bunyan* belongs with *Les Illuminations*, the *Seven Sonnets of Michelangelo* and the later settings of poems by Hölderlin (in German) and Pushkin (in Russian). *Les Illuminations*, with its accompaniment for string orchestra which is as inventively handled as that of the *Frank Bridge Variations*, sets out to treat an elaborate French text in entirely idiomatic music, as a French composer would have set them. The *Michelangelo Sonnets* do the same for Italian poems, with a naturally Italianate grace of melody. Britten's natural melodic style is English, but in these works he adopts not merely the style of French and Italian composition but seemed almost to adopt the nationalities. In the same way, the phrasings and intonations of American speech, rather than those of English, appear unfalteringly in *Paul Bunyan*.

The music which Britten brought back from the United States caught something in the mood of wartime England. It has great charm of melody but controls the emotions it presents; it has a clean, firm, fluently moving eloquence of line and it says frankly what it has to say. This was quite simply beautiful and quite new. At the same time, he was almost dazzlingly prolific; the *Hymn to St Cecilia* and *A Ceremony of Carols* came in 1942, the Prelude and Fugue for string orchestra, *Rejoice in the Lamb*, the *Serenade for Tenor, Horn and Strings* and *The Ballad of Little Musgrave and Lady Barnard* in 1943, two smaller choral pieces in 1944, and *Peter Grimes*, *The Holy Sonnets of John Donne*, the Festival *Te Deum* and the Second String Quartet in 1945.

Britten was convinced that the composer's duty to society is to be useful, therefore he was ready to accept commissions and to treat the compositions they entailed extremely seriously, matching his composition to the requirements and possibilities of whomever was to perform his work but taking for granted their wish to be involved in ambitious music-making and composing to stimulate their ambition. *Rejoice in the Lamb* is a festival cantata written to celebrate the fiftieth anniversary of the dedication of St Matthew's Church, Northampton; *The Ballad of Little Musgrave and Lady Barnard* was composed for the 'music festival' of British prisoners of war in a German prison camp and sent to them almost sheet by sheet.

In 1948, with Peter Pears, he inaugurated the Aldeburgh Festival, which involved him as composer and pianist as well as organizer and in growing measure as conductor. Plain as it was that Britten was never really comfortable in front of an audience, he was a fine pianist, a rare but magnificent soloist in Mozart's music, and he rapidly developed into an equally outstanding conductor. The musicians who worked with him at Aldeburgh during the festival stimulated his creativity; over the years he wrote music for Julian Bream, Osian Ellis, Dietrich Fischer-Dieskau and Msitslov Rostropovitch, among others; his mind responded to music he loved so that he became one of the greatest of pianists in Schubert's songs, and in the same way, it responded to the personalities and gifts of those with whom he made music. It was natural that such a versatile musician should become the leader of the musical profession in London. The success of *Peter Grimes* in 1945 consolidated his position. The taut intensity of the music, its leanness and muscularity, its closeness to popular English traditions which it sees through twentieth-century eyes, and its richness of melody as well as its immediate sense of character and stage effectiveness (even down to a not untraditional 'mad scene' untraditionally allotted to a tenor) established the opera in all the world's opera houses. The doctrine of social usefulness sent Britten immediately to chamber opera which can fit into theatres too small for full-size orchestras and large choirs—the choirs of *Peter Grimes* is so to speak, the population of Aldeburgh—and thus became available to audiences where full-scale opera cannot be accommodated. Despite a libretto that even with familiarity seems pretentious, and an unconvincingly Christian slant on the ancient tragedy, Britten's *The Rape of Lucretia* gives an entirely convincing musical form to the action and creates a great deal of music of moving beauty and gentleness. *Albert Herring*, a comic opera which gives a happy ending to de Maupassant's almost brutally grim story of the young man appointed May King because of the quietness, sobriety and chastity of his life—in the opera a single debauch releases him from the inhibitions imposed on him by an over-possessive mother, whilst in de Maupassant's original he falls into debauchery and degradation—has equally magical moments of colour and beauty.

Britten was one of those composers to whom strict discipline is a stimulus. Certain effects do not appeal to him, and we can listen in vain for the usually thrilling sound of voices doubled by a halo of strings negotiating some wide arch of melody. The orchestra of *Peter Grimes* reaches a tremendous climax in the storm between the two scenes of act one, but it remains a lean, muscular orchestra with a minimum of the doublings that gives it weight. Reduced to four strings and eight other players, in *The Rape of Lucretia* and *Albert Herring* it concerns itself with beauties of colour and rare subtleties of effect though both are capable of sweeping along with surprising power. At the same time, he is perhaps too ready to imply importances rather than dwell on them. Albert Herring, the greengrocer's down-trodden son, appears to live until his emancipation in a state of such uncertainty that he is rarely sure whether his music expresses itself in the major or in the minor. The emancipated Albert of the conclusion simply has a single line of text, set to a single musical phrase of a note to a syllable—"And I'm more than grateful to you all for kindly providing the wherewithal." The point could, perhaps, have been expressed in a rounded quatrain and a complete melody without suffering from being laboured. Albert's simplicity is not, perhaps, as sophisticated as Britten makes it.

The popular styles that were always near enough to his music to ensure that we kept in touch with him, and the music capacity for simple joy in an age when joy was not the easiest emotion to capture, continued in his work. *Billy Budd* (1951), the second full-scale opera, has no extended sea pieces like the 'Interludes' of *Peter Grimes*, but the sea and the wind, and the life they impose upon the ship and its *dramatis personae*, are never out of the score, as though they have taken possession of Britten's imagination. The opera has its set-pieces—the lament after the flogging of the boy simply called 'The Novice', the soliloquy of Claggart, the villainous Master-at-Arms, the scene in which the crew sings shanties in a mood of happy relaxation, the uncanny scene on an empty stage in which, to a procession of unrelated common chords, Billy accepts his fate and is reconciled to it, his final, entirely typical ballad and the fierce, savage scene of near-meeting after his hanging. But the greatest triumph of *Billy Budd* is really the exactitude with which the work is integrated; what at a first hearing sounds like recitative designed simply to carry entirely naturalistic dialogue reveals itself more and more to be thematic music referring to phrases and musical statements the great importance of which is made explicit by some powerful statement elsewhere in the opera.

There seems to be not a bar in *The Turn of the Screw* (1954) which does not shine with the beauty, intensity and emotional truth which the exactitudes of Britten's craftsmanship won from the severe economy of statement and effect to which he submitted his art. *A Midsummer-Night's Dream* (1960), apart from the sense of cheek involved in an English composer's daring to trim and set the words of Shakespeare, is in a sense Britten's return to comedy in a tragic world. The *War Requiem* (1961), another occasional work—it was written for the consecration of the new Coventry Cathedral—links the war poems of Wilfred Owen with the Latin Mass for the dead and finally weaves the two together into a reconciling beauty. The Latin words are set to music of rich textures and beauty, the war poems are treated for the most part with almost violent rhetoric. The world heard it as a true statement about war.

It was after the *War Requiem* that Britten's output slowed down and his music became intellectualized. Throughout his work there is a great mastery of technical device. Canons and double canons, for example, abound at the dictates of expression, but a series of works as powerfully thought out as any he had written before, and as fascinating in their cleverness and ingenuity, seemed to be searching in un-Brittenesque directions for something which seems not to have revealed itself clearly.

Abundantly as he had reaped an artistic profit from the severe economies of chamber opera, he reached for a further simplicity in the three operas which he called 'Parables for Church Performance'. They reflected concerns which had been revealed in earlier of the pressure of society on the individual and the corruption of innocence; they risked, and did not always succeed in avoiding, aridity and monotony. The three works, with a small number of instruments and singers and all naturalism of setting and action banished, take their musical materials from the plain-song hymn with which each begins. All three are dazzlingly clever and the second, *The Burning Fiery Furnace*, contains in the procession and march to King Nebuchadnezzar's golden image an evocation of barbarism as stirring and frightening as anything in music. The 'Parables' are written with great concentration but without any external joy. Britten was always inclined to Puritanism; voices, we noted, never sail superbly on luscious washes of string tone and there are few or no points at which the music comes to rest and to take its ease. Like Tippett, Britten finds happiness in activity, and the passages in his music which are most lovingly beautiful are not passages in which emotion is enjoyed for its own sake. The sense of dryness which he admitted into his music in the 'Parables for Church Performance', the apparent attempt to find a static style of performance with gesture and music conventionalized, seems to have encouraged him to move away from the naturalness and direct simplicity of communication which makes so much of his music—the boys' song in the *Spring Symphony*, the sublime victory reached at the end of *The Holy Sonnets of John Donne*, the Latin mnemonics of the lesson scene in *The Turn of the Screw*, the music of redemption which ends *Noyes Fludde*—unique among modern works in their poignancy.

In 1969, the period of apparently self-imposed aridity reached his piece for boys' voices, *The Children's Crusade*. Listening to its first performance it was natural to wonder if the terrible story of

Bertolt Brecht's poem, in which a crowd of children wander across a war-tormented world in search of a land "where there was peace", can only be told by a dry-eyed composer in total command of his work; too intense an emotion can have an inhibiting effect upon the listener. But *The Children's Crusade* follows the emotional road down which Britten had begun to travel perhaps before the 'Parable' operas. It seems to chill the intellectual mastery of *Owen Wingrave*, the television opera first seen in 1970, where intellectual, spiritual and emotional conviction are reached but denied any conclusively melodic statement. In his final work, *Death in Venice*, the aridity ends and the series of 'Parables for Church Performance' seems to fall into place as three extensive studies in which the composer explored ways of liberating the music and its performers from various conventions, of rhythmic organization and from scores which impose an unyielding dictatorship on them. *Death in Venice* could be seen as Britten's return to melodic richness and fluency, and thus to the true nature of his genius.

Everything that Britten wrote is calculated as exactly as his technique allowed. All the music of his last ten years looks towards aleatoric procedures by which the performer is given a certain limited freedom of action; the limits which control this freedom, however, are so designed that they cannot be further relaxed. In the same way, his awareness of twelve-note music had met his ineradicable sense of tonality and made it plain that, effective as serial methods of composition can be, to Britten they were useful only insofar as he could use them within the bounds of tonality. *The Turn of the Screw*, perhaps the greatest of his operas, is a set of variations on a twelve-note theme, in which all the twelve semitones of the chromatic scale are deployed in what could be regarded as a completely orthodox way; what follows is not twelve-note music but eloquent and lucid tonality with a wide range of expression from the childishly light-hearted to the sinister and the tragic. The *Cantata Academica* was composed for Basel University to a Latin text taken from the University Statutes; as befits an 'academic' work, one movement reconciles itself to twelve-note organization, and it may be Britten's sense of humour which made him use this close and often difficult type of organization for the jolly movement he called *Canto Popolare*. Britten, never becoming a Schoenbergian, remained a craftsman who could make use of Schoenberg's methods when they seemed appropriate, and he was never anything other than a 'modern' musician. He did not, as young rebels often do, mature into respectable conservatism.

Britten's undisputed leadership of English music was not that of a composer who found the way ahead for his contemporaries and juniors, pioneering the route along which they chose to follow him; what others learned from him was an attitude to music and to composition; he made respectable the doctrine of usefulness and the composing of the music that people wanted. There are, of course, times enough when we realize that certain phrases, and the method chosen to deal with some problem of composition, seem to have been chosen because something or other in Britten's work seems to lead to them, but it is Britten's sense of social commitment, of his eagnerness to be useful to his age and its people, which have most profoundly affected other composers. Music proceeds from him, so to speak, centrifugally.

Naturally, the new musical climate of England after the Second World War and the modern demand for music which has transformed English operatic and concert life encourages composition. Sometimes it seems that the Isle is not simply full of voices but really overcrowded with music, and the sense that with his work not simply English music but music in general and everywhere has reached the end of an age and is looking for a new direction or waiting rudderless for a compelling tide is not simply the result of Britten's enormously effective moral example and prodigious output as a composer, accompanist, conductor, organizer and public personality. The truth is that there is no generally accepted way forward for us to go .

After the BBC's exploration of the music of Mahler and Bruckner, the investigation, even though it turned out to be somewhat partial, of the music of Schoenberg, Webern, Berg and the 'Second Viennese School' was inevitable. English Schoenbergians, like the indomitable Elisabeth Lutyens (b. 1906) and Humphrey Searle began to seem less eccentric and isolated than they had previously done. Searle, educated at Winchester and Oxford and then trained at the Royal College of Music, the New Vienna Conservatory and by private studies under Webern, signalled his arrival among the general concert-going public with his Piano Concerto in 1944; this work, like the *Night Music* he had composed a year earlier, demonstrates an attitude to tonality so uncertain and ambiguous that it seemed no more than natural that after 1946 he should write in the twelve-note system. Apart from the modern revolutionary masters, however, Searle was actively involved in the Society for the Promotion of New Music and the whole, complex, modern musical scene. He was, too, from the start an enthusiast for the music of Liszt and for the ballet. Twelve-note composers tended, when Searle arrived, to write music of great, puritanical intensity; Webern reduced music to no more than its skeletal necessities, abjuring orchestral colour for its own sake and sacrificing everything to the sense that nothing but the essential and inevitable should reach paper. Searle, however, even as a twelve-note composer, is a romantic, a lover of rich colour and powerfully emotive sound conveying impassioned emotions.

Searle's reputation was established immediately after the Second World War. Large-scale choral and orchestral works—*Gold Coast Customs* (words by Edith Sitwell), and *The Riverrun* (words from *Finnegan's Wake*, by James Joyce)—delivered by a speaker and richly accompanied by an urgently emotional orchestra, as well as a powerful, colourful setting of verses from Matthew Arnold's *Sohrab and Rustum* showed how immediately colourful and directly communicative twelve-note music can be. His symphonies are equally direct and eloquent although they give the listener no verbal props to aid him on his way.

Twelve-note music equally forceful and direct comes from the symphonies of Benjamin Frankel (1906–1974). Until the end of the Second World War, much of Frankel's life was spent writing and arranging music for London shows and writing for films with unusual craftmanship, wit and adaptability, and always with real musical inventiveness. It may be that the amount of time he spent on such work explains the intense, tragic seriousness of the chamber and orchestral music which he wrote from the middle 1940s onward. The first of his larger concert works to win an enthusiastic audience was his Violin Concerto (1951). It was followed, among other works, by seven symphonies, all closely and intensively worked out and all introverted, tending towards a tragic view of life; the clarity and thoroughness of their presentation is always impressive, and the string quartets which occupied him during the same years have similar emotional qualities but a sense of music remaining closer to tonality and traditional values, finding no need to present his ideas rhetorically.

The Spanish Roberto Gerhard (1896–1970) settled in England after the Spanish Civil War. His early training under Granados and Felipe Pedrell was followed by five years of study with Schoenberg in Vienna and Berlin. Before he left Spain he spent a great deal of time editing the works of eighteenth-century Spanish composers, and his compositions after he arrived in England remain Spanish in various imponderables of atmosphere rather than in melodic or rhythmic idioms, though their technique is never strictly Schoenbergian or dogmatically twelve-note. The music is beautifully refined and precise. His Violin Concerto (1942, Piano Concerto (1951) and symphony combine unorthodox ways of thought with remarkable subtleties of harmony and orchestral colour. Naturally his opera, a treatment of Sheridan's play *The Duenna*, comes closer to conventional idioms and the normally conventional thoughts of audiences.

Richard Arnell (b. 1917) studied at the Royal College of Music—he was one of John Ireland's many pupils—and his music began to attract attention during the Second World War, while he was living in the United States of America. His ballet *Punch and The Child* had a remarkable success, and the music of his five symphonies is thoughtful and colourful, accessibly written within the symphonic tradition.

Peter Racine Fricker (b. 1920), another one-time pupil of John Ireland at the Royal College of Music, leapt into prominence with a closely argued, uncompromisingly dissonant First Symphony in 1949, and followed it a year later with a second of equally unrelaxed severity and equally compelling argument. His earlier work had been chamber music, written with consideration for the nature of the instruments it demands rather than for the players, but never uninteresting, and his later symphonies have been heard with respect if with less excitement than greeted the first two. Fricker's music is always tense and intellectually convincing within a comparatively limited though tragic emotional range; it is always obedient to the logic implicit in the materials it uses, concerned with serious matters which are precisely equated with the forms he adopts. *The Vision of Judgement*, a large work for choir and orchestra is, in his own view, "the most English work I have ever written", for in his view the change that came over English music after the Second World War is that "we've become aware that Europe exists".[46] The English tradition, perhaps, assists *The Vision of Judgement* to gather the power to deal effectively with a large choir, although the choir is occupied by music in a far from traditional style, for his natural tendency seems to be towards instrumental music, but not towards the concerto or the display of solo instruments. From the Hungarian Matyas Seiber (1905–1960), the teacher who had most influence on his style, he found his way to a sort of English approximation to the style of Bartók, and thence to some sympathy with Stravinsky and Schoenberg, though his attitudes are eclectic, as though varieties of technique exist to be used whenever they are appropriate.

The arrival of Malcolm Arnold (b. 1921) suggested that there are other ways forward in directions other than that of later European modernism, through which the symphony can expand. Arnold was a scholarship winner at the Royal College of Music, where he won the Cobbett prize for composition. In 1941 he joined the London Philharmonic Orchestra as a trumpeter, and later played with the BBC Symphony Orchestra. His music grows partly from an expert, affectionate and completely intimate knowledge of the orchestra and its instruments; he writes little for voices, and the piano plays little part in his output though he has written sonatas for flute and piano and violin and piano.

Arnold is by wish and by will a communicator who accepts it as his duty to appeal to as wide an audience as possible and rarely writes twelve-note music because he has no wish "to lock himself up in a narrow personal idiom". His experience of the orchestra and a wide, catholic taste which embraces jazz and popular music are elements in compositions which, so to speak, are happy to celebrate the natural life of men and women, their social pleasures and anxieties; he has said that to write music like the tortured intensities of Bartók's string quartets would be a sign of mental disturbance. His music is often witty, sometimes frankly comical; he has a vivid gift for melody and a sense of rhythm that can be racily boisterous and is always powerfully alive. It was Arnold who provided a revised version of Henry Wood's *Fantasia on British Sea Songs* for the end of a Promenade season, slipping an extra beat into the bars of the hornpipe as though it were danced by a three-legged sailor and doing so to the confusion of the audience which likes to clap out the rhythm of the dance during its performance.

Arnold's Overture, *Beckus the Dandipratt*, in 1943, won him an immediate audience; its clarity, boisterous high-spirits and expert knowledge of how to achieve every effect he had imagined struck a new note in English music. His first two symphonies show the artistic ends to which his view of life could be put with a greater range of reference; the Second Symphony has a finale which is a beautifully worked-out rhythmic joke, but Arnold is not simply a musical jester; he has, as well as great orchestral skill and a mastery of vivid rhythms, a capacity for serious thought, for contentment, moments of touching nostalgia and, at times, the experience of sadness. What he does not give to his listeners is the indulgence in tortured intensities of feeling that have become almost inseparable from advanced modern music, though his harmonic style is as radical as a harmonic style can be within the boundaries of tonality. What he often offers as bountifully as Britten is the possibility of a creative reconciliation between what nowadays is often called 'serious' music and current popular styles—indeed his determination to remain in touch with the mass of listeners is, to him, a fruitful discipline. His Sixth Symphony (1967) has a first movement that was written in homage to Charlie Parker, the American saxophonist of the 1940s who was part of the revolution in jazz style known as 'Bebop', and the second movement is, according to the composer, "a lament for a pop style which will be dead before this symphony is performed". What it laments is the syncopated, sentimental popular song of the years between the two world wars, and it does so with a rueful nostalgia which the finale tries to banish with a display of high-spirits which become rather strained as the nostalgia refuses to be sent away.

It was inevitable in the 1950s that 'serious' composers should pay attention to the revolution in popular music. In the 1920s it was specialists, so to speak, like Stravinsky, or like Walton in *Façade* or Lambert in the nostalgic pyrotechnics of *The Rio Grande* who could find a legitimate use for current popular idioms. Tippett and Britten could not, however hard they tried, avoid them any more than composers born in the 1960s will find it possible to avoid the bland boredom of 'muzak'. There are jazz-influenced passages in

A Child of Our Time just as there are in the later Tippett symphonies; Britten's *Sinfonia da Requiem* and the climax of the 'Storm' Interlude in *Peter Grimes* quite obviously come from a composer not only aware of but also naturally able to use jazz idioms. But by the late 1960s, the dance-music styles of the years before the Second World War had become no more than a source of nostalgia for Peter Maxwell Davies (b. 1934), whose *St Thomas Wake* treats it as his music often treats medieval and early Renaissance music, as a stimulus for new composition, with far less reverence than Stravinsky, for example, had treated music by Pergolesi in *Pulcinella* (composed in 1920). By the end of the 1950s, the style of the sentimental syncopated song had been so enfeebled by clichés and convention that a younger generation simply put it to death to release it from its pitiful state.

The masters of the older style, the American composers George Gershwin, Jerome Kern, Cole Porter and Irving Berlin, among others, were dead or had nothing new to say. Composers like Duke Ellington and astonishing jazz virtuosi like the trumpeter Louis Armstrong were exploiting a style that had grown over-familiar. New ensembles, like the Modern Jazz Quartet (themselves heirs and successors of earlier experimentalists) were engaged in intellectualizing what had always been almost purely instinctive music and travelling down a road on which they could hardly avoid a head-on collision with Jacques Loussier, who plays Bach with drums and a plucked double-bass with a pleasant tightening of rhythms. The American musical, with new ambitions and no noticeable loss of energy, had become in and since *Oklahoma!* closer to modern folk opera than to the lavish musical comedy of the 1920s. Its real father may be Kurt Weill (1900–1950), driven from Germany by the Nazis for his Jewish descent and left-wing sympathies; Weill's 'students' opera' *Down in the Valley* even more than his early works to texts by Bertolt Brecht may have been the seminal work from which a new American musical form sprang.

The revolution in entertainment music pure and simple came in the United States with 'Rock'n'Roll, mechanically rhythmic, noisy, and an almost complete rejection of the luke-warm jazz-orientated style of the immediate past. It was not enough to make music noisily, with the basic rhythms pounded out inescapably by drums and electric guitars; musical performance became an act to entertain the not very musical; it was not enough to play an instrument, because it seemed more amusing, if not more musical, to clown as one played and to combine instrumental playing with the business of minor acrobatics. It is not that Rock'n'Roll could not be good in a musical sense; it is that its premises regarded musical quality as a relatively minor matter. A more hopeful future opened with Skiffle, the music which people made for themselves with whatever portable instruments that were available, including tea-chest basses and corrugated wash boards. A large number of skiffle musicians, in search of the music that was both within their technical range and entirely relevant to their lives, turned to folk music, in particular to the folk music of the industrial town of the early nineteenth century; in the hands of such people, particularly in America, Skiffle became a new folk-song revival inspired by the music of social protest.

The home-spun simplicities of Skiffle were quickly wiped out in the 1960s by the rise of 'pop'. Skiffle groups were usually contented with acoustic guitars and whatever other instruments were available, but 'pop' demanded electric guitars, drums heard through amplifiers, and the electronic amplification of whatever harmonies other instruments used. Its dynamic levels never altered from the almost unendurably loud with the rhythms, always simple, pounded out remorselessly. Its subject matter was at first nothing more than the inevitable, universal experience of the young, but the emergence of the Beatles in the early 1960s brought a group with a wider awareness of life and a wider musicality into the field, singing pleasant songs of matters of more than juvenile concern and finding good tunes for them, with the result that their achievements and abilities were often exaggerated even by literate musicians who should have known better. The acclaim that greeted them has meaning only in terms of the generality of pop music and its sadly restricted language. The Liverpool musicians who, for fun, organized a number of Beatles' tunes for string orchestra and called it *Eine kleine Beatlesmusik* made a pleasant little work but incidentally destroyed the Beatles' claim (made for them rather than by them) to be musical revolutionaries of great importance.

'Pop' became a youth movement because the young were sensibly tired of an outworn musical style, but it fell quite innocently into hands eager to exploit it. The young, newly affluent, bought vast quantities of gramophone records, both '7-inch singles' and '12-inch albums'. The adolescent world, in an age of full employment, spends about £500,000,000 a year on its pleasures. In this situation, whatever is latest is best because many people have not got it and can be induced to buy it, so that new movements have succeeded the Beatles but have had little or nothing to say that is new and musical. The Beatles themselves quite rapidly moved beyond the early stage of songs sung to three guitars and drums which had won them their altogether amazing popularity; their later records, which brought some of their best as well as their most ambitious songs, call on the services of 'session musicians', freelance players often quite distinguished in other walks of musical life and whose appearance on the platform to be occupied by four young men who had become idols would have been greeted with a singular lack of enthusiasm. Pop music was not in itself a restrictive influence upon the musical development, the developing sympathies and the sensitivity to life of the young who made the four defiantly regional, proudly unassuming young men who for some years were its most outstanding exponents and creators into heroes and idols. But it would be instructive and perhaps painful to discover how much harm the commercial exploitation of pop has done both to its audiences and to the performers. The doctrine that the latest is best naturally leads to more or less new pop fashions, 'classical rock', 'progressive pop' and other departures from the norm remain so close to standard that it grows extremely difficult to discover in what way the new can be distinguished from the old. Even 'punk rock', at the time of writing the latest and most sensational brand of deviation, popularized and publicized as an anti-social music designed for the rebellious young, restricts its deviation to the wearing of unorthodox, expensively shabby clothes ostentatiously patched and the use of lyrics which show only a rude distaste for all established authority in music of naïvely noisy simplicity which, submitted to any analysis, would probably repel its adherents won by publicity rather than by the musical achievements of its creators.

Music Ho!, which Constant Lambert wrote in the mid-1930s, lamented the absence of the musicians and music lovers whom he called "the disappearing middle brow". "So far as I can see," he wrote, "music written by composers whose individualism links them with the great composers of the past and whose work, being a result of concentration, requires at least a modicum of concentration from the listener, will become a specialized art like poetry, appreciated with the same intensity by an equally small public. Apart from that, music will be a definitely popular form of art, revolving round the concert hall but adapting itself to wireless and the films."[47] Time has made fun of many of Lambert's prophecies: Schoenberg and his fellow revolutionaries are familiar names and it has become clear that whatever future awaits their music, what they did has proved an enrichment to the traditional mainstream of music. Later rebels —Boulez, Nono, Berio, Stockhausen among them—are leading a new revolt in a variety of directions, while a new generation which grew up during the Second World War is moving with equal determination, but every one in his own direction. No composer today would write for the music lover whom Lambert, in the language of the 1930s, called the "middle brow"; it would not be worth the labour to a new Elgar to perpetrate a *Salut d'Amour* or to a new Sibelius to write a *Valse Triste*, for nobody listens to salon music or plays it, and the number of composers who discipline themselves to write within the traditions once generally accepted is growing smaller year by year.

The gulf between 'serious' music and the 'pop' world is not, of course, unbridgeable, and a considerable number of young listeners step from one world to the other with no apparent difficulty; how long they will be able to do so, or will wish to do so, may be very doubtful. But pop creates a new problem. The most successful pop artists are to be heard on gramophone records, not in the concert hall or the theatre; the Beatles did not appear in public with the considerable band of 'session' musicians who play in their later records. Pop publicity made the personality of performers on the platform far more important than anything they did, so that their work in public was usually inaudible, drowned by the screams of ecstatic delight which was the feminine reaction to the presence of the divinity, who was simply not listened to. Whatever the sort of music we consider, it is almost impossible to make sense of its position in the world.

Malcolm Williamson (b. 1931), Australian by birth but now Master of the Queen's Musick, is prodigiously prolific, influenced by jazz and pop rhythms and able to use them with conviction, aware of twelve-note music and the techniques it involves, including the techniques of total serialism which developed from twelve-note music for a comparatively short time before it proved to be too limited for general use. Williamson, like Malcolm Arnold, is a determined communicator, whose technique, like Arnold's, is designed to make his music and its purposes clear to the widest available audience, to whom he is ready to offer luscious tunes and succulent harmonies. His operas, both for adult audiences and those for children, have a real theatrical grip and an often unconventional choice of subject matter; Graham Greene's novel *Our Man in Havana* is not the sort of novel which its readers expect to find dramatized in the opera house though, like *The Violins of St Jacques*, it demonstrates Williamson's enjoyment of the musically exotic. *Julius Caesar Jones*, a children's opera about the fantasy life of a group of children, its total incomprehensibility to their parents and its potentialities for tragedy and terror, spends much of its time in the 'Fortunate Isle' of the children's hectic imagination; naturally this gives rise to music that might not unworthily accompany a film or television 'travelogue' or welcome radio listeners to the 'Desert Island' to which celebrities are asked week by week to take their eight favourite records. The only doubt about *Julius Caesar Jones* is the extent to which the children who take part in it or who see it can grasp the disturbing moral which it promulgates. Williamson's music—concertos, a Sinfonietta and a large scale *Mass of Christ the King*—can always be listened to with pleasure and interest, though it may be that the listener's pleasure is sometimes too easily won.

John Tavener (b. 1944) has written music that makes an equally effective approach to popular musical styles and thought, but not in the 1930-ish, cinematic style which Williamson adopts at times. His cantata *The Whale* deals with the Old Testament story of Jonah, whose three-day sojourn in the whale's belly is orchestral pop music grown quite menacing. His music has involved the singing of children's rhymes and game-songs, and Tavener plainly loves Victorian hymn tunes. He has, in other words, his direct lines of communication with his audience, and his general style is colourful and emotional.

Richard Rodney Bennett (b. 1931), a pupil of Pierre Boulez, is a very effective jazz pianist and accompanist whose interest in this musical field hardly affects his compositions. He is a master of precise craftsmanship who has written children's music in an idiom never noticeably conservative but close enough to tradition never to bore its players or baffle their expectations; it attracts and is accessible to the players and listeners for whom it was designed, but it takes them to strange places and involves them with new ideas. *All the King's Men* (1969), the better known of his children's operas, deals cleanly, tunefully and without any sense of patronizing its performers with an incident in the English Civil War, and it is perhaps only incidental to the work that it contains a calypso which, in different circumstances, might be described as 'show-stopping'; and it condemns war. The first of Bennett's adult operas, *The Mines of Sulphur*, is a work of unsparing grimness which creates an inescapable atmosphere of terror. It succeeded with its audiences more powerfully than the more cheerful *A Penny for a Song* (1968) or his treatment of Conrad's novel *Victory* (1970). His orchestral works—concertos for guitar and piano, *Actaeon*, a work of spectacular difficulty for horn and orchestra, a symphony and a number of songs and smaller works—are all exactly thought out and precisely written. Bennett is, too, one of the most efficient and successful of composers for the cinema, and to film music he gives the scrupulous craftsmanship that marks all his work, so that the films he handles gain considerably from his remarkable power to evoke place and atmosphere.

Manchester Royal College of Music, in the 1950s, gave a training to Alexander Goehr (b. 1932), Peter Maxwell Davies and Harrison Birtwistle (b. 1934), who have shown a sufficient unity of aim to make it possible at times to think of them as a Manchester School analogous to Schoenberg and his first disciples of the 'New Vienna' School. Goehr is nearer than the others to what might well be called the classic Schoenbergian position, with something of Schoenberg's technical determination and an ability to express himself lyrically in his natural idiom. His opera *Arden Must Die*, based on the Elizabethan play *Arden of Feversham*, was staged at Hamburg with considerable success, and a choral work, *Sutter's Gold*, first heard at the Leeds Festival, followed the tradition inaugurated by *Belshazzar's Feast* of bringing a tough score to realization at the Festival. But Goehr, the son of a much admired German conductor, who came to England to escape the Nazis, is by nature a cosmopolitan for all the skill and sympathy with which he handles English texts.

Birtwistle is not in any sense bound by the laws of twelve-note grammar; his compositions are not technically thematic or serial but depend upon free juxtapositions of colour, contrast and on the transformation and variation of often anonymous, fugitive motives and figurations. The sense of discontinuity which rises from much of his work does not preclude recognition of his great imaginative power, and when it is overcome by some driving force that our present techniques hardly enable us to analyse, his music has considerable power. Works like *The Triumph of Times* and the *Grimethorpe Aria,* written for the brass band of Grimethorpe Colliery in Yorkshire, have a sufficient technical force to carry an audience along with their idiosyncratic ways. Like many composers of the generation which came to maturity late enough to be influenced by the techniques developed on the continent after the Second World War, Birtwistle uses voices in music that adopts the style of wide intervals athletically leaping and has little regard for anything that tradition has always held to be naturally vocal. Birtwistle and Peter Maxwell Davies together organized a group, or small, elastically composed orchestra, which they called Pierrot Players, in 1967; the group later changed its name, apparently preferring to be known as The Fires of London, and satisfying the need for an ensemble of musicians who can handle difficult avant-garde music without hesitancy or any lack of conviction. One of the first successes of the Pierrot Players was Goehr's stage piece *Naboth's Vineyard*.

Maxwell Davies is the most prolific, and perhaps the most imaginative, of the Manchester School. He was known to the naturally limited audience for advanced modern music as the composer of some difficult piano and instrumental works before his reputation spread among the generality of music lovers. As music master at Cirencester Grammar School he wrote a lengthy piece in several movements which he called *O Magnum Mysterium* and published in 1966; it consists of instrumental music in the attenuated textures of advanced music depending on the style of thematic transformation and variation and having some affinity with medieval compositional techniques; these instrumental movements are interspersed with choral movements, 'carols' with words largely as archaic as the medieval techniques, and music as spare, muscular and dissonant as his adult style demands. That Davies should write a magically effective work in this style for schoolboy and schoolgirl musicians, and train them to perform it effectively, not only bears witness to his creativity and imaginative power but also shows that he must have unusual qualities as a teacher.

The occasion and performers of *O Magnum Mysterium* were, perhaps, a valuable discipline from which Davies has since withdrawn himself; at least, it was not written without a necessary sense that performers and their satisfaction matter. His opera *Taverner*, based on the life of the Tudor composer and produced at Covent Garden, naturally approached its audience through words and stage production, though the events on the stage moved from naturalism to fantasy and symbolism. As though he felt the need for such crutches to the listener's imagination, *Eight Songs for a Mad King*, for voice and small, eccentrically organized orchestra, is written for a singing actor who wears costume; its adherence to the avant-garde conventions of vocal writing, however, means that the listener would do better to look for personality, style and expression in the often freakish orchestral parts than in the vocal line. A work for large symphony orchestra, *Worldes Bliss*[48], produced as much puzzlement as enthusiasm at a Promenade Concert, and sufficient performances to provoke mature judgement are overdue. In 1978 a symphony, though it exploits advanced textural schemes and thematic techniques, seemed to come nearer to normal symphonic style and orchestral practice than anything we had heard from him before. Davies's later work is influenced by the scenery and atmospere of the Orkney Islands, and has resulted in a treatment of the medieval *Hymn to St Magnus*, an operatic treatment of the story of the martyred King, *The Martyrdom of St Magnus*, and a children's opera, *Two Fiddlers*.

At this point, the historian stops. He could decide to change his aim and function and act as a compiler of lists or as an annalist. There are a number of composers and works which he has not treated because they seem to lead his work no further and give him no assistance in creating his account of the development of music towards its present situation. He has said nothing, for example, about the work of Lennox Berkeley (b. 1903), whose musical studies followed normal university education and were undertaken with Nadia Boulanger, a teacher whose enormous influence and prestige among musicians have otherwise not impinged on this history. Berkeley's operas, *Nelson*, *A Dinner Engagement* and *Ruth*, have an apparent modesty of aim—Berkeley never says more than is necessary—which aids conviction. Apparent modesty is a quality of all Berkeley's music, and it means that his music, carefully worked, cleanly constructed and economical, is music that listeners can live with because of its naturalness and interest. He strikes no poses. His oratorio *Jonah*, his *Stabat Mater* and his *Four poems by St Theresa of Avila* are marked by deep religious devotion that is intense without hysteria. Berkeley, in the 1930s, collaborated with Britten in *Mont Juic*, a suite of Catalan dances, and his symphonies and chamber music have the typically Berkeleyan sense of proportion and neatness of craftsmanship in an age when such qualities are, alas, not the most highly valued.

The case of Havergal Brian (1876–1973) is far more surprising. Born in Staffordshire and largely self-taught, between 1905 and 1921 Brian won a good deal of attention, and some performances, with the encouragement of conductors such as Wood, Hamilton Harty and Beecham. Among his early works is his Second Symphony, the *Gothic*; the three conductors each projected a performance of the work, to be baffled by the impossibility of financing a performance of a symphony more extensive and more demanding than Mahler's Eighth. Brian's music was then forgotten until the 1960s, when Robert Simpson (b. 1921), himself a composer of well-made, thoughtful and convincing symphonies, used his position in the Music Department of the BBC to bring Brian's work back into notice. Among the works which Brian had written in complete obscurity and without, apparently, any idea of performance were thirty-six symphonies as well as operas and a violin concerto. With the passing of time, Brian's music had grown terser, more economical and more elliptical, changing gear, so to speak, often with a disconcerting jerk at points where another composer would have provided a smooth transition guiding the listener forward. In an isle overfull of voices, not every item on the aural landscape can be charted and described on a map which can hope to do no more than try to show generalities of structure and lay-out.

Such a map is, perhaps, less happy in its results than a mere chronicle of the achievements of British composers and their standards normally maintained in a very wide repertory by English players and singers. From the Renaissance to yesterday, it is possible for music to be an open book with comparatively few uncut pages. There is still too much music by Purcell left to gather dust on the library shelves, and his contemporaries, like Handel, are totally neglected. We have had our attention drawn to medieval music. Much of what we know from radio performances and gramophone records is music that we cannot hope to hear at concerts and recitals or in the opera house. The gramophone record, however, is a mixed blessing to the listener, and it shares some of its dangerous elements with the radio. A recording of any work, however good it is, is only one of an infinite number of possible legitimate performances, but it is too often accepted as a definitive statement; consequently, the record tends to set up rules and dogmas where none should be. Perhaps more dangerously, it tends to make music too accessible: should we be able to hear the great overwhelming masterpieces whenever we want to? To be able to hear a work whenever we want to do so is not essentially to know it intimately but to find oneself beginning to treat it as no more than a familiar piece of furniture. The gramophone record rapidly mops up our remaining corners of ignorance. All the operas of Mozart and Handel, all the concertos of Vivaldi, all the cantatas of Bach, possibly all the odes of Purcell, seem inevitably to be on their way to us, so that it will be impossible to find room for everything that we should like to have.

To complain about abundance seems both ungrateful and ungracious. But the truth of the matter is twofold; music is becoming a secret indulgence as reprehensible as secret drinking; music is or should be, a social pleasure, and part of the secret of the success of the London Promenade Concerts is that they recreate the almost forgotten sense of community. The other aspect of the truth is that our age is without any musical style of our own. What musical age do we live in? Is it the age of Pierre Boulez or the age of Karlheinz Stockhausen? It might be the age of Maxwell Davies or of Harrison Birtwistle. Or is it the age of Britten, Tippett, Shostakovitch? Or the age of the rediscovery of medieval music? And the world of pop music is no less rent asunder by schism and distressed by heresy. Perhaps we are entering the age when the musicologist becomes more important than the musician, and the musicologist will continue to demand that everything be played on the instruments its composer knew even when modern instruments are patently more effective. This is a new concern arising because, for the first time in history, we do not know what we want from the music of the past or in what way we should listen to it. Our grandfathers, and even our fathers, knew what they wanted from the music of the past and, getting it, found that the music of the past endorsed their present and its essential attitudes. We know more but enjoy less and find that there is more to worry about than to enjoy.

This is the age of everything, and therefore an age of hopeless self-contradiction. It is an age with no musical identity of its own. It is without a genuine artistic aim because it has no generally accepted social identity and no sure artistic home. There cannot, therefore, be a sort of music which adequately expresses the character and aspirations of the English people in the way that the trio of the first of Elgar's *Pomp and Circumstance* marches did even before it was fitted with words for which Elgar seems to have cared little. The melody expressed a mood which made the English people feel that A. C. Benson's words "Land of Hope and Glory" belonged naturally to that princely tune. Nobody, from Benjamin Britten to the Beatles, has so caught the mind of the general public despite the vast popularity of many of the Beatles' songs and the equal popularity of the 'Audience Songs' in Britten's *The Little Sweep*. For one thing, the Beatles' admirers seem rarely to have sung the songs they admired, for singing is, in the world of pop music, an activity usually left to professional entertainers.

The composers who represent traditional musical values could once expect to succeed with the generality of critical opinion, and the readers of music criticism could take it for granted that the music critics are the determined, learned champions of tradition. Now it is critical opinion, and not the general public, which tends to dismiss composers as powerful and wide-ranging as Walton, as inventive as Arnold and as active as Williamson because they do not wholeheartedly cast their vote with a radical avant-garde but are listened to by the majority of audiences who can follow their trains of thought. The musical world, in step with other worlds co-existent in our age, rejects the necessity of a train of thought but pins its faith to a possibly spurious doctrine of originality. Originality for its own sake was never the first priority of the masters in the past; it was something for which composers were inclined to apologise and to explain that despite their efforts to find a traditional way of doing something, they had found themselves unwillingly forced into becoming original; the traditional language had failed them. Musical logic, with other logics, has been discarded. Schoenberg and his disciples evolved a musical grammar which appeals to the analytical eye before it manifests itself to the receptive ear, but later styles have abandoned Schoenbergian twelve-note grammar as completely as they have abandoned the style of the Renaissance or the *Ars Nova*, so that to the listener, even to the practised listener, composers seem to have abandoned all the continuities of logic and grammar and left us with no criteria beyond our personal pleasure in this or that combination or succession of sounds. Dissonances of any intensity are free to the composer, just as thematic composition is frowned upon, and dissonance, emancipated by Schoenberg, has not given us a wider and more liberal musical vocabulary; the stringing together of a succession of dissonant chords with no guidance beyond the composer's own quite subjective taste has denied our vocabulary the use of combinations which offer relaxation, peace, mere enjoyment or fun, all of which are elements of life which music has splendidly expressed in the past. Music, like many other aspects of human life, seems to have lost faith in the validity of reason, as though reason is no longer able to express what we wish to communicate.

Possibly this means no more than that we are in an age of transition, and that the anxieties voiced here are no more than those voiced over the centuries by critics of Monteverdi, Wagner, Richard Strauss and others; the same sort of anxiety greeted every step of Stravinsky's career even when he was determinedly moving backwards. At the present moment, English music is no longer engaged in its traditional role of panting along behind the European leaders; it is still trying to transform what is idiomatically English into the style of today. For the first time since the early Renaissance, English composers are walking along in step with the continental leaders through our age of transition. To what the transition leads it is, of course, impossible to say. It may find its way to a new age of consolidation; it may be that the Great Schism will become a further split, with the new and experimental minds occupying an advanced position in which they no longer speak to the world but only to those who share their experimental interests. Another possibility, of course, arises, for it may be that what is chronicled here is the end of Western Music in any sense in which we have always known it. In that case, all we can say, with gratitude, is that it will still last for our time.

Notes and Sources

1 Joseph Addison: *The Spectator*, 30 April, 1711.
2 John Milton: *Paradise Lost*, Book I.
3 Reproduced in Hans Tischler: *A Medieval Motet Book*, No. 18. New York—London, 1973.
4 Constance Bullock-Davies: *Minstrellorum Multitudo, Minstrels at a Royal Feast.* Cardiff, 1978.
5 Translated by Gustave Reese: *Music in the Middle Ages,* London, 1964.
6 Erasmus: *Commentary of 1 Corinthians XIV.*
7 Richard Hooker: *The Laws of Ecclesiastical Polity.* 1593 edition.
8 Thomas Whythorne: *Autobiography*, edited by James M. Osborne. Oxford, 1951. pp. 241–243.
9 Thomas Morley: *A Plaine and Easie Introduction to Practicall Musicke.* London, 1597. 1952 edition edited by Alec Harman, London.
10 ibid.
11 ibid.
12 A. L. Lloyd: *Folk-Song in England.* London.
13 Foakes and Rickert (editors): *Philip Henslowe's Diary.* Cambridge, 1961.
14 William Kemp: *The Nine Dayes Wonder, Kemps Morris to Norwiche.* London (Bodley Head edition), 1923.
15 William Prynne: *Histrio-Mastix.* London, 1633 edition.
16 J. Dover Wilson: *Life in Shakespeare's England.* London, 1944. p.189.
17 Samuel Pepys: *Diary*, 17 December, 1660.
18 ibid. November, 1667.
19 John Evelyn: *Diary*, 25 October, 1660.
20 Samuel Pepys: *Diary*, 14 October, 1660.
21 Joseph Addison: *The Spectator*, 7 April, 1711.
22 Aaron Hill: *Works.* Quoted in *Handel: A Documentary Biography* by O. E. Deutsch. London, 1955. p. 299.
23 Lord Chesterfield: *Letters to His Son.* London.
24 Sir John Hawkins: *A General History of the Science and Practice of Music*, Volume II. 1875 edition. p. 257.
25 Charles Dibdin: *The Professional Life of Mr Charles Dibdin*, Volume I. London, 1803.
26 Sir John Hawkins: *A General History of the Science and Practice of Music*, Volume II. 1875 edition. p. 886.
27 Hector Berlioz: *Evenings in the Orchestra*, translated by C. R. Fortescue. London, 1963. p. 222.

28 John Ella: *Musical Sketches.* London, 1878. p. 107.
29 G. Bernard Shaw: *London Music in 1888–1889*, as heard by Corno di Bassetto. London, 1937. p. 51.
30 J. F. Sterndale Bennett: *The Life of William Sterndale Bennett.* Cambridge, 1907. p. 101.
31 Hector Berlioz: *Memoirs*, translated by David Cairns. London, 1968. p. 448 *et seq.*
32 A. E. Dobbs: *Education and Social Movements, 1700–1900.* London, 1919.
33 William Gardiner: *Music and Friends*, Volume II (3 volumes). London. 1832. p. 511 *et seq.*
34 Richard Wagner: *My Life*, authorized English translation. London, 1963. p. 634.
35 John Ella: op. cit. p. 141.
36 Charles Dickens: *Sketches by Boz*, Chapter 2. 1838.
37 Charles Dickens: *Bleak House*, Chapter 11. 1853.
38 J. B. Priestley: *Bright Day*, Chapter 3. London, 1946.
39 Arnold Bennett: *Clayhanger*, Chapter 10. London, 1928.
40 Ivor Newton: *At the Piano—Ivor Newton.* London, 1966. p. 83.
41 G. Bernard Shaw: *Music In London, 1890–1894.* Volume II (3 volumes). London, 1932. p. 297 *et seq.*
42 R. Vaughan Williams: *A Musical Autobiography*, in *National Music and Other Essays.* Oxford, 1934.
43 ibid.
44 Constant Lambert: *Music Ho! A Study of Music in Decline.* London, 1934 (paperback, 1948). p. 198.
45 Henry J. Wood: *My Life of Music.* London, 1938. p. 96.
46 Interview in *The Times* (London), 7 September, 1958.
47 Constant Lambert: op. cit. pp. 198–199.
48 *See* Example 3, p. 31.

BIBLIOGRAPHY

A. L. Bacharach (editor): *British Music of Our Time*. Penguin Books, Harmondsworth, 1946.
J. R. Sterndale Bennett: *The Life of William Sterndale Bennett*. Cambridge University Press, 1907.
William Boosey: *Fifty Years of Music Publishing*. Ernest Benn, London, 1931.
Noel Boston: *The Musical History of Norwich Cathedral*. Friends of Norwich Cathedral, Norwich, 1963.
Neville Cardus: *Sir Thomas Beecham*. Collins, London, 1961.
Christopher Dearnley: *English Church Music, 1650–1750*. Herbert Jenkins, London, 1969.
E. J. Dent: *The Foundations of English Opera*. Cambridge University Press, 1928.
O. E. Deutsch: *Handel: A Documentary Biography*. A. & C. Black, London, 1955.
Robert Elkin: *Old Concert Rooms of London*. Edward Arnold, London, 1956.
John Ella: *Musical Sketches*. London, 1878.
Roger Fiske: *English Theatre Music in the Eighteenth Century*. Oxford University Press, 1976.
Carl Fuchs: *Recollections of Carl Fuchs, Cellist*. St Anne's Press, Manchester, 1937.
A. W. Ganz: *Berlioz in London*. Quality Press, London, 1956
Wilhelm Ganz: *Memories of a Musician*. John Murray, London, 1913.
William Gardiner: *Music and Friends* (3 volumes). London, 1832.
C. L. Graves: *Hubert Parry: His Life and Works* (2 volumes). Macmillan, London, 1926.
Cecil Gray: *Peter Warlock*. Jonathan Cape, London, 1938.
A. Plunkett Green: *C. V. Stanford*. Edward Arnold, London, 1935.

W. H. Hadow: *English Music*. Longman, London, 1931.

C. E. Hallé and Marie Hallé: *The Life and Letters of Charles Hallé*. Smith Elder, London, 1896.

John Harley: *Music in Purcell's London*. Dobson, London, 1969.

Frank Lloyd Harrison: *Music in Medieval Britain*. Routledge & Kegan Paul, London, 1968.

Phyllis Hartnoll (editor): *Shakespeare in Music*. Macmillan, London, 1964.

Frank Howes: *The English Musical Renaissance*. Secker & Warburg, London, 1966.

George Hogarth: *Musical History, Biography and Criticism*. London, 1835.

A. K. Holland: *Henry Purcell and the English Musical Tradition*. London, 1938; Penguin Books, 1948.

Gervase Hughes: *The Music of Arthur Sullivan*. Macmillan, London, 1960.

Peter le Huray: *Music and the Reformation in England*. Herbert Jenkins, London, 1967.

Arthur Hutchings: *English Church Music in the Nineteenth Century*. Herbert Jenkins, London, 1967.

Alan Kendall: *Benjamin Britten*. Macmillan, London, 1973.

Michael Kennedy: *Barbirolli*. MacGibbon & Kee, London, 1972.
The Hallé Tradition. University of Manchester Press, Manchester, 1966.
Portrait of Elgar. Oxford University Press, 1968.
The Works of R. Vaughan Williams. Oxford University Press, 1964.

Sylvia W. Kenney: *Walter Frye and the Contenance Anglois*. Yale University Press, 1964.

Constant Lambert: *Music Ho! A Study of Music in Decline*. Faber, London, 1934; Penguin Books, Harmondsworth, 1948.

George Lowe: *Josef Holbrooke and His Work*. Kegan Paul, London, 1920.

Benjamin Lumley: *Reminiscences of the Opera*. Hurst and Blackett, London, 1864.

E. D. Mackerness: *A Social History of English Music*. Routledge & Kegan Paul, London, 1964.

Diana McVeagh: *Edward Elgar: His Life and His Music*. Dent, 1955.

John Manifold: *The Music in English Drama: Shakespeare to Purcell*. Rockliffe, London, 1956.

Ernest H. Meyer: *English Chamber Music*. Lawrence and Wishart, London, 1946.

Donald Mitchell and Hans Keller (editors): *Benjamin Britten*. Rockliffe, London, 1952.

Robert Etheridge Moore: *Henry Purcell and the Restoration Theatre*. Macmillan, London, 1961.

Thomas Morley: *A Plaine and Easie Introduction to Practicall Musicke*; edited by Alec Harman. J. M. Dent, London, 1952.

R. Nettel: *The Englishman Makes Music*. Dobson, London, 1952.
The Orchestra in England: A Social History. Jonathan Cape, 1956.

Ivor Newton: *At the Piano—Ivor Newton*. Hamish Hamilton, London, 1966.

Novello & Company: *A Century and a Half in Soho*. Novello, London, 1961.

James M. Osborne: *The Autobiography of Thomas Whythorne*. Oxford University Press, 1961.

Ronald Pearsall: *Victorian Popular Music*. David and Charles, Newton Abbot, 1973.

W. H. Reed: *Elgar as I Knew Him*. Gollancz, London, 1936.

John F. Russell and J. H. Elliott: *The Brass Band Movement*. J. M. Dent, London, 1936.

Stanley Sadie: *Concert Life in Eighteenth-Century England*. Proceedings of the Royal Musical Association, 1958–9.

Percy A. Scholes: *The Puritans and Music in England and New England*. Oxford University Press, 1974.

G. Bernard Shaw: *London Music in 1888–1889*. Constable, London, 1937.
Music In London, 1890–1894 (3 volumes). Constable, London, 1932.

Richard Sheard: *Constant Lambert*. Simon Publications, London, 1973.

Denis Stevens: *Tudor Church Music*. Faber, London, 1961.

C. S. Terry: *Johann Christian Bach*. Oxford University Press, 1964.

Richard Wagner: *My Life* (authorized translation). Kegan Paul, London, 1963.

R. Vaughan Williams: *National Music and Other Essays*. Oxford University Press, 1934.

R. Vaughan Williams and Gustav Holst: *Heirs and Rebels*. Oxford University Press, London, 1959.

Ursula Vaughan Williams: *R.V.W.: A Biography of Ralph Vaughan Williams*. Oxford University Press, 1964.

John Wilson: *Roger North on Music*. Novello, London, 1959.
Henry J. Wood: *My Life of Music*. Gollancz, London, 1938.
Percy M. Young: *Elgar, O.M.: A Study of A Musician*. Collins, London, 1955.
Franklin B. Zimmerman: *Henry Purcell, 1659–1695*. Macmillan, London, 1967.

Index